THE OCCUPATION OF THE CAPITAL OF MEXICO BY THE AMERICAN ARMY.

The Mexican War
and
Its Warriors

*Comprising a Complete History
Of all the Operations of the American
Armies In Mexico*

J. Frost L.L.D.

HERITAGE BOOKS
2008

HERITAGE BOOKS
AN IMPRINT OF HERITAGE BOOKS, INC.

Books, CDs, and more—Worldwide

For our listing of thousands of titles see our website
at
www.HeritageBooks.com

Published 2008 by
HERITAGE BOOKS, INC.
Publishing Division
100 Railroad Ave. #104
Westminster, Maryland 21157

Copyright © 1850 J. Frost, L.L.D.

Entered, according to Act of Congress,
by H.Mansfield,
in the Clerk's Office of the District of Connecticut

All rights reserved. No part of this book may be reproduced or transmitted in any form or by any means, electronic or mechanical, including photocopying, recording or by any information storage and retrieval system without written permission from the author, except for the inclusion of brief quotations in a review.

International Standard Book Numbers
Paperbound: 978-1-55613-276-6
Clothbound: 978-0-7884-7129-2

PREFACE.

THE recent contest between the United States and Mexico has called forth the military energies of this country, and has led to displays of valour and military science which have astonished the whole civilized world. In a succession of battles, sieges, marches, and skirmishes, lasting through a period of nineteen months, the arms of the United States have been uniformly triumphant. Wherever our armies have met the enemy they have conquered.

Of such a contest the history cannot but prove interesting to the whole body of the American people. The scattered details which have been furnished by the public journals, although they have served to allay anxiety for the moment, are quite insufficient to satisfy the lively curiosity which such events are well calculated to awaken. "A round unvarnished tale" of the whole progress of the war is necessary to form a portion of the historical library of every family; and it is due to the heroic officers and men who have served in this war, that their claims to the gratitude of their country should be distinctly recorded and preserved in a permanent form.

It is with these views that the following history, and the biographical sketches which accompany it, have been written. The author's aim has been to do justice to all, and he hopes that this intention will atone for any imperfections to which this, in common with every work of its class, is necessarily liable.

LIST OF ILLUSTRATIONS

Bombardment of Vera Cruz,	
Ornamental Headpiece,	
Point Isabel,	28
Fort Brown,	32
Battle of Palo Alto,	41
American army entering Marin,	69
Bishop's Palace,	73
Cavalry Charge,	87
Storming of the Bishop's Palace,	93
Paredes,	99
Santa Anna,	101
Battle of Buena Vista,	107
Death of Colonel Clay,	117
Commencement of the Guerilla Warfare,	125
American fleet saluting the castle at Vera Cruz	141
Battle of Cerro Gordo,	147
Jalapa,	152
Northern extremity of Puebla de los Angelos,	163
General Butler,	166
Battle of Churubusco,	175
The City of Mexico,	183
Chapultepec,	191
Capture of Tuspan,	208
Capture of Panuco,	212
Loss of the Somers,	215
General Taylor,	224
Headpiece,	225
General Worth,	238
Worth at Monterey,	239
Storming of Federation Hill,	242
View from Tacubaya,	247
Headpiece,	255
Headpiece,	259
Tailpiece,	264
Headpiece,	265

LIST OF ILLUSTRATIONS.

Headpiece,	271
Street fight at Monterey,	273
General Kearny,	280
Headpiece,	281
Headpiece,	285
Colonel McCulloch,	292
Headpiece,	293
Captain Walker,	298
Headpiece,	299
Colonel Hays,	304
Headpiece,	305
Headpiece,	311
General Scott,	314
Headpiece,	315
General Shields,	322

Bombardment of Vera Cruz.

THE WAR AND ITS WARRIORS

THE WAR.

Though several subjects of dispute existed between this country and Mexico, previous to the annexation of Texas, yet the latter event was the immediate cause of the war between the two countries. As soon as Mexico understood that a project of union was entertained between the United States and Texas, she endeavoured to defeat it; and when the act was consummated, her minister protested against it as "an act of

Annexation of Texas.

aggression the most unjust which can be found recorded in the annals of modern history; namely, that of despoiling a friendly nation, like Mexico, of a considerable portion of her territory." Immediately after, the minister demanded his passports, and from that time all efforts at amicable negotiation entirely failed.

On the 21st of March, 1845, orders were issued for General Zachary Taylor, commandant at Fort Jessup, Louisiana, to prepare his forces for marching into Texas, whenever orders to that purpose should be issued. The reasons for this were given by President Polk in his message of December, 1845. "Both the congress and the convention of the people of Texas, invited this government to send an army into their territory to protect and defend them against a menaced attack. The moment the terms of annexation offered by the United States were accepted by Texas, the latter became so far a part of our country as to make it our duty to afford such protection and defence. I therefore deemed it proper, as a precautionary measure, to order a strong squadron to the coasts of Mexico, and to concentrate an efficient military force on the western frontier of Texas."

Agreeably to instructions received from government, General Taylor concentrated his forces at Corpus Christi, in the eastern part of Texas. Here he remained until March, 1846, when he received from the president orders to the following effect:

"Instructions have been issued to the general in command to occupy the left bank of the Del Norte. This river which is the south-west boundary of the state of Texas, is an exposed frontier. From this quarter invasion was threatened; upon it, and in its immediate

Taylor leaves Corpus Christi.

vicinity, in the judgment of high military experience, are the proper stations for the protecting forces of the government. In addition to this important consideration, several others have occurred to induce this movement. Among these are the facilities afforded by the ports at Brazos Santiago, and the mouth of the Del Norte, for the reception of supplies by sea; the stronger and more healthful military positions; the convenience for obtaining a ready and a more abundant supply of provisions, water, fuel, and forage; and the advantages which are afforded by the Del Norte, in forwarding supplies to such ports as may be established in the interior, and upon the Indian frontier." General Taylor left Corpus Christi on the 11th of March, and marched toward the Rio Grande.* The troops marched through a sandy desert, infested by venomous reptiles, until they

* In this march, says a late writer, the army encountered the most appalling hardships, both from the heat of the sandy deserts over which they passed, and the want of food and water. The discipline acquired in camp, where large portions of the troops had for the first time an opportunity of seeing and learning the evolutions of the line, was here amply tested; and it should be recorded to the honour of the soldiers, that throughout their whole march they bore their hardships with patience and cheerfulness.

The sufferings on this march were rendered the more painful by contrast with the agreeable sojourn of the army at Corpus Christi, which is described by Captain Henry in his entertaining Campaign Sketches, as one of the most delightful regions in the world. "From the top of the bluff," he says, "the view is magnificent in the extreme. Far off to the east the scene was bounded by the white caps of the beautiful bay; to the south-east, the Flower Bluffs stood out in bold relief; in the north-east, the distant highlands of Maylone's Bluff were dimly visible; to the northwest, the land near the mouth of the Nueces; in the west, one unlimited plain presented itself, extending to the mountains, the home of the mustang and buffalo."

reached the Arroya Colorado, thirty miles eastward of the Rio Grande. On the opposite bank of this river a body of soldiers and rancheros was stationed, apparently for the purpose of disputing the passage. This place was favourable for opposing the passage of the army, and General Taylor expected that war was now about to begin. He made his preparations for crossing, however, but soon after received a message from the governor of Matamoras, stating that an attempt to cross the Colorado woul be considered a signal for war.

Notwithstanding these warlike demonstrations, General Taylor crossed the river in face of the foe. He experienced no opposition, although an excellent opportunity was afforded from the position in which the Mexicans were stationed.

Being thus unexpectedly delivered from a disagreeable collision, General Taylor spent a day in refreshing his troops, and then [March 22d] resumed his march for the Rio Grande. On the 24th, news was received that the Mexicans had taken possession of Point Isabel, on the Brazos Santiago, which place the general had previously selected as a military depot. Knowing the advantages to be derived from this station, General Taylor determined to occupy it; and accordingly, leaving his main army with General Worth on the Matamoras road, he pushed toward the Brazos with the dragoons and artillery train. Wh n near the place, he was met by the prefect of Tamaulipas, and other citizens, who protested against the occupation of their territory, and intimated that their government considered it a declaration of war. While General Taylor was considering this protestation, he observed a column of smoke in the

Excitement in Matamoras.

direction of Point Isabel, and conjecturing that the Mexicans had fired it, he dismissed the prefect, with the promise of an answer when the Americans would arrive near Matamoras. Colonel Twiggs was sent forward with the dragoons to stop the conflagration, and arrest those who had caused it. He found the station deserted by the soldiery and many of the citizens, and succeeded in saving a few of the burning houses. General Taylor arrived soon after, and commenced the construction of a fortification subsequently known as Fort Polk. Major John Munroe was intrusted with the command. Six brass six-pounders, two long eighteens, large quantities of powder and ball with about four hundred and fifty men, were left for its defence.

Having completed such other arrangements as were thought necessary, in order to guard against attack, General Taylor continued his march with the main army, and reached the Rio Grande opposite Matamoras on the 28th.

At the first appearance of the American army the city of Matamoras was thrown into the greatest excitement. Exaggerated reports both of its strength and intentions had preceded its coming; and our troops were regarded as lawless banditti, whose sole intention was spoil and plunder. In a few days, however, this feeling seems to have subsided; the good behaviour of the American troops dissipated previous fears; and the citizens at least became willing to wait for the result of the natural course of events, rather than immediately rush upon the American army, as was at first their intention.

The Americans were now situated in a beautiful coun-

Description of the Country.

try—the more grateful after their fatiguing march. "Far as the eye can reach," says a volunteer, "one level surface presents itself to view, dotted with cotton and sugarcane fields, interspersed with lovely gardens after the Spanish fashion, the whole cut up and divided in all sorts of ways, by groves of the finest trees, among which the lignum vitæ figures largely; and the entire picture is cut in twain by the muddiest, crookedest, and swiftest river in North America. Neither mountain, hill, nor elevation of any sort, varies the everlasting level of the country around. The scene is rich and peaceful, with nought to mar its appropriate character save the armies of the two nations. Our nights here, for the most part, are remarkable for their serenity. The stars stand forth in numerous crowds, with rare brilliancy; not a leaf is moved, not a cloud is seen; while ever and anon a meteor of surpassing brightness shoots across the azure vault."

When the army reached the Rio Grande, and had planted the American flag upon its banks, General Worth crossed to the Mexican side, in order to have an interview with the city authorities, and deliver to them despatches from General Taylor. He was met by General la Vega, the Licenciado Casares, Juan Garza, an interpreter, and two officers, who had been appointed by the authorities to confer with him. After considerable altercation, the reception of the despatches was refused, and a like result attended a request for an interview with the American consul. Worth then returned to the camp.

After this event, the Mexicans, withheld all supplies from General Taylor, and commenced the erection of

Mexican Proclamation Inviting Deserters.

batteries and fortifications opposite his position. He had previously begun the construction of a fort, intended to defend his camp and afford a depot for such stores as would be drawn from time to time from Point Isabel. A gloom now settled over both armies, and speculations upon a dark and uncertain future filled the mind of both friend and foe.

The following proclamation of "The commander-in-chief of the Mexican army, to the English and Irish under the orders of the American General Taylor," was distributed in the American camp, in the early part of April. It was the first display of that unmanly craft, for which the Mexicans seem to be characteristically adapted:

"Know ye:—That the government of the United States is committing repeated acts of barbarous aggression against the magnanimous Mexican nation; that the government which exists under the flag of the stars, is unworthy of the designation of Christian. Recollect that you were born in Great Britain; that the American government looks with coldness upon the powerful flag of St. George, and is provoking to a rupture the war-like people to whom it belongs. President Polk boldly manifesting a desire to take possession of Oregon, as he already has done of Texas. Now, then, come with all confidence to the Mexican ranks; and I guarantee to you upon my honour, good treatment, and that all your expenses shall be defrayed until your arrival in the beautiful capital of Mexico.

"Germans, French, Poles, and individuals of all nations! Separate yourselves from the Yankees, and do not contribute to defend a robbery and usurpation, which, be assured, the civilized nations of Europe look upon with the utmost indignation. Come, therefore, and array yourselves under the tricoloured flag, in the confidence that the God of armies protects, and that it will protect you equally with the English."

This inglorious appeal was not unattended with success. Several desertions took place, until it became necessary to issue orders to shoot every soldier, who should attempt this crime. Two or three being thus dealt with, the evil was stopped.

The situation of the two armies became every day more critical. By order of General Taylor, strong guards of foot and mounted men were established on the margin of the river, for the purpose of preventing all intercourse. The Mexican pickets extended above and below his camp for several miles, but were watched by strong and vigilant guard, so as to prevent the possibility of surprise under disadvantageous circumstances. A field-work was also erected, together with a strong battery, a number of buildings for the security of supplies, and several respectable works for their protection. Fronting each other, for an extent of more than two miles, were batteries shotted, within range of each other, and watched by officers and men who were impatiently waiting for orders to apply their matches.

But both armies still seemed unwilling to interrupt the peace which had ever existed between the two republics. Neither army was very well prepared for active hostilities. Taylor's entire force was small, separated into two portions, and ill provided with artillery and ammunition; the Mexicans were waiting for rein-

Murder of Colonel Cross.

forcements, both of men and supplies, and were uncertain as to a proper point of attack.

On the 10th of April, an event occurred, which, on account of its being the first of the kind, created great sensation in the American camp. This was the death of Colonel Truman Cross. Early in the morning he had ridden into the country, to his usual exercise, but did not return at his customary time. As the country was known to be infested with plunderers and rancheros, his non-appearance caused much uneasiness in camp, and several parties were despatched in quest of him. General Taylor then wrote to the commandant of Matamoras upon the subject, but that officer disclaimed all knowledge of his fate, and the army was left to the most painful conjectures. This continued until the 21st, when a Mexican strolled into camp, and stated that the body of an American soldier was lying in the chaparral at some distance. A party was immediately sent with him, and, among some thick bushes, they found a body, which, by fragments of the dress and several other marks, was recognized as the remains of Colonel Cross. The spot was a short distance from a road leading to the river. He had been deprived of his watch, pistols, and clothing, and the flesh was picked off his body by the vultures. The account given of his death by a Mexican appears worthy of credit. He stated that he was taken by a band of lawless Mexican soldiers, commanded by Romano Falcon, who murdered him with his own hands, after he had been robbed, although his band were in favour of taking him a prisoner to Matamoras. General Taylor caused the body to be interred with full military honours.

Correspondence between Taylor and Ampudia.

On the 11th, the arrival of General Ampudia in Matamoras, caused many demonstrations of joy on the part of the citizens and soldiers in that city, and the Americans expected an early attack. On the following day, however, General Ampudia sent a messenger to General Taylor with a despatch, requiring him, "in all form and at the latest in the peremptory term of twenty-four hours, to break up his camp and retire beyond the Neuces," assuring him, that in the event of a refusal, arms, and arms alone, must decide the question," and advising him that, in that case, the Mexicans accepted the war to which he provoked them.

General Taylor in reply to this letter, informed him that he had been ordered by his government to take a position on the left bank of the Rio Grande, which he had done, and from which he could not recede, except under directions from the same quarter with those which brought him there. He further stated that the movement in question was expected by his government to be a peaceful one, and that he (Ampudia) was fully at liberty to make it otherwise, at any moment he might see fit to do so; in which case he would be responsible for all the consequences resulting from the same. The allotted time expired without being followed by any occurrence of interest, notwithstanding the definite form of General Ampudia's notice.

On the 17th, Lieutenant T. H. Porter, and Lieutenant Dobbins, started from camp for the purpose of discovering if possible, the murderers of Colonel Cross, a step induced by the rumour that Romano Falcon was prowling in the vicinity with his command. Each commanded a detachment of two non-commissioned officers

Death of Lieutenant Porter.

and ten privates. They took opposite directions. During the night it rained hard. On the second day, Lieutenant Porter met a party of Mexicans, one of whom snapped his piece at him. Lieutenant Porter answered by firing a double barrel. The Mexican took to flight, whilst Lieutenant Porter took possession of the camp of the marauders, containing ten horses, blankets, &c. He then immediately mounted his men, and started for head-quarters. It shortly after commenced raining with the violence known only in tropical climates. While passing through a clump of chaparral, Lieutenant Porter was fired upon. He instantly ordered his men to dismount, but their arms were useless from the rain, while the enemy continued to pour in a galling fire. One of Lieutenant Porter's men was shot down, and he himself received a ball in the thigh and fell, exclaiming, "Fight on, boys! Take care of yourselves." The men then separated into three parties as they retreated into the chaparral, but they all finally reached the camp. As they retired, the Mexicans, yelling like Indians, rushed upon Lieutenant Porter and the wounded soldier, and plunged their knives into their breasts. The gallant young officer whose life was thus early lost to his country, was a son of Commodore David Porter. It has been said of some families that chivalry runs in the blood, and of none can it be more true than of the Porters. The brother of Lieutenant Porter, who held a similar rank in the navy, is reported to have said, when he heard of his brother's death, that his father had given him a sword as his only bequest, and with that sword he would avenge his brother's fall or share his fate. His *American* mother had written to him, " come not to

Blockade of the Rio Grande.

me—but go the other way, to avenge your brother and defend your country."

On the 19th of April, General Taylor learned that two vessels from New Orleans, laden with supplies for the Mexicans in Matamoras, were off the mouth of the Rio Grande, he ordered the United States brig Lawrence, with the revenue cutter St. Anna, to cut off the communication by water with that place. A letter from Ampudia followed the establishment of this blockade, in which that step is complained of, and a demand made for the release of two Mexicans, falsely alleged to be held as prisoners by the American general. The letter of General Taylor in reply is of great interest, and is worthy of preservation as an evidence of the dignified yet firm bearing of that officer at this critical period.

"HEAD-QUARTERS, ARMY OF OCCUPATION,
Camp near Matamoras, Texas, April 22, 1846.

"SIR:—I have had the honour to receive your communication of this date, in which you complain of certain measures adopted by my orders to close the mouth of the Rio Bravo against vessels bound to Matamoras, and in which you also advert to the case of two Mexicans supposed to be detained as prisoners in this camp.

"After all that has passed since the American army first approached the Rio Bravo, I am certainly surprised that you should complain of a measure which is no other than a natural result of the state of war so much insisted upon by the Mexican authorities as actually existing at this time. You will excuse me for recalling a few circumstances to show that this state of war has not been sought by the American army, but has been forced upon it, and that the exercise of the rights incident to such a state cannot be made a subject of complaint.

"On breaking up my camp at Corpus Christi, and moving forward with the army under my orders to occupy the left bank of the Rio Bravo, it was my earnest desire to execute my instructions in a pacific manner; to observe the utmost regard for the personal rights of all citizens residing on the left bank of the river, and to take care that the religion and customs of the people should suffer no violation. With this view, and to quiet the minds of the inhabitants, I issued orders to the army, enjoining a strict observance of the rights and interests of all Mexicans residing on the river, and caused said orders to be translated into Spanish, and circulated in the several towns on the Bravo. These orders announced the spirit in which we proposed to occupy the country, and I am proud to say that up to this moment the same spirit has controlled the operations of the army. On reaching the Arroyo Colorado I was informed by a Mexican officer that the order in question had been received in Matamoras; but was told at the same time that if I attempted to cross the river it would be regarded as a declaration of war. Again, on my march to Frontone I was met by a deputation of the civil authorities of Matamoras, protesting against my occupation of a portion of the department of Tamaulipas, and declaring that if the army was not at once withdrawn, war would result. While this communication was in my hands, it was discovered that the village of Frontone had been set on fire and abandoned. I viewed this as a direct act of war, and informed the deputation that their communication would be answered by me when opposite Matamoras, which was done in respectful terms. On reaching the river I despatched an officer, high in rank, to convey to the commanding general in Matamoras the expression of my desire for amicable relations, and my willingness to leave open to the use of the citizens of Matamoras the port of Brazos Santiago until the question of boundary should be definitively settled. This officer received for reply, from the officer selected to confer with him, that my advance to the Rio Bravo was considered as a veritable act of war, and he was absolutely refused an interview with the American consul, in itself an act incompatible with a state of peace.

"Notwithstanding these repeated assurances on the part of the Mexican authorities, and notwithstanding the most obviously hostile preparations on the right bank of the river, accompanied by a rigid non-intercourse, I carefully abstained from any act of hostility—determined that the onus of producing an actual state of hostilities should not rest with me. Our relations remained in this state until I had the honour to receive your note of the 12th instant, in which you denounce war as the alternative of my remaining in this position. As I could not, under my instructions, recede from my position, I accepted the alternative you offered me, and made all my dispositions to meet it suitably. But, still willing to adopt milder measures before proceeding to others, I contented myself in the first instance with ordering a blockade of the mouth of the Rio Bravo by the naval forces under my orders—a proceeding perfectly consonant with the state of war so often declared to exist, and which you acknowledge in your note of the 16th instant, relative to the late Colonel Cross. If this measure seems oppressive, I wish it borne in mind that it has been forced upon me by the course you have seen fit to adopt. I have reported this blockade to my government, and shall not remove it until I receive instructions to that effect, unless indeed you desire an armistice pending the final settlement of the question between the governments, or until war shall be formally declared by either, in which case I shall cheerfully open the river. In regard to the consequences you mention as resulting from a refusal to remove the blockade, I beg you to understand that I am prepared for them, be they what they may.

"In regard to the particular vessel referred to in your communication, I have the honour to advise you that, in pursuance of my orders, two American schooners, bound for Matamoras, were warned off on the 17th instant, when near the mouth of the river, and put to sea, returning probably to New Orleans. They were not seized, or their cargoes disturbed in any way, nor have they been in the harbour of Brazos Santiago to my knowledge. A Mexican schooner, understood to be the 'Juniata,' was in or off that harbour when my instructions to block the river were issued, but was driven to sea in a gale, since which time I have had no report concerning her. Since the receipt of your communication, I have learned that two persons, sent to the mouth of the river to procure information respecting this vessel, proceeded thence to Brazos Santiago, when they were taken up and detained by the officer in command, until my orders could be received. I shall order their immediate release. A letter from one of them to the Spanish vice-consul is respectfully transmitted herewith.

"In relation to the Mexicans said to have drifted down the river in a boat, and to be prisoners at this time in my camp, I have the pleasure to inform you that no such persons have been taken prisoners or are now detained by my authority. The boat in question was carried down empty by the current of the river, and drifted ashore near one of our pickets and was secured by the guard. Some time afterwards an attempt was made to recover the boat under the cover of darkness; the individuals concerned were hailed by the guard, and, failing to answer, were fired upon as a matter of course. What became of them is not known, as no trace of them could be discovered on the following morning. The officer of the Mexican guard directly opposite was informed next day that the boat would be returned on proper application to me, and I have now only to repeat that assurance.

"In conclusion, I take leave to state that I consider the tone of your communication highly exceptionable, where you stigmatize the movement of the army under my orders as 'marked with the seal of universal reprobation.' You must be aware that such language is not respectful in itself, either to me or my government; and while I observe in my own correspondence the courtesy due to your high position, and to the magnitude of the interests with which we are respectively charged, I shall expect the same in return.

"I have the honour to be, very respectfully, your obedient servant,

"Z. TAYLOR,
"*Brevet Brig. Gen. U. S. A., Commanding.*
" Sr. Gen. D. Pedro de Ampudia, *Commanding in Matamoras.*"

Taylor's account of his preparations for defense.

On the 20th of April, an artfully-worded address was issued by General Arista, offering lands to all who should desert from the American army and become citizens of Mexico, three hundred and twenty acres being fixed as the price of a private, and others in proportion. Any services to Mexico were to be properly rewarded. The state of things at this time is well described by General Taylor in a letter written on the 25th of April. He says, "strong guards of foot and mounted men are established on the margin of the river, and thus efficient means have been adopted on our part to prevent all intercourse. While opposite to us, their pickets extend above and below for several miles, we are equally active in keeping up a strong and vigilant guard to prevent surprise or attacks, under disadvantageous circumstances. This is the more necessary while we are to act on the defensive, and they are at liberty to take the opposite course whenever they think proper to do so. Nor have we been idle in other respects; we have a field-work under way, besides having erected a strong battery, and a number of buildings for the security of our supplies, in addition to some respectable works for their protection. We have mounted a respectable battery, four pieces of which are long eighteen-pounders, with which we could batter or burn down the city of Matamoras, should it become necessary to do so. When our field-work is completed—which will soon be the case—and mounted with its proper armament, five hundred men could hold it against as many thousand Mexicans. During the twenty-seven days since our arrival here, a most singular state of things has prevailed all through the outlines of the two armies, which, to a certain extent, have

Capture of Captain Thornton.

all the feelings as if there were actual war. Fronting each other for an extent of more than two miles, and within musket range, are batteries shotted, and the officers and men, in many instances, waiting impatiently for orders to apply the matches, yet nothing has been done to provoke the firing of a gun or any act of violence." In the postscript to this letter, General Taylor adds, " since writing the above, an engagement has taken place between a detachment of our cavalry and the Mexicans, in which we are worsted. So the war has actually commenced and the hardest must fend off."

This significant language has reference to the defeat of Captain Thornton. General Taylor's scouts had brought in intelligence on the 23d, that twenty-five hundred Mexicans had crossed the river to the Texas side, above the American fort, and fifteen hundred below. A squadron of dragoons was despatched to each place of crossing to reconnoiter them and learn their position. The squadron ordered below was commanded by Captain Ker; that above, commanded by Captain Thornton, consisted of Captain Hardee, Lieutenants Kane and Mason, and sixty-one privates and non-commissioned officers. Captain Ker found that the report of the crossing below was false. Captain Thornton, however, proceeded up the country some twenty-six miles, where he fell into an ambuscade, and found himself surrounded by about two thousand five hundred of the enemy concealed in the chaparral. The command behaved with great gallantry, but the number of the enemy was so overwhelming that they surrendered as prisoners of war. Lieutenant George Mason, who was killed in the rencounter, is said to have maimed Romano Falcon for life, in

Point Isabel.

a close personal contest. He was a gallant young officer-
and his death is much regretted. Though the force
which obtained this success was about fifteen to one, it
filled the Mexican army with ecstacy, and General Arista
addressed to General Torrejon an eloquent letter of con-
gratulation on his great and glorious victory. The reserve they had hitherto manifested was now cast wholly
aside. They came across the river in great numbers;
all intercourse between General Taylor's camp and Point
Isabel was cut off, and there was imminent danger of
the fall of that place with all the military stores it contained. Nothing of interest had occurred at Point Isabel up to this time. Major Munroe, who commanded,
had completed his arrangements for defense, and armed
some five or six hundred men, among whom were fifty
or sixty sailors, collected from the vessels in port. Captain Walker of the Rangers, and some small parties of
Texans had arrived there, and was speedily engaged
upon important duties. Some teams having returned
to Point Isabel, on account of the obstructions of
the roads by the Mexicans, Captain Walker went out on
the 28th with a number of men to reconnoiter. He was
driven back to Point Isabel with great loss, having been
attacked when midway between that place and the camp,
by an overwhelming force of the enemy. His raw troops
fled in confusion, and he was obliged to retreat. He
returned with only two men; seven afterwards came in.
He estimated the force of the enemy at fifteen hundred,
and thought that many of them must have fallen in the
skirmish. Notwithstanding this repulse, Captain Walker
volunteered to carry a message to General Taylor. Major Munroe having accepted the offer, he started on the

evening of the 29th and, after encountering many imminent dangers, reached the camp in safety. As soon as General Taylor had received Major Munroe's statement, he determined upon a movement that would release him from the embarrassment of having the communication cut off. Accordingly, on the morning of the 1st of May, 1846, he took up the line of march for Point Isabel, with the main body of his army, leaving the seventh regiment of infantry and two companies of artillery under Captain Lowd and Lieutenant Bragg, to complete the works in the fort, and defend it if it was attacked. The whole was put under command of Major Brown. As the army passed out, the banks of the river on the Matamoras side were crowded with spectators of the departure of what they thought our discomfited army, whilst General Arista employed himself in announcing the "retreat" of General Taylor and his army to his government, taking care to pay to himself and his brave men the tribute so signal a triumph deserved.

The Mexicans, however, evinced great judgment by refraining from attacking him on the way to Point Isabel, as it afforded them an opportunity of attacking and trying to capture his fortified camp with a weakened garrison, by which, if successful, they would have a vast advantage over him when he returned, and also they would have more advantage and probability of success in annoying and harassing his forces, or in fighting a pitched battle on his return route, encumbered as he would be by two or three hundred loaded wagons.

The Mexicans were too sagacious to delay improving these advantages. On the morning of the 3d, a battery of seven guns placed in the town, opened a brisk fire upon the fort. It was returned, and shortly silenced. They then fired shells and shot from the lower fort and a mortar battery, which was continued with a short intermission till midnight. During all this time a part of the troops laboured to complete the fortifications, although exposed to the full range of the enemy's guns. By the fifteen hundred shot fired during this first day, but one man was killed. The Americans stopped firing about ten o'clock in the forenoon, as they were wasting ammunition and doing no injury, except to the town. This silence was mistaken by the enemy as a symptom of fear or despair, they momentarily expected a surrender.

The noise of this cannonading having reached Point Isabel, General Taylor despatched Captain May with Captain Walker and a hundred men, to learn something of the garrison, and reconnoiter the country. They avoided the enemy, and penetrated to within a few miles of the fort. Captain May there concealed his party in the chaparral, and Captain Walker with six rangers proceeded to the fort. Walker not having returned to the detachment, May feared that he had fallen a victim to the enemy, and as the Mexican scouts had discovered his own position, he decided to return. He reached the camp in safety, having on the way put to flight and pursued for three miles, a very superior body of the enemy's cavalry. The supposed loss of Captain Walker, who was a general favourite, cast a gloom over the whole army, which, however, was speedily dispelled by the appearance of that gallant officer, bearing the gratifying intelligence that Major Brown was able to maintain his position. Captain Walker had returned to the place

Preparations for assault on Fort Brown.

Fort Brown.

where he had left Captain May, and finding him gone, returned to the fort, stating that the Mexicans had blocked the game on him this time, but that he would give them another turn when it was dark. Starting from the fort at night with his party, his superior knowledge of the country only enabling him to avoid the numerous parties of the enemy who were aware of his mission, and on the alert to capture him.

At the fort, during the 4th, the fire of the enemy was not renewed, and the soldiers laboured with energy to complete the works. On the following day, large parties of the enemy, both horse and foot, were discovered in the rear of the fort. These thousands were supported by a battery that had been erected in the night, and which the garrison named for the sake of distinction, "the Battery in the country." This battery, with those in Matamoras, opened with shot and shell in the afternoon, and kept up a galling cross fire. At nine o'clock, Lieutenant Hanson, after a gallant reconnoisance, reported the erection of a new battery at the cross roads. On Wednesday morning, the 6th, a spirited fire was kept up against the fort, the shot and shells being well directed. The balls falling into the fortress afforded considerable merriment to the soldiers, who were sitting idly about, reserving their ammunition in case of need under an assault. An old soldier, who prided himself on his culinary skill, had made some coffee, and was stooping to pour it into the cups of his mess, when a ball flying over the parapet, struck in the ashes near him and overturned the beverage into the fire. The disciple of Careme and votary of Mars, shocked at the disrespect, gave the ball a kick, while in a dolorous voice he cursed the rascally Mexicans for knocking over his coffee.

In compliance with the directions given by General Taylor to be pursued in case the fort was surrounded, the eighteen-pounders were fired at stated intervals. The enemy, as if conscious that this was a call for relief, reopened their fire upon the fort. The officers of the garrison, however, reserved their ammunition for the expected assault. The bomb proofs were built at points convenient for the soldiers to retreat into, and the sentinel on the look out could name the battery from which a ball or shell was fired, as soon as he saw the smoke of the discharge, and the soldiers would have time to get under cover before the balls reached them. Shells were frequently allowed to explod harmlessly in the air, by the soldiers falling flat on their faces, when one was fired, a measure which a Mexican, elevated to a considerable height in a tall tree, with a glass in his hand, reported to his comrades as being what it seemed to him, a mark of the destruction produced by their fire.

The lamented death of Major Brown occurred at this time, May 6th.* We give the following graphic account of it, taken from "Our Army on the Rio Grande," by T. B. Thorpe, Esq. He says, "After the cross firing, called forth with so much energy by our signal eighteen pounders, had continued for three hours and a half, the noble-minded Major Brown, commander of the fort, with his adjutant-lieutenant by his side, took his usual round to see that officers and men were at their posts. He stopped for a moment to give directions to some of the soldiers who were busily employed at one of the bomb proofs. Every instant the men were engaged in dodging to avoid the ball and bursting shell. One of the latter, from "the battery in the country," struck in the parapet, burying itself in the sand without exploding; a cloud of dust rose into the air, amid which the gallant commander was seen to fall, mortally wounded, He was immediately taken to the hospital tent, and,

---

* The death of Major J. Brown was a severe loss to the army. He was a native of Vermont, and at the age of twenty-four years entered the army as a common soldier, in the 7th infantry, at the commencement of the war of 1812. His merit soon raised him to the rank of ensign, lieutenant, and finally major. He did good service in the Florida war; and was selected by General Taylor to command at the fort where he fell, in consequence of the general's high opinion of his courage and ability. General Taylor says cf him: "The pleasure (*of victory*) is alloyed with profound regret at the loss of the heroic and indomitable Major Brown. His loss would be a severe one to the service at any time, but to the army under my orders, it is indeed irreparable."

In the case of Major Brown we see the importance of occasional promotions of common soldiers to the rank of officers.

Summons to Surrender.

while being borne in the arms of two of his men, he exhorted those about him never to give up the fort. His right leg had been shot off, exhibiting the torn muscles, and jagged crushed bones to the pained sight of his command. Although suffering the most excruciating tortures, he remained perfectly calm, and said to those who were sympathizingly standing about him, "Men, go to your duties, stand by your posts; I am but one among you." While suffering under the operation of having his leg amputated above the knee, which was most skilfully done, he congratulated his country that the misfortune had befallen him, and not been meted out to a younger man.

Attempts were next made by the enemy to bring musketry into play upon the garrison, but those who approached for the purpose were scattered with some loss by a few rounds of canister. The bombardment then grew still more severe, and continued till noon. In the afternoon, a few shells were thrown. At four P.M., two Mexican officers approached with a white flag, bearing a communication from General Arista, which proved to be a summons to surrender, the humanity of the Mexicans being given as a reason for the demand, although he is asserted to have had a band of men organized and instructed to slaughter the garrison as soon as the surrender was made. Captain Hawkins, who had succeeded Major Brown in the command, summoned a council of the commissioned officers, and stated the purport of the message, (the want of a good Spanish interpreter making it difficult to be fully understood,) adding that though he knew there was but one sentiment upon the point, he thought it proper that all the officers should

Answer.

be represented in the reply. It was then unanimously voted to defend the fort to the death. The following reply was therefore prepared and despatched to General Arista, within the hour that had been allowed for a reply.

"Sir:—Your humane communication has just been received, and, after the consideration due to its importance, I must respectfully decline to surrender my forces to you.

The exact purport of your despatch I cannot feel confident that I understand, as my interpreter is not skilled in your language; but if I have understood you correctly, you have my reply above," &c., &c.

The reception of this answer was the signal of a general burst of heavy shot upon the fort; but the Americans saved their ammunition and doubled their sentinels during the night, in expectation of an attack. During the 7th, much activity was manifested, a heavy cannonade being maintained all day, and various parties firing with muskets into the fort from every position. The garrison, however, were directed not to return the fire unless they advanced within eighty yards, and they therefore preserved silence. In the evening, the gallant Major Mansfield advanced with a small party into the plain, and leveled the traverse formerly occupied by the Americans, and which now served to shelter the enemy while firing on the fort. A large quantity of chaparral, used in a similar manner, was also cut down. At midnight the garrison were roused by a terrible discharge of musketry, and the sound of bugles, but the anticipated assault did not follow. On the 8th, the cannonade was recommenced at daybreak, and continued till the afternoon. The bombardment had hardly ceased when a severe cannon-

Death of Major Brown.

ading was heard in the direction of Point Isabel, so sudden and so rapidly that it seemed to be one continuous volley of field-pieces. The soldiers in the fort answered it by hearty cheering; the men of Matamoras, by a renewal of the firing from four mortar batteries at once. Yet the gallant defenders knew that General Taylor was on his way to succour them, and they stood upon the parapet to listen to the far distant firing, while the terrific rain from the enemy's batteries poured unheeded around them. Towards night, they learned from a Mexican the events of the field of Palo Alto, and the knowledge that the victory rested with their friends made the quiet night, their nearer enemies permitted them to enjoy, the more refreshing. On the morning of the 9th, an officer of the 7th regiment went outside of the fort to the flagstaff, for the purpose of arranging the halyards, which had become unrigged on the previous day. He succeeded in lowering the topmast of the staff and rigging the halyards, the enemy playing upon him with round shot and shell from all their batteries. He was not strong enough to raise the flagstaff to its proper place, he therefore coolly lashed it in its position, and gave the flag to the breeze.

On this day Major Brown expired. At the time of his death every thing in the fort was perfectly still, and the silence was unbroken until the report of Ridgely's batteries on the field of the Resaca de la Palma were heard. "No language," says Mr. Thorpe, "can describe the intense interest with which the raging battle was listened to: each man was at his post, and every booming gun called forth an almost agonizing interest to learn its nationality and effects. Meanwhile the bom-

Flight of the enemy seen from the Fort.

bardment opened simultaneously with the firing on the field, and continued to increase with unprecedented severity; but it was not to the batteries of the Mexicans that attention was directed. Our eighteen-pounders were occasionally fired, to let General Taylor know that all was still well in the fort. The firing on the battle-field was now growing less and less powerful, and the discharges were becoming irregular. 'They have charged on the guns!' shouted one of the officers! Another and another was silenced. 'They have carried them!' shouted another, in uncontrollable ecstacy; all cannonading ceased; volleys of musketry were next heard, then all was still. How eloquently the silence spoke of the hand-to-hand conflict, and how the blood in the hearts of these brave men went and came from excitement to be engaged in it! The victorious result of our arms was now almost certain. General Taylor and his brave men would either conquer or die. No bells were now ringing in Matamoras, and the noisy music that was wont to belabour the air had been silenced since the evening of the 8th. This, to the heroes of the fort, was full of meaning, and the tale was soon told. At a little before six a confused rush of cavalry and straggling infantry towards the Rio Grande, announced the victory of the Americans, at sight of which, an officer of the 7th regiment jumped upon the parapet, beside the regimental flagstaff, and gave three cheers, which were responded to so loudly and heartily by all in the fort, that they silenced the enemy's batteries, for from that moment they ceased firing. The news had reached Matamoras, that to Mexico the day was lost." Besides Major Brown, one non-commissioned officer killed, and ten

March from Point Isabel.

men wounded was the amount of loss that the garrison sustained during one hundred and sixty hours severe bombardment.

General Taylor had left Point Isabel on the evening of the 7th of May, and moved with the main body of the army towards the Rio Grande. After marching seven miles, they bivouacked on their arms, and resumed the march on the following morning. At noon they discovered the enemy, prepared to oppose their progress, stretched out on the flat prairie more than a mile.

We give here the clear and concise account of this battle, given by General Taylor in his official despatches, reserving for another portion of the work more minute details and personal anecdotes.

"About noon, when our advance of cavalry had reached the water hole of 'Palo Alto,' the Mexican troops were reported in our front, and were soon discovered occupying the road in force. I ordered a halt upon reaching the water, with the view to rest and refresh the men, and to form deliberately our line of battle. The Mexican line was now plainly visible across the prairie, and about three-quarters of a mile distant. Their left, which was composed of a heavy force of cavalry, occupied the road, resting upon a thicket of chaparral, while masses of infantry were discovered in succession on the right, greatly outnumbering our own force.

Our line of battle was now formed in the following order, commencing on the extreme right:—5th infantry, commanded by Lieutenant-Colonel McIntosh; Major Ringgold's artillery; 3d infantry, commanded by Captain L. N. Morris; two eighteen-pounders, commanded

Battle of Palo Alto.

by Lieutenant Churchill, 3d artillery; 4th infantry, commanded by Major G. W. Allen; the 3d and 4th regiments composed the third brigade, under command of Lieutenant-Colonel Garland; and all the above corps, together with two squadrons of dragoons under Captains Ker and May, composed the right wing under the orders of Colonel Twiggs. The left was formed by the battalion of artillery commanded by Lieutenant-Colonel Childs. Captain Duncan's light artillery, and the 8th infantry, under Captain Montgomery—all forming the first brigade, under command of Lieutenant-Colonel Belknap. The train was packed near the water, under direction of Captains Crossman and Myers, and protected by Captain Ker's squadron.

At two oclock we took up the march by heads of columns, in the direction of the enemy—the eighteen-pounder battery following the road. While the columns were advancing, Lieutenant Blake, topographical engineer, volunteered a reconnoisance of the enemy's line, which was handsomely performed, and resulted in the discovery of at least two batteries of artillery in the intervals of their cavalry and infantry. These batteries were soon opened upon us, when I ordered the columns halted and deployed into line, and the fire to be returned by all our artillery. The 8th infantry on our extreme left, was thrown back to secure that flank. The first fires of the enemy did little execution, while our eighteen-pounders and Major Ringgold's artillery soon dispersed the cavalry which formed his left.—Captain Duncan's battery, thrown forward in advance of the line, was doing good execution at this time. Captain May's squadron was now detached to support that battery, and

Battle of Palo Alto.

the left of our position. The Mexican cavalry, with two pieces of artillery, were now reported to be moving through the chaparral to our right, to threaten that flank, or make a demonstration against the train. The 5th infantry was immediately detached to check this movement, and supported by Lieutenant Ridgely, with a section of Major Ringgold's battery and Captain Walker's company of volunteers, effectually repulsed the enemy—the 5th infantry repelling a charge of lancers, and the artillery doing great execution in their ranks. The 3d infantry was now detached to the right as a still farther security to that flank yet threatened by the enemy. Major Ringgold, with the remaining section, kept up his fire from an advanced position, and was supported by the 4th infantry.

The grass of the prairie had been accidentally fired by our artillery, and the volumes of smoke now partially concealed the armies from each other. As the enemy's left had evidently been driven back and left the road free, as the cannonade had been suspended, I ordered forward the eighteen-pounders on the road nearly to the position first occupied by the Mexican cavalry, and caused the first brigade to take up a new position still on the left of the eighteen-pounder battery. The 5th was advanced from its former position and occupied a point on the extreme right of the new line. The enemy made a change of position corresponding to our own, and after the suspension of nearly an hour the action was resumed.

The fire of artillery was now most destructive—openings were constantly made through the enemy's ranks by our fire, and the constancy with which the Mexican

Death of Major Ringgold,

infantry sustained the severe cannonade was a theme of universal remark and admiration. Captain May's squadron was detached to make a demonstration on the left of the enemy's position, and suffered severely from the fire of artillery to which it was for some time exposed. The 4th infantry, which had been ordered to support the eighteen-pounder battery, was exposed to a most galling fire of artillery, by which several men were killed, and Captain Page dangerously wounded. The enemy's fire was directed against our eighteen-pounder battery, and the guns under Major Ringgold, in its vicinity. The major himself, while coolly directing the fire of his pieces, was struck by a cannon ball and mortally wounded.*

In the mean time the battalion of artillery under Lieutenant-Colonel Childs, had been brought up to support the artillery on our right. A strong demonstration of cavalry was now made by the enemy against this part of our line, and the column continued to advance under a severe fire from the eighteen-pounders. The battalion was instantly formed in square, and held ready to receive

* The death of Major Ringgold was universally lamented. He was a native of Washington county, Maryland, born in 1800. He was educated at the Military Academy, West Point; graduated in 1818; entered the army as lieutenant; promoted to the rank of first lieutenant in 1822, and to that of captain in 1834. His brevet rank of major was the reward of severe service in the Florida war. To his exertions in perfecting the discipline of the light artillery, the country is chiefly indebted for the efficiency of that important arm of the national defense.

Major Ringgold's connections were of the first respectability. His father was General Samuel Ringgold, and his mother was a daughter of General John Cadwalader, who was greatly distinguished in the war of the Revolution. His conduct and character as an officer and a gentleman were in every respect worthy of so highly honourable a descent.

Loss, &c., at Palo Alto.

the charge of cavalry; but when the advancing squadrons were within close range a deadly fire of canister from the eighteen-pounders dispersed them. A brisk fire of small arms was now opened upon the square, by which one officer, Lieutenant Luther, 2d artillery, was slightly wounded; but a well-directed volley from the front of the square silenced all farther firing from the enemy in this quarter. It was now nearly dark, and the action was closed on the right of our line, the enemy having been completely driven back from his position, and foiled in every attempt against our line.

While the above was going forward on our right, and under my own eye, the enemy had made a serious attempt against the left of our line. Captain Duncan instantly perceived the movement, and by the bold and brilliant manœuvering of this battery, completely repulsed several successive efforts of the enemy to advance in force upon our left flank. Supported in succession by the 8th infantry and Captain Ker's squadron of dragoons, he gallantly held the enemy at bay, and finally drove him, with immense loss, from the field. The action here and along the whole line, continued until dark, when the enemy retired into the chaparral in rear of his position.

Our loss this day was nine killed, forty-four wounded, and two missing. Among the wounded were Major Ringgold, who has since died, and Captain Page dangerously wounded, and Lieutenant Luther slightly so. I annex a tabular statement of the casualties of the day.

Our own force engaged is shown by the field report, herewith transmitted, to have been one hundred and seventy-seven officers and two thousand one hundred

Arista's Despatch.

and eleven men; aggregate, two thousand two hundred and eighty-eight. The Mexican force, according to the statement of their own officers, taken prisoners in the affair of the 9th, was not less than six thousand regular troops, with ten pieces of artillery, and probably exceeded that number—the irregular force not known. Their loss was not less than two hundred killed, and four hundred wounded—probably greater. This estimate is very moderate, and founded upon the number actually counted on the field, and upon the reports of their own officers.

As already reported in my first brief despatch, the conduct of our officers and men was every thing that could be desired. Exposed for hours to the severest trials—a cannonade of artillery—our troops displayed a coolness and constancy which gave me throughout the assurance of victory. I purposely defer the mention of individuals until my report of the action of the 9th, when I will endeavour to do justice to the many instances of distinguished conduct on both days."

The Mexicans evinced great determination in this first day's battle, and remained almost within sight of the American army during the night. General Arista employed the night in writing a despatch to the minister of war and marine, giving an eloquent account of what he claimed as his victory, and at daybreak on the 9th, slowly moved into the chaparral, leaving General Taylor in possession of the battle-field. Fearing that the enemy might dispute his progress towards Fort Brown, as the fortification opposite Matamoras was now named, he ordered the train to be strongly parked. An intrenchment was thrown up, and the artillery battalion, with two eighteen-pounders and two twelve-pounders were assigned to its defence.

The army then moved over the plain in line of battle with lively music, marking every where around them the evidences of the terrible destruction produced by the American artillery on the previous day. Wounded soldiers, dying of thirst and hunger, received relief from their generous enemies. The ground was covered with torn clothing, military caps, gun-stocks, and large quantities of cartridges for muskets and artillery. On the edge of the chaparral, the army halted at a place convenient to water. A detachment under Captain McCall was sent forward into the chaparral to ascertain the position of the enemy. General Taylor then rode back to the train, accompanied by Lieutenant J. E. Blake of the topographical corps, who had displayed the utmost gallantry on the previous day. At the train, Lieutenant Blake dismounted from his horse to procure some refreshment, and expressed gratification at the prospect of a little rest, his labours during the previous twenty-four hours having been very arduous. He unbuckled his holsters and threw them on the ground, when one of the pistols unaccountably exploded, throwing the ball upwards into his body. He was mortally wounded, and expired shortly after, expressing his regret that he had not died on the battle-field on the preceding day.

Captain McCall with the advance guard found the enemy intrenched at La Resaca de la Palma, the Dry River of Palms, a strong position entirely commanding the approach to Fort Brown. At this place the road crosses a ravine sixty yards wide and nearly breast high, the bottom being wet, forming long and serpentine ponds

Gallantry of Ridgely.

through the prairie. Along the banks of this dry river, and more particularly on the side then occupied by the Mexicans, the chaparral grows most densely, and at this time, save where it was broken in by the passage of the road, formed almost a solid wall. The enemy occupied this ravine in double line; one behind and under the front bank, and the other intrenched behind the wall of the chaparral on the top of the rear ridge. A battery was placed in the centre of each line on the right and left of the road, and a third battery was on the right of the first line. Six or seven thousand troops were thus strongly fortified in a form resembling a crescent, between the horns of which the army had to pass, while the Mexican batteries were enfilading and cross firing, the narrow road which formed the only unobstructed approach to their position. Lieutenant Ridgely, the successor of Ringgold, was ordered forward on the road, while the 3d, 4th, and 5th regiments of infantry were ordered forward as skirmishers to cover the battery and engage the infantry of the enemy. General Taylor and his staff came up with Captain McCall and his party at four o'clock. He immediately deployed Captain McCall to the left of the road, and Captain C. F. Smith to the right, with orders to bring on the action.

Having received orders to advance, Lieutenant Ridgely moved cautiously forward with Captain Walker, who was charged with assisting him to find the enemy's batteries. At the instant they discovered them, they received a fire from them, which Ridgely, moving about a hundred yards to the front, returned with spirit. This contest was maintained for some time, their balls filling the air, and passing through Ridgely's battery in every direc-

Action Commences.

tion. His men worked at their guns with invincible determination, and he himself sighted them with all the coolness and certainty of ordinary target practice. These well-directed charges were necessary to keep off the enemy who were constantly charging upon him, and whom he had sometimes to beat back with his own sword. The rapid firing of the artillery on both sides produced an unintermitted roar. Colonel Duncan's battery was at the edge of the ravine, but he could not use it; Lieutenant Ridgely holding the only position from which the enemy could be assailed without galling our troops. These had come into the action in the most extraordinary manner, the firing of their musketry being heard at almost the same instant that Ridgely opened his fire in the centre.* The 6th regiment under Lieutenant-Colonel McIntosh supported Ridgely's battery. The 3d

---

* It is to be observed that the artillery, during the whole course of the present war, has proved the most efficient arm of the service in determining the fate of battles, with, perhaps, the exception of the rifle corps in the recent battles near the city of Mexico. Nothing can exceed the efficiency and bravery of the rifle corps. General Scott's pointed eulogy of their conduct was richly deserved.

The efficiency of this arm of the national defense, as we have had occasion to remark in another place, is greatly owing to the indefatigable exertions of Major Ringgold. In this important service the major was aided by Captain Duncan, whose battery rendered most efficient service in the battles of the 8th and 9th of May, as well as in the other most important engagements of the war. The batteries of Sherman, Bragg, and Washington have also become famous, especially by their efficient service at Buena Vista.

The services of the artillery in the battle of Buena Vista were so essential, that it is considered by all military men, that the absence of a small portion of it would undoubtedly have occasioned the loss of the battle.

regiment with a part of the 4th came up on the enemy's right, and the other portion of the 4th joined with the 5th on the left. The 3d and 4th were separated by the chaparral, through which the soldiers literally pushed each other into squads of five or six, and they were obliged to form in the ravine. The 8th, under Captain Montgomery, with Smith's light and other corps, faced to the right. The best troops of Mexico were now contending with the greatest bravery for victory. The contest with artillery and musketry, the sword and the bayonet, at the end of two hours, resulted in the Americans gaining possession of the ravine in which the enemy were posted at the beginning of the action. Yet the batteries in the centre still stood firm, pouring a perfect shower of grape and shells into the American front, and prevented General Taylor from reaping the advantages which the bravery of his troops would otherwise have secured. Captain May rode back to the general, and asked if he should charge the battery on the other side of the ravine. "Charge, captain, nolens volens," was the reply, and away dashed the gallant fellow.* He rode to the head of his command; every rein and sabre was tightly grasped. Raising himself in the saddle, he shouted to his command, "We are ordered to take that battery—follow!" In columns of fours, they dashed along the narrow road, until they came to where Lieutenant Ridgely obstructed their advance. "I am ordered to charge those batteries," said May, coming to a halt. Ridgely knowing the perilous nature of the duty, said, "Wait, Charley, till I draw their fire!" All begrimed

---

* Henry's Campaign Sketches.

Capture of La Vega.

with powder and labouring with his own hands, he fired his pieces slowly and with the usual deadly effect. A storm of copper balls came whizzing and crushing among the artillerists in reply, while Ridgely and his men limbered up, jumped on their pieces, and cheered as May dashed forward. An overwhelming discharge of grape and bullets from the other battery destroyed his first and second platoons, but he was unhurt, and with those who lived swept to the left of the road leaped over the battery and drove the Mexicans from their guns. But they seemed determined to retain their pieces or die: they rushed back to them with the bayonet, and commenced to load them again with grape. May then charged back upon our own lines, and the enemy shrunk in terror from the stroke of his sword. One man, General La Vega, alone maintained his ground, and tried to rally his men; but was made a prisoner by Captain May, and carried under a galling fire from his own countrymen to our lines. The infantry now gathered round the batteries in masses, crossing bayonets for their possession, over the very muzzles of the guns. In a short time, Captain Belknap, with the 8th infantry, and Captain Martin Scott, with the 5th, were engaged in a hand-to-hand conflict with the far-famed Tampico veterans, who had been in twenty battles and were never defeated. The battery was carried, and the 8th and the 5th charged up the ravine amidst a terrible fire from the enemy's right and front. The battery of Colonel Duncan now came into the front, and the retreat of the enemy was hastened by his deadly fire. While the centre battery of the enemy was being carried, Lieutenants Ruggles and Crittenden, with a small command of the 5th and

Capture of Arista's Despatches.

the 8th infantry, all under Captain Montgomery, routed the right wing and carried the right battery. Between this and the centre battery, the Tampico regiment had been posted, all of whom, except seventeen, are said to have fallen at their posts. Their tri-colour was the last Mexican flag waving on the field, and the gallant fellow who bore it, when all hope was lost, tore it from the staff, and concealed it about his person while he attempted to fly. He was ridden down by the dragoons, however, and made a prisoner, and his flag was a trophy of the victory.

The hurry of the Mexicans to escape was so great, that many of them were drowned in the river. Immense quantities of baggage, military stores, and camp equipage fell into the hands of the Americans; the personal, public, and private property of Arista, and all his despatches being among the spoils. The American army passed the night on the battle-field, in the enjoyment of the festival which had been prepared by the followers of the Mexican camp to regale their friends after the anticipated victory. In his despatch after this brilliant victory General Taylor says:

" The loss of the enemy in killed has been most severe. Our own has been very heavy, and I deeply regret to report that Lieutenant Inge, 2d dragoons, Lieutenant Cochrane, 4th infantry, and Lieutenant Chadbourne, 8th infantry, were killed on the field. Lieutenant-Colonel Payne, 4th artillery, Lieutenant-Colonel McIntosh, Lieutenant Dobbins, 3d infantry, Captain Hooe and Lieutenant Fowler, 5th infantry; and Captain Montgomery, Lieutenants Gates, Selden, McClay, Burbank, and Jordan, 8th infantry were wounded. The extent of

General Taylor's Despatch.

our loss in killed and wounded is not yet ascertained, and is reserved for a more detailed report.

The affair of to-day may be regarded as a proper supplement to the cannonade of yesterday; and the two taken together, exhibit the coolness and gallantry of our officers and men in the most favourable light. All have done their duty and done it nobly. It will be my pride, in a more circumstantial report of both actions, to dwell upon particular instances of individual distinction.

It affords me peculiar pleasure to report that the field-work opposite to Matamoras has sustained itself handsomely during a cannonade and bombardment of one hundred and sixty hours. But the pleasure is alloyed with profound regret at the loss of its heroic and indomitable commander, Major Brown, who died to-day from the effect of a shell. His loss would be a severe one to the service at any time, but to the army under my orders, it is indeed irreparable. One officer and one non-commissioned officer killed, and ten men wounded, comprise all the casualties incident to this severe bombardment.

I inadvertently omitted to mention the capture of a large number of pack-mules left in the Mexican camp."

"So confident," says Captain Henry, in his interesting work, 'Campaign Sketches of the War with Mexico,' "were the Mexicans of victory, that Ampudia, speaking to Captain Thornton, who was then their prisoner, said, 'it was utterly impossible it could be otherwise; that their numbers alone were sufficient, independent of those *veteran* regiments.' General La Vega said, that 'if he had any sum of money in camp he should have considered it as safe as if at the city of Mexico; and he would have bet any amount that no ten thousand men could have driven them off.'"

Our loss in this action was three officers and thirty-six men killed, and twelve officers and fifty-nine men wounded. The loss of the enemy in killed, wounded, and missing, was not less than two thousand, taking the two days fighting together.

On the morning after the battle, General Taylor, with characteristic humanity, sent to Matamoras for Mexican surgeons to attend to their wounded, and for men to bury their dead. The American army was occupied at the same time upon the same mournful duty.

On the 11th General Taylor again left Fort Brown for Point Isabel, in order to arrange with Commodore Conner the plan of a combined land and naval attack upon the Mexican posts on the Rio Grande. While at the Point, he despatched a hasty letter to Washington, from which we make the following extracts: "I avail myself of this brief time at my command to report that the main body of the army is now occupying its former position opposite Matamoras. The Mexican forces are almost disorganized, and I shall lose no time in investing Matamoras, and opening the navigation of the river." * * * "I have exchanged a sufficient number of prisoners to recover the command of Captain Thornton. The wounded prisoners have been sent to Matamoras; the wounded officers on their parole. General Vega and a few others have been sent to New Orleans, having declined a parole, and will be reported to Major-General Gaines. I am not conversant with the usages of war in such cases, and beg that such provision may be made for these prisoners as may be authorized by law Our own prisoners

Capture of Barita.

have been treated with great kindness by the Mexican officers."

On the morning of the 13th he started for camp with an escort of dragoons, but having been met by an express with the information that large bodies of fresh troops had arrived at Matamoras, and that the enemy was concentrating troops at Barita, he returned to the Point. Here he found a newly arrived detachment of troops from New Orleans, including regulars and volunteers from Louisiana and Alabama, an accession which enabled him to withdraw from the Point a force of six hundred men with a train of artillery, two hundred and fifty wagons, and a large quantity of military and other stores. With this force he set out on the morning of the 14th for Fort Brown. He had previously arranged a plan for an attack upon Barita, a small town near the mouth of the Rio Grande, on the Mexican side of the river. This was executed by Lieutenant-Colonel Wilson, who captured the place without opposition. It speedily became a place of importance as the depot of the new base of operations, being the first high land reached in ascending the river above hurricane tides, and in a military point of view, commanding every thing around it, and commanded by nothing.

Want of the necessary means of transportation prevented General Taylor from crossing the Rio Grande to attack Matamoras until the 17th. On that day Colonel Twiggs was ordered to cross above the city, whilst Colonel Wilson was to make a demonstration from Barita. The Mexicans then attempted to induce General Taylor to agree to an armistice, that they might be able to carry off the public stores and munitions of war with which

Matamoras was filled, but General Taylor was too well versed in Mexican cunning to be cajoled. He stated that he had offered an armistice a month before, which Ampudia had declined; that he had neither invited nor provoked hostilities, but that he would not now suspend them while he was receiving large reinforcements; that the possession of Matamoras was now necessary to his troops, but that the Mexican army might retire, leaving behind them public property of every description. The Mexican General Reguena promised to return with an answer at three o'clock but failed to keep his word; the time of his mission and the interval allowed for his answer, being employed by Arista in throwing the public stores into the river, burying artillery in wells, and concealing other portions of the public property in and about the city. In the evening, General Taylor, finding that no answer had been returned, finished his preparations for crossing early in the morning, while Arista retreated from the city, taking with him two pieces of artillery and four thousand men, and leaving behind his sick and wounded.

On the morning of the 18th Captain Bliss had an interview with the prefect of the town, and demanded its surrender, and all the public stores therein. The prefect replied to the demand "that General Taylor could march his troops into the town at any time that might suit his convenience." While this conversation was going on, Colonel Twiggs was crossing with his troops above the town, his band playing "Yankee Doodle." The other troops crossed at Matamoras, and the star-spangled banner speedily waved over the walls of Fort Paredes.

Description of Matamoras.

The best description of the taking of Matamoras that has yet appeared is given in the following sketch, by an officer of the army, who like many of the gallant warriors now in Mexico, wields a pen with no less ability than he wears his sword. He says, "We reached this point on the 25th of May. The country through which we passed was lovely in the extreme—being as level as a ball-room floor, and full of little chaparrals and muskeet groves. Our road, though not exactly following the meanderings of the river, touched its banks often enough to obtain water every mile or two. The citizens were friendly to us, and showed little displeasure at the invasion. In fact, some of them expressed their wish that the country should be governed by Americans or some other people, that would guaranty them a liberal or stable government, so much had they been annoyed by the internal convulsions of their own. At every house we found three or four men, which induced me to believe that the press-gang had met with very poor success among them. They say that it is not their disposition to play the soldier at any time, particularly the present, and when the call is made for troops they leave their homes in possession of the women, and find business in the chaparral. They are a happy, simple people, whose aim seems to be to make provision for to-day, leaving to-morrow to look out for itself. All along the road they were found waiting with milk, a sort of bread, which they call *tortillias*, cheese, *poloncas*, or maple sugar, and a sort of liquor resembling, in looks and taste, San Croix rum. We paid them liberally for all we obtained, which to them must have presented a strong contrast to the Mexican soldiery, who spread dismay and devastation among their own people wherever they go. It seems to have been the desire of every man in our ranks to make the line of disparity between the American and Mexican soldier as palpable as possible; and the good effect of such conduct, if not immediately developed, will in the course of time be more apparent. Our march was very heavy, particularly during the day we left the Baritas, and some of our young men were very much used up. Two from company A were so much affected by the scorching sun as to be unable to proceed farther, and stopped at the house of a Mexican, where they received the utmost kindness and attention during the night, and were furnished with horses in the morning to catch up with us.

It was about ten o'clock in the morning when we reached the town of Matamoras, though its white buildings, so different from those we had passed on the route, had attracted the eyes long before that time. There was something far more attractive to the eye than the white buildings of the town—something to awaken a thrill of pleasure in the breasts of the whole regiment—the *stripes* and *stars* were majestically floating in the breeze from the highest point in Matamoras, and between the river and the town hundreds and hundreds of white tents were pitched in such admirable order as to induce the beholder to think it a great town.

As we entered the town at the east end, thousands of people sallied out of their houses to look upon us, whose looks more bespoke a welcome to their own army than to that of the invaders. At many a half-opened door or window was to be seen the head of a senora, whose timidity or modesty (albeit they allow so little to the

Mexicans) forbade their emerging into the streets. Some of these women are indeed beautiful, though a great majority are indolent, slovenly, and destitute of that female delicacy which characterizes our own women. Their common dress is a white muslin skirt, tied quite loosely around the body, without any bodice; their chemise being the only covering for their breasts, in which they wear their jewelry and cross. I did not see one pair of stockings in all the town. From this style of dressing you will infer that pride of dress gives way to comfort and ease, and that, too, in a greater degree than I think the largest liberty would warrant them indulging in. I went into a house yesterday evening, occupied by an old man and two daughters, both speaking a sufficiency of English to be understood. After being seated for a few moments, the eldest of the daughters went to the bed and brought to me a lovely and interesting child, as white almost as any of our own people. She informed me that she was married about two years ago to a Texan prisoner, and that he had been killed whilst fighting under General Taylor. She spoke in the highest terms of her deceased lord, and seemed to worship his image in the child. She is a lovely creature, and, I think, deeply devoted to our cause.

Matamoras is a much handsomer place than I expected to find it. It covers two miles square, though by no means as compact as an American city—every house except those around the public square, has a large garden attached. The houses in the business part of the town are built after the American fashion, though seldom exceeding two stories in height. All the windows to these buildings are grated from top to bottom with iron bars, and half of the door only opens for admittance, which gives them the appearance of prisons more than business houses. The public square is in the centre of the town, and must have been laid off by an American or European, for the Mexicans never could have laid it out with such beauty and precision. On the four sides of the square, the houses are built close together, as in block, and are of the same size and height, with the exception of the cathedral, which, though unfinished, still towers above the others. In these houses are sold dry goods, groceries, and every kind of wares, with now and then an exchange or coffee-house. They are principally occupied by Europeans, and you can hear French, English, Spanish, and German spoken at the same time. After leaving the public square on either side, the houses decrease in size and beauty for two or three squares, when the small reed and thatched huts commence, and continue to the extreme limits of the place.

In walking through the streets, my attention was attracted to a house, in the door of which stood, or leaned, two half-naked Mexicans, so wobegone as to cause me to halt. On my nearing the door, a most disagreeable stench almost induced me to recede. I mustered courage to enter the door. On the floor, lying upon mats, without covering, were near fifty Mexicans, wounded in the late engagements, attended by some ten or twelve women. The smell of the place was insufferable, and I had to leave it. The next door was the same, and so on for about twenty houses. A friend of mine called my attention to a room in which there were at least forty of these miserable objects, and this room was scarcely twelve feet square. There was not positively room for the nurses

Colonel Twiggs governor of Matamoras.

to attend them. Some had lost a leg, others an arm, and some both legs and arms. I noticed one who will certainly get well, whose legs were shot off within two or three inches above the knees, and he seemed to me to have a greater flow of spirits than some who had only flesh wounds. I said to him that had his wounds been made by a Mexican shot, he would have been dead, to which he replied, 'The American shot was very good— no poisonous copper in them!' One had died just before I had entered the room, and they were making preparations to carry him out. He had been shot in the mouth by a rifle ball, which passed under the left ear, and he had lived from the 9th up to this time. There are between three hundred and fifty and four hundred of these horrid objects in this place, and the sight of them would induce many a stout heart to lament the horrors of war. These men give the number of killed and wounded on the 9th much greater than the Americans ever claimed,—some say twelve hundred, and some, fifteen hundred,—but enough of them."

Colonel Twiggs was appointed governor of Matamoras, and immediately afterwards the prefect or former governor retired in disgust. Don Jesus Cardenus, for that was his name, appears to have been distinguished for his tyranny and his hatred to foreigners. The only care he expressed in surrendering the city was whether he could retain his office; the privileges or interests of the citizens being matters of no consequence to him.

General Taylor issued orders to his men to respect strictly the private property of the citizens, and permitted the latter to go on with their business as usual, prohibiting only the sale of intoxicating liquors. "The people had been told," says Captain Henry, in his Campaign Sketches, "they would be persecuted 'for conscience' sake;' that we would tolerate no religion but the protestant; and their priests have added all the fuel to the flame they could to produce the impression among these poor, ignorant creatures that we were a set of savage barbarians. Our acts, both civil and military, and now religious, will prove the contrary, and will open their eyes to the magnitude of the attempted deception.

The behaviour of our army after the victory is as highly honourable as the victories themselves. In taking possession of Matamoras we have not interfered with either the civil or religious rights of the inhabitants. Their courts of justice are still held, the most perfect respect is paid to law and order, and every infraction of either is severely punished. The army instead of entering the city as conquerors, encamped quietly in the suburbs. Instead of taking possession of their houses for our men, we remain under *miserable* canvass, which affords no protection from the storm, and scarcely shade to protect the soldier from the noonday sun. Many have *no tents*, and yet, under these circumstances no building is occupied: those taken for storehouses and public offices are regularly rented. By such conduct we have restored confidence to the people; the citizens mingle freely among us, walk through our camp, and feel sure of protection. Such conduct should make our countrymen proud of their army."

On the day following the taking of Matamoras, Lieutenant-Colonel Garland, with all the cavalry of the army, about two hundred and fifty dragoons and Rangers,

Pursuit of Arista.

started in pursuit of the retreating Mexicans, with orders to harass their march, and to capture prisoners and baggage. He succeeded in capturing a small rear party, after a skirmish, in which two Mexicans were killed and twenty-two taken prisoners, and one wagon with ammunition and clothing of an artillery company. The army of Arista was twenty-four hours in advance of this pursuing party, retreating in good order. The Americans having stopped at a *ranche*, the proprietor asked Captain Graham, with some appearance of astonishment, whither they were going. He was told that they were pursuing the retreating Mexican army. His astonishment was now still more increased, as he asserted that General Arista had stopped at his house on the night before, and had informed him that he had conquered the Americans, and was then on his way to Mexico to bear the news. The scarcity of water, with the barrenness of the country, and the jaded condition of the horses, compelled Colonel Garland to return on the 22d, and his pursuit of Arista closes the history of the opening of the war on the banks of the Rio Grande.

Large numbers of volunteers, called out by the government to reinforce the gallant commander, having arrived on the Rio Grande, General Taylor determined to move forward into Mexico, that they might not become dispirited by inaction. He despatched Colonel Wilson to scour the country in advance, and if possible to capture some of the Mexican towns near the river. This party soon got possession of Mier, Reynosa, and Camargo. The last named town, it had been directed, should be entered by a party of Texan Rangers from the rear, while a small party of regulars should approach it in front. The steamer containing the regulars was groping along at night a little south of the town, the pilot being altogether ignorant of the river, and the commander equally doubtful as to his reception by the townsmen. A light was seen glimmering on shore. The pilot neared it, and demanded to know in Spanish, "De quien es ese rancho?"

"'Tis my rancho," answered a good Yankee voice from out the chaparral. "'Tis my rancho, and who has any claims against it?"

"If you are an American, come on board."

"I will at once, soldier," said a stalwart man, stepping on the deck of the steamer. "I hail you in these parts, for I have been sleeping out some dozen nights, afraid of the treachery of the Mexicans; not that I fear them in a *fair fight*, of a dozen or more at me at once, but I could not stand five hundred."

Here was an enterprising American, full of patriotism, on "the search for town sites on the Rio Grande;" he knew the people well, and ere the day had fairly dawned, he had completed all the preliminaries of the surrender of Camargo, and at the head or the heel of our troops, as suited his humour best, he entered the city.*

Captain Duncan was sent forward on the 14th of August, with a small command, to Seralvo, sixty miles above Mier, for the purpose of making a reconnoissance. On the road, half way to Seralvo, he entered Punta Aguada, a town of four hundred inhabitants, said to be the head-quarters of Canales, and in which Captain Duncan expected to find some of his robber band. His

---

* Our Army at Monterey.

Captain Duncan's adventure, and Capture of Seralvo.

force was divided, marched into the town from all sides, and met in the centre, without alarming the people, who were now found to be engaged in an absorbing fandango. The consternation caused by the entrance of the Rangers into the ball-room, can be better imagined than described. The gallant captain, however, ordered the music to proceed, led off the dance with the belle of the room, and then, bidding them adieu, gained quiet possession of Seralvo before daybreak.

On the 18th of August, General Taylor having learned the nature of the route from Captain Duncan, organized the regular army, and ordered General Worth to take up the line of march for Seralvo on the next day.

The first division of the army, commanded by General Twiggs, consisted of the second dragoons, first, second, third, and fourth regiments of infantry, and Bragg's and Ridgely's artillery. The second division, under General Worth, consisted of the artillery battalion serving as infantry, the fifth, seventh, and eighth infantry, Duncan's battery, and Captain Blanchard's Louisiana volunteers.

On the 6th of August, General Taylor moved to join the advance under General Worth at Seralvo, leaving General Patterson in command at Camargo. At Seralvo it was first learned definitely that Ampudia had arrived at Monterey with a large force, and that the city was perfectly fortified, and would make a stout defense. The march to Monterey was now arranged in every particular. Major-General Butler arrived, and the volunteer division was concentrated in the vicinity of Seralvo. It was composed of the first Mississippi regiment, under Colonel Jefferson Davis, the first Tennessee, under

Arrangements of Forces.

Colonel Campbell, the first Ohio, under Colonel A. M. Mitchell, the Baltimore battalion, under Lieutenant-Colonel W. H. Watson. On the 11th September, the following order was issued:

"1. As the army may expect to meet resistance in the further advance towards Monterey, it is necessary that its march should be conducted with all proper precaution to meet attack and secure the baggage and supplies.

From this point, the following will be the order of march, until otherwise directed:

2. All the pioneers of the army consolidated into one party, will march early to-morrow on the route to Marin, for the purpose of repairing the roads, and rendering it practicable for artillery and wagons. The pioneers of each division will be under a subaltern, to be especially detailed for the duty, and the whole be under command of Captain Craig, third infantry, who will report to head-quarters for instructions. This pioneer party will be covered by a squadron of dragoons, and Captain McCulloch's company of Rangers. Two officers of topographical engineers, to be detailed by Captain Williams, will accompany the party for the purpose of examining the route. Two wagons will be provided by the quartermaster's department for the transportation of the tools, provisions, and knapsacks of the pioneer party.

3. The first division will march on the 13th instant, to be followed on successive days by the second division and field division of volunteers. The head-quarters will march with the first division. Captain Gillespie, with half of his company, will report to Major-General Butler; the other half, under the first lieutenant, to Brigadier-General Worth. These detachments will be

employed for outposts and videttes, and as expresses between the columns and head-quarters.

4. The subsistence supplies will be divided between the three columns, the senior commissary of each division receipting for the stores and being charged with their care and management. The senior commissaries of divisions will report to Captain Waggaman for this duty.

5. Each division will be followed immediately by its baggage train and supply train, with a strong rear-guard. The ordnance train under Captain Ramsay will march with the second division, between its baggage and supply train, and will come under the protection of the guard of that division. The medical supplies will, in like manner, march with the first division.

6. The troops will take eight days' rations and forty rounds of ammunition. All surplus arms and accoutrements, resulting from casualties on the road, will be deposited with Lieutenant Stewart, left in charge of the depot at this place, who will give certificates of deposit to the company commanders.

7. The wagons appropriated for transportation of water, will not be required, and will be turned over to the quartermaster's department for general purposes.

8. Two companies of the Mississippi regiment will be designated for the garrison of this place. All sick and disabled men, unfit for the march, will be left behind, under charge of a medical officer to be selected for this duty by the medical director."

The first division accordingly took up the line of march on the 13th, the army finding the Mexican general, Torrejon, with a large cavalry force constantly in

Arrival of General Henderson with Texas troops.

their vicinity. On the 14th General Ampudia issued from Monterey an address to his soldiers—in which he promised them certain victory, and volunteered for them the assurance to the government that they were worthy sons of the immortal Hidalgo, Morelo, Iturbide, and others who knew how to die combating for the independence of their cherished country." On the following day he issued another address, holding out inducements to General Taylor's troops to desert. On the 16th and 17th the army was concentrated at Marin, and rested there from the fatiguing march. The Spanish consul at Monterey sent a messenger to General Taylor to know if the property of foreigners would be respected. General Taylor informed him that he would be responsible for nothing in case the town was taken by an assault. On the 18th the army resumed its march, and reached the town of San Francisco. On this day General Henderson joined General Taylor with Wood's and Hays' regiment of mounted Texans, which numbered eleven hundred men. The old padre of the village of San Francisco informed General Taylor that the most determined opposition would be made at Monterey, General Ampudia having determined only to surrender the city with his life.

On the 19th of September the army reached the vicinity of Monterey. The troops marched in order of battle; first General Taylor and staff, with a number of officers; then followed the advanced guard, McCulloch's and Gillespie's rangers. The brigade of General Henderson came next; then the first division under General Twiggs, and the second under General Worth, and lastly the volunteer division under General Butler. We

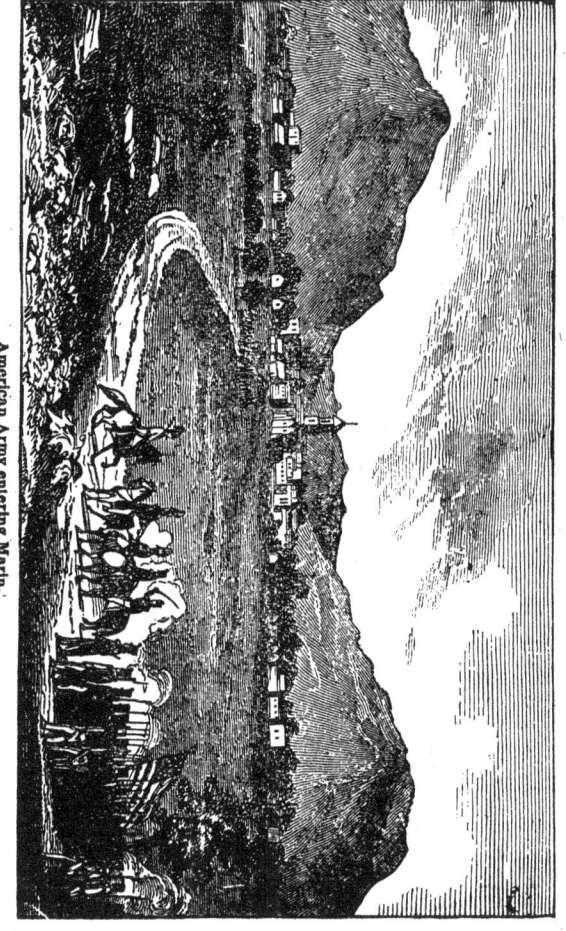

American Army entering Marin.

Account of arrival at Monterey.

give an extract respecting the arrival at Monterey, from Mr. Thorpe's valuable work, " Our Army at Monterey."

" The beautiful grove of St. Domingo was passed, when the city burst upon the sight in all its splendour. The mists still clung around the turrets of its churches, and enveloped its commanding heights; but the ascending sun constantly dissipated the veil, until palace and hill, barricade and fort, with long lines of tents and pendent flags presented themselves, as if floating in the pure ether with which they were surrounded. All was silent; not a breath of air stirred; dewy softness rested upon every thing. Suddenly a hot sulphurous smoke rose quickly from one of the bastions of the citadel, a heavy cannon-shot cleared the air with its hissing sound, and long before its booming sound was heard, two more in quick succession followed; one of the deadly missiles ricochetted directly over General Taylor's head, and, just beyond him, ploughed deeply in the earth.

A cry of exultation followed from those who witnessed it, which was taken up by the long lines of advancing troops, until it was carried miles in the rear, the shouts mingling strangely with the ten thousand echoes that were awakened among the mountains, by the firing of the heavy artillery that announced that the battle of Monterey had begun.

The first division accelerated its speed, and quickly arrived where General Taylor had halted, when it formed into order of battle; while this was being done, the gallant chieftain, surrounded by his staff, coolly, through his glass, examined the defenses of the city, when orders were issued for the army to encamp at the beautiful grove of St. Domingo, so recently passed.

General Taylor's despatch.

The attack upon Monterey was arranged to be made by two divisions of the army, acting separately and independently. General Taylor, assisted by General Butler, commanded that directed against the city itself while General Worth was detached to storm the Bishop's Palace, and the other forts outside of Monterey.

For the account of the conduct and achievements of the division under General Taylor, we have his own despatch, clear, succinct, and satisfactory, as are all the papers he has written concerning his operations.

"Sir:—I have now the honour to submit a detailed report of the recent operations before Monterey, resulting in the capitulation of that city.

The information received on the route from Seralvo, and particularly the continual appearance in our front of the Mexican cavalry, which had a slight skirmish with our advance at the village of Ramas, induced the belief, as we approached Monterey, that the enemy would defend that place. Upon reaching the neighbourhood of the city on the morning of the 19th of September, this belief was fully confirmed. It was ascertained that he occupied the town in force; that a large work had been constructed commanding all the northern approaches; and that the Bishop's Palace, and some heights in its vicinity near the Saltillo road, had also been fortified, and occupied with troops and artillery. It was known, from information previously received, that the eastern approaches were commanded by several small works in the lower edge of the city.

The configuration of the heights and gorges in the direction of the Saltillo road, as visible from the point attained by our advance on the morning of the 19th, led

View of the Bishop's Palace, Monterey.

me to suspect that it was practicable to turn all the
works in that direction, and thus cut off the enemy's
line of communication. After establishing my camp at
the 'Walnut Springs,' three miles from Monterey, the
nearest suitable position, it was, accordingly, my first
care to order a close reconnoissance of the ground in
question, which was executed on the evening of the
19th, by the engineer officers under the direction of
Major Mansfield. A reconnoissance of the eastern approaches was at the same time made by Captain Williams, topographical engineer. The examination made
by Major Mansfield proved the entire practicability of
throwing forward a column to the Saltillo road, and thus
turning the position of the enemy. Deeming this to be
an operation of essential importance, orders were given
to Brevet Brigadier-General Worth, commanding the
second division, to march with his command on the
20th ; to turn the hill of the Bishop's Palace : to occupy
a position on the Saltillo road, and to carry the enemy's
detached works in that quarter, where practicable. The
first regiment ef Texas mounted volunteers, under command of Colonel Hays, was associated with the second
division on this service. Captain Sanders, engineers,
and Lieutenant Meade, topographical engineers, were
also ordered to report to General Worth for duty with
his column.

At two o'clock P. M. on the 20th, the 2d division took
up its march. It was soon discovered, by officers who
were reconnoitering the town, and communicated to
General Worth, that its movement had been perceived,
and that the enemy was throwing reinforcements towards
the Bishop's Palace, and the height which commands it.

General Taylor's despatch.

To divert his attention as far as practicable, the 1st division, under Brigadier-General Twiggs, and field division of volunteers, under Major-General Butler, were displayed in front of the town until dark. Arrangements were made at the same time to place in battery, during the night, at a suitable distance from the enemy's main work, the citadel, two twenty-four-pound howitzers, and a ten-inch mortar, with a view to open a fire on the following day, when I proposed to make a diversion in favour of General Worth's movement. The 4th infantry covered this battery during the night. General Worth had in the mean time reached and occupied, for the night, a defensive position just without range of a battery above the Bishop's Palace, having made a reconnoissance as far as the Saltillo road.

Before proceeding to report the operations of the 21st and the following days, I beg leave to state that I shall mention in detail only those which were conducted against the eastern extremity of the city, or elsewhere, under my immediate direction, referring you for the particulars of General Worth's operations, which were entirely detached, to his own full report transmitted herewith.

Early on the morning of the 21st, I received a note from General Worth, written at half past nine o'clock the night before, suggesting what I had already intended, a strong diversion against the centre and left of the town, to favour his enterprise against the heights in rear. The infantry and artillery of the 1st division, and the field division of volunteers, were ordered under arms, and took the direction of the city, leaving one company of each regiment as a camp guard. The second dragoons, under Lieutenant-Colonel May, and Colonel Woods' regiment of Texas mounted volunteers, under the immediate direction of General Henderson, were directed to the right to support General Worth, if necessary, and to make an impression, if practicable, upon the upper quarter of the city. Upon approaching the mortar battery, the 1st and 3d regiments of infantry, and battalion of Baltimore and Washington volunteers, with Captain Bragg's field battery—the whole under the command of Lieutenant-Colonel Garland—were directed towards the lower part of the town, with orders to make a strong demonstration, and carry one of the enemy's advanced works, if it could be done without too heavy loss. Major Mansfield, engineers, and Captain Williams and Lieutenant Pope, topographical engineers, accompanied this column, Major Mansfield being charged with its direction, and the designation of points of attack.

In the mean time, the mortar, served by Captain Ramsay, of the ordnance, and the howitzer battery under Captain Webster, 1st artillery, had opened their fire upon the citadel, which was deliberately sustained, and answered from the work. General Butler's division had now taken up a position in rear of this battery, when the discharges of artillery, mingled finally with a rapid fire of small arms, showed that Lieutenant Garland's command had become warmly engaged. I now deemed it necessary to support this attack, and accordingly ordered the 4th infantry, and three regiments of General Butler's division, to march at once, by the left flank, in the direction of the advanced work at the lower extremity of the town, leaving one regiment (1st Kentucky) to cover the mortar and howitzer battery. By some mistake, two companies of the 4th infantry did not receive this order, and, consequently, did not join the advance companies until some time afterwards.

Lieutenant-Colonel Garland's command had approached the town in a direction to the right of the advanced work (No. 1,) at the north-eastern angle of the city, and the engineer officer, covered by skirmishers, had succeeded in entering the suburbs and gaining cover. The remainder of this command now advanced and entered the town under a heavy fire of artillery from the citadel and the works on the left, and of musketry from the houses and small works in front. A movement to the right was attempted, with a view to gain the rear of No. 1, and carry that work, but the troops were so much exposed to a fire which they could not effectually return, and had already sustained such severe loss, particularly in officers, that it was deemed best to withdraw them to a more secure position. Captain Backus, 1st infantry, however, with a portion of his own and other companies, had gained the roof of a tannery, which looked directly into the gorge of No. 1, and from which he poured a most destructive fire into that work and upon the strong building in its rear. This fire happily coincided in point of time with the advance of a portion of the volunteer division upon No. 1, and contributed largely to the fall of that strong and important work.

The three regiments of the volunteer division, under the immediate command of Major-General Butler, had in the mean time advanced in the direction of No. 1. The leading brigade, under Brigadier-General Quitman, continued its advance upon that work, preceded by three companies of the 4th infantry, while General Butler, with the 1st Ohio regiment, entered the town to the right. The companies of the 4th infantry had advanced within short range of the work, when they were received by a fire that almost in one moment struck down one-third of the officers and men, and rendered it necessary to retire and effect a conjunction with the two other companies then advancing. General Quitman's brigade, though suffering most severely, particularly in the Tennessee regiment, continued its advance, and finally carried the work in handsome style, as well as the strong building in its rear. Five pieces of artillery, a considerable supply of ammunition, and thirty prisoners, including three officers, fell into our hands.

Major-General Butler, with the 1st Ohio regiment, after entering the edge of the town, discovered that nothing was to be accomplished in his front, and at this point, yielding to the suggestions of several officers, I ordered a retrograde movement; but learning almost immediately from one of my staff, that the battery No. 1 was in our possession, the order was countermanded, and I determined to hold the battery and defenses already gained. General Butler, with the 1st Ohio regiment, then entered the town at a point farther to the left, and marched in the direction of the battery No. 2. While making an examination with a view to ascertain the possibility of carrying this second work by storm, the general was wounded and soon after compelled to quit the field. As the strength of No. 2, and the heavy musketry fire flanking the approach, rendered it impossible to carry it without great loss, the 1st Ohio regiment was withdrawn from the town.

Fragments of the various regiments engaged were

General Taylor's despatch.

now under cover of the captured battery and some buildings in its front and on the right. The field battery of Captains Bragg and Ridgely was also partially covered by the battery. An incessant fire was kept on this position from battery No. 2, and other works on its right, and from the citadel on all our approaches. General Twiggs, though quite unwell, joined me at this point, and was instrumental in causing the artillery captured from the enemy to be placed in battery, and served by Captain Ridgely, against No. 2, until the arrival of Captain Webster's howitzer battery, which took its place. In the mean time, I directed such men as could be collected of the 1st, 3d, and 4th regiments and Baltimore battalion, to enter the town, penetrating to the right, and carry the second battery if possible. This command, under Lieutenant-Colonel Garland, advanced beyond the bridge 'Purisima,' when, finding it impracticable to gain the rear of the second battery, a portion of it sustained themselves for some time in that advanced position; but as no permanent impression could be made at that point, and the main object of the general operation had been effected, the command, including a section of Captain Ridgely's battery, which had joined it, was withdrawn to battery No. 1. During the absence of this column, a demonstration of cavalry was reported in the direction of the citadel. Captain Bragg, who was at hand, immediately galloped with his battery to a suitable position, from which a few discharges effectually dispersed the enemy. Captain Miller, 1st infantry, was despatched with a mixed command to support the battery on this service. The enemy's lancers had previously charged upon the Ohio and a part

G neral Taylor's despatch.

of the Mississippi regiments, near some fields at a distance from the edge of the town, and had been repulsed with considerable loss. A demonstration of cavalry on the opposite side of the river was also dispersed in the course of *.ne afternoon by Captain Ridgely's battery, and the squadrons returned to the city. At the approach of evening all the troops that had been engaged were ordered back to the camp, except Captain Ridgely's battery and the regular infantry of the first division, who were detailed as a guard for the works during the night, under command of Lieutenant-Colonel Garland. One battalion of the 1st Kentucky regiment was ordered to reinforce this command. Intrenching tools were procured, and additional strength was given to the works, and protection to the men, by working-parties during the night, under the direction of Lieutenant Scarritt, engineers.

The main object proposed in the morning had been effected. A powerful diversion had been made to favour the operations of the 2d division, one of the enemy's advanced works had been carried, and we now had a strong foot-hold in the town. But this had not been accomplished without a very heavy loss, embracing some of our most gallant and accomplished officers. Captain Williams, topographical engineers; Lieutenants Terrett and Dilworth, 1st infantry; Lieutenant Woods, 2d infantry; Captains Morris and Field, Brevet Major Barbour, Lieutenants Irwin and Hazlitt, 3d infantry; Lieutenant Hoskins, 4th infantry; Lieutenant-Colonel Watson, Baltimore battalion; Captain Allen and Lieutenant Putnam, Tennessee regiment, and Lieutenant Hett, Ohio regiment, were killed, or have since

General Taylor's despatch.

died of wounds received in this engagement, while the number and rank of the officers wounded gives additional proof of the obstinacy of the contest, and the good conduct of our troops. The number of killed and wounded incident to the operations in the lower part of the city on the 21st is 394.

Early in the morning of this day (21st) the advance of the 2d division had encountered the enemy in force, and after a brief but sharp conflict, repulsed him with heavy loss. General Worth then succeeded in gaining a position on the Saltillo road, thus cutting the enemy's line of communication. From this position the two heights south of the Saltillo road were carried in succession, and the guns taken in one of them turned upon the Bishop's Palace. These important successes were fortunately obtained with comparatively small loss: Captain McKavett, 8th infantry, being the only officer killed.

The 22d day of September passed without any active operations in the lower part of the city. The citadel and other works continued to fire at parties exposed to their range, and at the work now occupied by our troops. The guard left in it the preceding night, except Captain Ridgely's company, was relieved at midday by General Quitman's brigade. Captain Bragg's battery was thrown under cover in front of the town, to repel any demonstration of cavalry in that quarter. At dawn of day the height above the Bishop's Palace was carried, and soon after meridian the palace itself was taken, and its guns turned upon the fugitive garrison. The object for which the 2d division was detached had thus been completely accomplished, and I felt confident that with a strong

General Taylor's despatch.

force occupying the road and heights in his rear, and a good position below the city in our possession, the enemy could not possibly maintain the town.

During the night of the 22d the enemy evacuated nearly all his defenses in the lower part of the city. This was reported to me early in the morning of the 23d, by General Quitman, who had already meditated an assault upon those works. I immediately sent instructions to that officer, leaving it to his discretion to enter the city, covering his men by the houses and walls, and advance carefully so far as he might deem prudent.

After ordering the remainder of the troops as a reserve, under the orders of Brigadier-General Twiggs, I repaired to the abandoned works, and discovered that a portion of General Quitman's brigade had entered the town, and were successfully forcing their way towards the principal plaza. I then ordered up the 2d regiment of Texas mounted volunteers, who entered the city, dismounted, and, under the immediate orders of General Henderson, co-operated with General Quitman's brigade. Captain Bragg's battery was also ordered up, supported by the 3d infantry, and after firing for some time at the cathedral, a portion of it was likewise thrown into the city. Our troops advanced from house to house, and from square to square, until they reached a street but one square in rear of the principal plaza, in and near which the enemy's force was mainly concentrated. This advance was conducted vigorously, but with due caution, and although destructive to the enemy, was attended with but small loss on our part. Captain Ridgely, in the mean time, had served a captured piece in battery No. 1 against the city, until the advance of our men rendered it imprudent to fire in the direction of the cathedral. I was now satisfied that we could operate successfully in the city, and that the enemy had retired from the lower portion of it to make a stand behind his barricades. As General Quitman's brigade had been on duty the previous night, I determined to withdraw the troops to the evacuated works, and concert with General Worth a combined attack upon the town. The troops accordingly fell back deliberately in good order, and resumed their original positions, General Quitman's brigade being relieved after nightfall by that of General Hamer. On my return to camp I met an officer with the intelligence that General Worth, induced by the firing in the lower part of the city, was about making an attack at the upper extremity, which had also been evacuated by the enemy to a considerable distance. I regretted that this information had not reached me before leaving the city, but still deemed it inexpedient to change my orders, and accordingly returned to camp. A note from General Worth, written at eleven o'clock P. M., informed me that he had advanced to within a short distance of the principal plaza, and that the mortar (which had been sent to his division in the morning) was doing good execution within effective range of the enemy's position.

Desiring to make no farther attempt upon the city without complete concert as to the lines and mode of approach, I instructed that officer to suspend his advance until I could have an interview with him on the following morning, at his head-quarters.

Early in the morning of the 24th I received through Colonel Moreno, a communication from General Ampudia, proposing to evacuate the town; which, with the answer, were forwarded with my first despatch. I arranged with Colonel Moreno a cessation of fire until twelve o'clock, at which hour I would receive the answer of the Mexican general at General Worth's headquarters, to which I soon repaired. In the mean time, General Ampudia had signified to General Worth his desire for a personal interview with me, to which I acceded, and which finally resulted in a capitulation, placing the town and materiel of war, with certain exceptions, in our possession.

For the operations of General Worth, we have the following account by an intelligent eye witness.

"At two P. M. of the 20th, General Worth marched from the camp, east of the town, in the direction of the heights west, McCulloch's and Gillespie's companies of rangers forming the reconnoitering party. At night, the division bivouacked almost within range of the guns stationed upon the highest point of the hill on which the Bishop's Palace is situated. At daylight of the 21st, the column was again in motion, and in a few moments, was turning the point of a ridge, which protruded out toward the enemy's guns, bringing us as near to them as their gunners could desire. They immediately opened upon the column with a howitzer and twelve-pounder, firing shell and round-shot as fast as they could discharge their pieces.

The road now wound in toward a gorge, but not far enough to be out of range of their guns, which still played upon us. Another ridge lay about three-fourths of a mile beyond the first, around the termination of which the road wound, bringing it under the lofty summit of a height which rises between Palace Hill and the mountains, which arise over us on the west, When the head of the column approached this ridge, a body of Mexican cavalry came dashing around that point to charge upon our advance. Captain Gillespie immediately ordered his men to dismount and place themselves in ambush. The enemy evidently did not perceive this manœuver; but the moment they came up, the Texans opened upon them a most destructive fire, unsaddling a number of them. McCulloch's company now dashed into them. Captain C. F. Smith's camp, and Captain Scott's camp of artillery, (acting as infantry,) and Lieutenant Longstreet's company of the eighth infantry, with another company of the same regiment, likewise charged upon the enemy. The Texan horsemen were soon engaged with them in a sort of hand-to-hand skirmish, in which a number of them fell, and one Texan was killed and two wounded.

Colonel Duncan now opened upon them with his battery of light artillery, pouring a few discharges of grape upon them, and scattering them like chaff. Several men and horses fell under this destructive fire. I saw one horse and rider bound some feet into the air, and both fell dead and tumbled down the steep. The foot companies above named then rushed up the steep, and fired over the ridge at the retreating enemy, a considerable body of whom were concealed from our view, around the point of the hill. About thirty of the enemy were killed in this skirmish, and among them a captain, who, with two or three others, fell in the road. The captain was wounded in three places, the last shot hitting him in the forehead. He fought gallantly to the last, and I am sorry that I cannot learn his name.

Cavalry charge on the morning of the 21st.

Operations of General Worth.

The light batteries, one of which is commanded by Lieutenant Mackall, were now driven upon the slope of the ridge, and the howitzers opened upon the height of Palace Hill. A few shots only were thrown, before the enemy commenced firing with a nine-pounder from the height immediately over the right of the column, aiming at Duncan's batteries. The several regiments took positions, and a few more shells were thrown towards Palace Hill, but did no execution. The nine-pounder continued to throw its shot with great precision at our batteries, one ball falling directly in the midst of the pieces, but, fortunately, hitting neither men nor guns. Finding his batteries thus exposed, and unable to effect any thing, Colonel Duncan removed his command to a rancho about half a mile farther up the Saltillo road, where General Worth took up his position, after ordering the foot regiments to form along the fence near the point of the ridge. The artillery battalion, 5th, 7th, and 8th infantry, and the Louisiana volunteers, remained in this position about two hours, directly under fire of the enemy's guns. The balls fell directly in their midst all this time without wounding a man! To begin with, the Mexicans manage their artillery in battery as well as the Americans do—this, I believe, is now conceded by every officer.

At half-past ten, the column moved towards the general's position. At this time, Captain McKavett of the 8th infantry, was shot through the heart by a nine-pound ball, and a private of the 5th infantry was severely wounded in the thigh, and he died the next morning. About fifty Mexicans now appeared upon the side hill over the moving column, and fired at our troops some hundred musket-shot, without doing any harm. The division deployed into the position pointed out, and remained an hour or two, when Captain C. F. Smith of the artillery battalion, with his own company, and Captain Scott's, together with four companies of Texan Rangers on foot, were ordered to storm the second height. This the gallant officer cheerfully undertook, and was followed with enthusiasm by the officers and men of his command. It was considered on all sides to be a dangerous undertaking, and his party was regarded most emphatically as a *forlorn hope*. That the height would be taken no one doubted, but that many brave fellows would fall in the attempt seemed inevitable. The distance to be climbed, after reaching the foot of the hill, was about a quarter of a mile; a part of the way almost perpendicular, through thorn-bushes and over sharp-pointed rocks and loose sliding stones.

The 7th infantry commanded by Captain Miles, was ordered to support Captain Smith's party, and by marching directly to the foot of the height, arrived before Captain Smith, who had been ordered to take a circuitous route. Captain Miles sent up Lieutenant Gantt, with a detachment of men upon the hill-side, to divert the attention of the enemy from Captain Smith's command, which could not yet be seen. The 7th had already sustained a heavy fire of grape and round-shot, as they forded the San Juan, which winds round the foot of the height, and which fell like a shower of hail in their ranks without killing a man. Lieutenant Gantt's party were greeted with grape and round-shot, which cut the shrubs, and tore up the loose stones about the ranks, without killing any one; but the gallant young officer came within an inch of being killed by a cannon-shot, which ran down the steep and filled his face with fragments of rock, dust, and gravel. The fire was accompanied by a constant discharge of musketry, the enemy covering the upper part of the hill-side ; but the detachment continued to move up, driving the Mexicans back, until they were recalled.

Captain Smith's party now arrived and moved up the hill, the rangers in advance, and did not halt for an instant until the Mexicans were driven from the summit. Whilst this was going on, Colonel Persifer F. Smith, who commanded the 5th and 7th infantry—the 5th with Blanchard's Louisiana boys, under Major Martin Scott, had been ordered to support the whole—gave orders for these commands to pass around on each side and storm the fort, which was situated about half a mile back of the summit on the same ridge and commanded the Bishop's Palace. Such a foot-race as now ensued has seldom if ever been seen; the Louisiana boys making tremendous strides to be in with the foremost. Captain Smith had the gun which he took upon the height, run towards the breast-works, and fired into it. Then came Colonel P. F. Smith's men, with a perfect rush, firing and cheering— the 5th and 7th, and Louisianians, reaching the ridge above nearly at the same time. The Mexicans fired at us with grape, but it did not cause an instant's hesitation in our ranks. Our men ran and fired, and cheered until they reached the work, the foremost entering at one end while the Mexicans, about a thousand in number, left the other in retreat. The colours of the 5th infantry were instantly raised, and scarcely were they up before those of the 7th were alongside. The three commands entered the fort together—so close was the race—the 5th a little in advance. J. W. Miller, of Blanchard's company, was among the first four or five who entered. The three commands may be said to have come out even in the race, for the 7th was not five seconds behind. In less than five minutes the gun found in the fort was thundering away at the Bishop's Palace.

On the morning of the 21st, Colonel Childs of the artillery battalion, with three of his companies—one commanded by Captain Vinton, another by Captain J. B. Scott, and the third by Lieutenant Ayres—and three companies of the 8th infantry—company A, commanded by Lieutenant Longstreet and Wainright; company B, by Lieutenant Halloway and Merchant; company D, by Captain Schrivner and Lieutenant Montgomery—was ordered to take the summit of Palace Hill.

The colonel left the camp at three o'clock A.M., and climbed the mountain through the chaparral, and up the steep rocks, with such secrecy, that at daybreak he was within one hundred yards of the breastwork of sandbags before he was discovered. Three of the artillerymen having rushed ahead too fast, found themselves in the hands of the Mexicans. They surrendered, and were shot down with the very pieces they had given up. I saw the poor fellows lying there.

Colonel Staniford went up at daylight with the balance of the 8th, and Major Scott led up the 5th. The Louisiana troops were on the hill, with the 5th, at 8 A.M. One of Duncan's howitzers, in charge of Lieutenant Rowland, was dragged up, or rather *lifted* up, and opened on the palace, which was filled with troops. The Mexicans charged on the howitzer, but were driven back. A constant firing was kept up for several hours, particu-

Storming of the Bishop's Palace.

farly by Blanchard's men, who left a dozen Mexicans dead upon the hill-side. At length a charge was ordered, and our men rushed down upon the palace, entered a hole in a door that had been blocked up, but opened by the howitzer, and soon cleared the work of the few Mexicans who remained. Lieutenant Ayres was the lucky one who first reached the halyards and lowered the flag. One eighteen-pound brass piece, a beautiful article, manufactured in Liverpool in 1842, and a short brass twelve-pound howitzer, were captured, with a large quantity of ammunition, and some muskets and lances.

The fort adjoining the palace walls is not complete, but is very neatly constructed as far as it is built. The killed on our side, in taking the palace, were seven— wounded, twelve. Lieutenant Wainright was wounded in the side and arm by a musket-ball. Colonel Childs, Captain Vinton, Captain Blanchard, Lieutenant Longstreet, Lieutenant Clark, (adjutant of the 8th,) Lieutenant Ayres, Lieutenant McCown, and the two Nicholls, seem to have been the heroes of the day. The two latter performed prodigies, and not only Judge Nicholls, but old Louisiana may well be proud of such sons. The Mexicans lost at least thirty killed.

Yesterday morning the whole division under General Worth entered the town on this side, and have been fighting there ever since. The heart of the city is nothing but one fortification, the thick walls being pierced for muskets and cannon, and placed so as to rake the principal streets. The roofs being flat, and the front walls rising three or four feet above the roof, of course every street has a line of breastworks on each side. A ten-inch mortar came around from General

Taylor last evening, and it is now placed in the largest plaza, to which our troops have fought step by step and from house to house. Duncan's batteries are in town, and the present impression is that the place will soon be taken. General Worth has gained all the strongholds that command the city, and has pushed the enemy as far as they can go without falling into General Taylor's hands on the other side of the city. All this has been done with the loss of only about seventy killed and wounded."

At noon on the 22d, while the American troops were closely engaged in the lower part of the city, General Taylor received by a flag a communication from the governor of the state of New Leon, asking him to grant a sufficient time for the inhabitants to leave the city; which General Taylor declined. Early on the morning of the 24th, a flag was received from the town, bearing a communication from General Ampudia, proposing an evacuation of the city and fort, with all the personel and materiel of war. General Taylor, in reply, declined the proposition, and demanded a complete surrender of the town and garrison, offering in consideration of the gallant defense that had been made, to allow the garrison to retire to the interior after laying down its arms, on condition of not serving again during the war. A cessation of hostilities, until twelve o'clock, was arranged.

Before that hour, however, General Ampudia had signified to General Worth his desire for a personal interview with General Taylor, for the purpose of making some definitive arrangement. An interview was accordingly appointed for one o'clock, and resulted in the

Terms of capitulation.

naming of a commission to draw up articles of agreement regulating the withdrawal of the Mexican forces, and a temporary cessation of hostilities. The commissioners named by the Mexican general-in-chief were Generals Ortega and Requena, and Don Emanuel M. Llano, governor of New Leon. Those named on the American side were General Worth, General Henderson, governor of Texas, and Colonel Davis, Mississippi volunteers.

This commission finally settled upon the articles of capitulation. The details of the negotiations are reserved as part of the personal history of the commissioners, and will be found in another place.

By the terms of capitulation, it was agreed that the Mexican officers should retain their side arms, and the infantry and cavalry their arms and accoutrements, the artillery one field battery of six pieces; that, surrendering the city, fortifications, cannon, munitions of war, and public stores, to General Taylor, they should evacuate the city and retire, within seven days, beyond the line formed by the pass of Rinconada, the city of Linares, and San Fernando de Presas; and that this line should not be crossed by the Americans before the expiration of eight weeks, unless the respective governments should refuse to ratify the terms of this truce.

Monterey and its fortifications were armed with forty-two pieces of cannon, well supplied with ammunition, and manned with a force of at least seven thousand troops of the line, and from two to three thousand irregulars. The force under General Taylor was four hundred and twenty-five officers, and six thousand two hundred and twenty men. Our artillery consisted of one ten-inch mortar, two twenty-four-pound howitzers, and four light field batteries of four guns each—the mortar being the only piece suited to the operations of a siege. The American loss was twelve officers and one hundred eight men killed, thirty-one officers and three hundred and thirty-seven men wounded. The loss of the enemy was much greater.

The storming of Monterey requires no comment. A city surrounded by high massive walls which supported strong redoubts, with every street swept by cross fires of artillery, and every house a fortification in itself, was attacked and carried by an army numbering scarcely more than half of the defenders, inferior in artillery and small arms, and obliged to divide its small force to resist the cannonade of another fortification, the Bishop's Palace, nearly as strong as the city itself.

Such an event can only be attributed to the national coolness and intrepidity of the assailants, aided by their good discipline, the example of their officers and the unsurpassed ability of their commanding general. The glory of the victors at Cuidad Rodrigo pales before that of the Americans at Monterey.

The troops of General Taylor proved themselves to be possessed of a still higher attribute of the soldier than the most fearless bravery: the finer feelings of men calm in the moment of victory, and possessed of minds principled of humanity, which the most desperate resistance could not excite to a single deed of cruelty. In their retreat from Monterey, the enemy destroyed every thing in their route that might be of service to the invading army. The water streams were stopped or filled up, **the wells destroyed, provisions carefully removed, and**

Paredes.

even private property ruthlessly consumed by the torch. Meanwhile, they made every effort to organize a new army in the interior, and declared that the loss of Monterey was owing only to the incapacity of Ampudia, who was ordered to be tried by court-martial. General Herrera had been president of Mexico when the war was first threatened, but his inclination to avoid hostilities had caused him to be deprived of power, and Paredes assumed the reins of government, and the responsibility of the war. Being unsuccessful, however, he lost caste with his countrymen, who now began to look for another ruler. Several leaders presented themselves, each at the head of a small

Santa Anna lands at Vera Cruz.

army, and each breathing implacable hostility to the United States. In the mean time a party had arisen favourable to the recall of Santa Anna, who had been exiled in 1844, and was living at Havana. A proclamation was issued at Mexico, inviting the return of all Mexicans faithful to their country, Santa Anna being named as one, and appointed general-in-chief; and calling for a meeting of a congress of representatives to be chosen according to the repudiated constitution of 1824, under which Mexico was a federal republic, similar to that of the United States. This was the production of General Salas, who was the avowed supporter of Santa Anna, and who had been elevated to the presidency.

On the 16th of August, Santa Anna landed at Vera Cruz, having been allowed to pass the American blockading squadron, in the British mail steamer Arab. On the 14th of September, when he had reached Ayotla, he received and accepted a commission appointing him supreme dictator. On the next day he entered the capital and was received with every demonstration of joy and confidence. He issued a proclamation calling upon the people to support him in defending the country. The American government had refused to sanction the conditional armistice of eight weeks, provided for by one of the articles of capitulation at Monterey, and directed General Taylor to resume hostilities. That officer therefore addressed a letter to Santa Anna notifying him of the renewal of hostilities, and making a request for the release of certain prisoners at San Luis Potosi. Santa Anna acknowledged the receipt of the letter in a courteous and dignified manner, acquiesced in the conclusion of the armistice, and complied in a liberal manner with

Taylor marches to Victoria.

Santa Anna.

the request concerning the prisoners. He soon found himself at the head of an army of twenty thousand men, who regarded him as invincible.

Meanwhile, the Americans were not idle. General Worth had moved with fifteen hundred men upon Saltillo and taken it, and Parras had fallen into the hands of General Wool. In December, General Santa Anna threatened to attack the American forces in Saltillo, and General Urrea was reported to be in the vicinity of Victoria. General Taylor marched to the latter place, which he reached on the 30th of December. Here he received a letter from General Scott, requesting a large detachment of his troops, which was to increase the army destined to capture Vera Cruz. No soldier could feel more keenly than General Taylor the di appointment to which he was thus subjected: to lose the veterans who had won for him so great glory, and be at the same time reduced from a victorious position to one of comparative inaction. Yet he cheerfully obeyed the command. At parting with his troops he issued the following address to them:

"It is with deep sensibility that the commanding general finds himself separated from the troops he so long commanded. To those corps, regular and volunteer, who have shared with him the active services of the field, he feels the attachment due to such associations, while to those who are making their first campaign, he must express his regret that he cannot participate with them in its eventful scenes. To all, both officers and men, he extends his heartfelt wishes for their continued success and happiness, confident that their achievements on another theatre will redound to the credit of their country and to them."

After they had left him, he again established his headquarters at Monterey, where he remained until February. In that month, his force was raised to nearly five thousand, by the arrival of a considerable number of volunteers. He then marched from Monterey to Agua Nueva, a place eighteen miles below Saltillo.

He retired, however, on the approach of Santa Anna, to Buena Vista, a strong position a few miles south of Saltillo. Here he was attacked by Santa Anna, on the 21st of February. That general seems to have been for a considerable time wavering as to the course he should pursue; at one time threatening to march to Vera Cruz, then turning to quell an insurrection at the capital, and again manœuvering in the vicinity of Saltillo. At length he issued an address to his companions in arms, which contained his real intentions. We quote a specimen of it.

"Soldiers! the entire world observes us, and will expect our acts to be heroic as they are necessary. Privations of all kinds surround us, in consequence of the neglect shown towards us for more than a month, by those who should provide your pay and provisions. But when has misery debilitated your spirits, or weak your enthusiasm? The Mexican soldier is well known by his frugality and patience under suffering, never wanting magazines in marches across deserts, and always counting upon the resources of the enemy to provide for his wants. To-day we shall undertake to march over a desert country, without succour or provisions. But be assured, that we shall be immediately provided from those of the enemy, and with them you will be sufficiently reimbursed. My friends, we go to open the campaign. What days of glory await us! What a flattering future for our country! How satisfactory, when we contemplate that we have saved its independence! How the world will admire us! How the nation will bless us! And when in the bosoms of our families we shall relate the risks and fatigues which we have endured, the combats with and triumphs over a daring and presumptuous enemy; and hereafter, when telling our children that we have saved our country a second time, the jubilee will be complete, and the sacrifices will then appear to us as nothing. Soldiers! Hurry forth in the defense of your country. The cause we sustain is a holy one; never have we struggled with more justice, because we fight for the honour and religion of our wives and children! What sacrifice, then, can be too great for objects so dear? Let our motto be—'CONQUER OR DIE!' Let us swear before the great Eternal, that we will not wait an instant in purging our soil of the stranger, who has dared to profane it with his presence. No treaty, nothing which may not be heroic and proud.''

We give the distinct and explicit account of the opperations which followed, from the official report of General Taylor, reserving, as before, our notices of individual gallantry for another portion of the work.

" The information which reached me of the advance and concentration of a heavy Mexican force in my front, had assumed such a probable form, as to induce a special examination far beyond the reach of our pickets, to ascertain its correctness. A small party of Texan spies, under Major McCulloch, despatched to the hacienda of Encarnacion, thirty miles from this, on the route to San Luis Potosi, had reported a cavalry force of unknown strength at that place. On the 20th of February, a strong reconnoissance under Lieutenant-Colonel May was despatched to the hacienda of Heclionda, while Major McCulloch made another examination of Encarnacion. The result of these expeditions left no doubt that the enemy was in large force at Encarnacion, under the orders of General Santa Anna, and that he meditated a forward movement and attack upon our position

As the camp of Agua Nueva could be turned on either flank, and as the enemy's force was greatly superior to

Official report of General Taylor.

our own, particularly in the arm of cavalry, I determined, after much consideration, to take up a position about eleven miles in rear, and there await the attack. The army broke up its camp and marched at noon on the 21st, encamping at the new position a little in front of the hacienda of Buena Vista. With a small force I proceeded to Saltillo, to make some necessary arrangements for the defense of the town, leaving Brigadier-General Wool in the immediate command of the troops.

Before those arrangements were completed, on the morning of the 22d, I was advised that the enemy was in sight, advancing. Upon reaching the ground it was found that his cavalry advance was in our front, having marched from Encarnacion, as we have since learned, at eleven o'clock on the day previous, and driving in a mounted force left at Agua Nueva to cover the removal of public stores. Our troops were in position, occupying a line of remarkable strength. The road at this point becomes a narrow defile, the valley on its right being rendered quite impracticable for artillery by a system of deep and impassable gullies, while on the left a succession of rugged ridges and precipitous ravines extends far back toward the mountain which bounds the valley. The features of the ground were such as nearly to paralyze the artillery and cavalry of the enemy, while his infantry could not derive all the advantage of its numerical superiority. In this position we prepared to receive him. Captain Washington's battery (4th artillery) was posted to command the road, while the 1st and 2d Illinois regiments, under Colonels Hardin and Bissell, each eight companies, (to the latter of which was attached Captain Conner's company of Texas volunteers,) and the 2d Kentucky, under Colonel McKee, occupied the crests of the ridges on the left and in rear. The Arkansas and Kentucky regiments of cavalry, commanded by Colonels Yell and H. Marshall, occupied the extreme left near the base of the mountain, while the Indiana brigade, under Brigadier-General Lane, (composed of the 2d and 3d regiments, under Colonels Bowle: and Lane,) the Mississippi riflemen, under Colonel Davis, the squadrons of the 1st and 2d dragoons, under Captain Steen and Lieutenant-Colonel May, and the light batteries of Captains Sherman and Bragg, 3d artillery, were held in reserve.

At eleven o'clock, a summons to surrender at discretion was received from General Santa Anna, which was declined. The enemy still forebore his attack, evidently waiting for the arrival of his rear columns, which could be distinctly seen by our look-outs as they approached the field. A demonstration made on his left caused me to detach the 2d Kentucky regiment and a section of our artillery to our right, in which position they bivouacked for the night. In the mean time the Mexican light troops had engaged ours on the extreme left, (composed of parts of the Kentucky and Arkansas cavalry dismounted, and a rifle battalion from the Indiana brigade, under Major Gorman, the whole commanded by Colonel Marshall,) and kept up a sharp fire, climbing the mountain side, and apparently endeavouring to gain our flank. Three pieces of Captain Washington's battery had been detached to the left, and were supported by the 2d Indiana regiment. An occasional shell was thrown by the enemy into this part of our line, but without effect. The skirmishing of the light troops was kept up

Battle of Buena Vista.

Official report of General Taylor.

with trifling loss on our part until dark, when I became convinced that no serious attack would be made before morning, and returned, with the Mississippi regiment and squadron of 2d dragoons, to Saltillo. The troops bivouacked without fires, and lay upon their arms. A body of cavalry, some fifteen hundred strong, had been visible all day in rear of the town, having entered the valley through a narrow pass east of the city. This cavalry, commanded by General Minon, had evidently been thrown in our rear to break up and harass our retreat, and perhaps make some attempt against the town if practicable. The city was occupied by four excellent companies of Illinois volunteers, under Major Warren, of the 1st regiment. A field-work, which commanded most of the approaches, was garrisoned by Captain Webster's company,* 1st artillery, and armed with two twenty-four-pound howitzers, while the train and head-quarter camp was guarded by two companies of Mississippi riflemen, under Captain Rogers, and a field-piece commanded by Captain Shover, 3d artillery. Having made these dispositions for the protection of the rear, I proceeded on the morning of the 23d to Buena Vista, ordering forward all the other available troops. The action had commenced before my arrival on the field.

During the evening and night of the 22d, the enemy had thrown a body of light troops on the mountain side, with the purpose of outflanking our left; and it was here that the action of the 23d commenced at an early hour. Our riflemen, under Colonel Marshall, who had been reinforced by three companies under Major Trail, 2d Illinois volunteers, maintained their ground handsomely against a greatly superior force, holding themselves under cover, and using their weapons with deadly effect. About eight o'clock, a strong demonstration was made against the centre of our position, a heavy column moving along the road. This force was soon dispersed by a few rapid and well-directed shots from Captain Washington's battery. In the mean time the enemy was concentrating a large force of infantry and cavalry under cover of the ridges, with the obvious intention of forcing our left, which was posted on an extensive plateau. The 2d Indiana and 2d Illinois regiments formed this part of our line, the former covering three pieces of light artillery, under the orders of Captain O'Brien—Brigadier-General Lane being in the immediate command. In order to bring his men within effective range, General Lane ordered the artillery and 2d Indiana regiment forward. The artillery advanced within musket range of a heavy body of Mexican infantry, and was served against it with great effect, but without being able to check its advance. The infantry ordered to its support had fallen back in disorder, being exposed, as well as the battery, not only to a severe fire of small-arms from the front, but also to a murderous cross-fire of grape and canister from a Mexican battery on the left. Captain O'Brien found it impossible to retain his position without support, but was only able to withdraw two of his pieces, all the horses and cannoneers of the third piece being killed or disabled. The 2d Indiana regiment, which had fallen back as stated, could not be rallied, and took no farther part in the action, except a handful of men, who, under its gallant colonel, Bowles, joined the Mississippi regiment,

Official report of General Taylor.

and did good service, and those fugitives who, at a later period in the day, assisted in defending the train and depot at Buena Vista. This portion of our line having given way, and the enemy appearing in overwhelming force against our left flank, the light troops which had rendered such good service on the mountain were compelled to withdraw, which they did, for the most part, in good order. Many, however, were not rallied until they reached the depot at Buena Vista, to the defense of which they afterward contributed.

Colonel Bissel's regiment, (2d Illinois,) which had been joined by a section of Captain Sherman's battery, had become completely outflanked, and was compelled to fall back, being entirely unsupported. The enemy was now pouring masses of infantry and cavalry along the base of the mountain on our left, and was gaining our rear in great force. At this moment I arrived upon the field. The Mississippi regiment had been directed to the left before reaching the position, and immediately came into action against the Mexican infantry which had turned our flank. The 2d Kentucky regiment and a section of artillery under Captain Bragg, had previously been ordered from the right to reinforce our left, and arrived at a most opportune moment. That regiment, and a portion of the 1st Illinois, under Colonel Hardin, gallantly drove the enemy, and recovered a portion of the ground we had lost. The batteries of Captains Sherman and Bragg were in position on the plateau, and did much execution, not only in front, but particularly upon the masses which had gained our rear. Discovering that the enemy was heavily pressing upon the Mississippi regiment, the 3d Indiana regiment, under

Colonel Lane, was despatched to strengthen that part of our line, which formed a crotchet perpendicular to the first line of battle. At the same time Lieutenant Kilburn, with a piece of Captain Bragg's battery, was directed to support the infantry there engaged. The action was for a long time warmly sustained at that point—the enemy making several efforts both with infantry and cavalry against our line, and being always repulsed with heavy loss. I had placed all the regular cavalry and Captain Pike's squadron of Arkansas horse under the orders of Brevet Lieutenant-Colonel May, with directions to hold in check the enemy's column, still advancing to the rear along the base of the mountain, which was done in conjunction with the Kentucky and Arkansas cavalry under Colonels Marshall and Yell.

In the mean time our left, which was still strongly threatened by a superior force, was farther strengthened by the detachment of Captain Bragg's and a portion of Captain Sherman's batteries to that quarter. The concentration of artillery fire upon the masses of the enemy along the base of the mountain, and the determined resistance offered by the two regiments opposed to them, had created confusion in their ranks, and some of the corps attempted to effect a retreat upon their main line of battle. The squadron of the 1st dragoons, under Lieutenant Rucker, was now ordered up the deep ravine which these retreating corps were endeavouring to cross, in order to charge and disperse them. The squadron proceeded to the point indicated, but could not accomplish the object, being exposed to a heavy fire from a battery established to cover the retreat of those corps. While the squadron was detached on this service, a

Official report of General Taylor.

large body of the enemy was observed to concentrate on our extreme left, apparently with the view of making a descent upon the hacienda of Buena Vista, where o r train and baggage were deposited. Lieutenant-Colonel May was ordered to the support of that point, with two pieces of Captain Sherman's battery under Lieutenant Reynolds. In the mean time, the scattered forces near the hacienda, composed in part of Majors Trail and Gorman's commands, had been to some extent organized under the advice of Major Munroe, chief of artillery, with the assistance of Major Morrison, volunteer staff, and were posted to defend the position. Before our cavalry had reached the hacienda, that of the enemy had made its attack; having been handsomely met by the Kentucky and Arkansas cavalry under Colonels Marshall and Yell. The Mexican column immediately divided, one portion sweeping by the depot, where it received a destructive fire from the force which had collected there, and then gaining the mountain opposite, under a fire from Lieutenant Reynolds' section, the remaining portion regaining the base of the mountain on our left. In the charge at Buena Vista, Colonel Yell fell gallantly at the head of his regiment; we also lost Adjutant Vaughan, of the Kentucky cavalry—a young officer of much promise. Lieutenant-Colonel May, who had been rejoined by the squadron of the 1st dragoons and by portions of the Arkansas and Indiana troops, under Lieutenant-Colonel Roane and Major Gorman, now approached the base of the mountain, holding in check the right flank of the enemy, upon whose masses, crowded in the narrow gorges and ravines, our artillery was doing fearful execution.

Battle of Buena Vista.

The position of that portion of the Mexican army which had gained our rear was now very critical, and it seemed doubtful whether it could regain the main body. At this moment I received from General Santa Anna a message by a staff officer, desiring to know what I wanted. I immediately despatched Brigadier-General Wool to the Mexican general-in-chief, and sent orders to cease firing. Upon reaching the Mexican lines, General Wool could not cause the enemy to cease their fire, and accordingly returned without having an interview. The extreme right of the enemy continued its retreat along the base of the mountain, and finally, in spite of all our efforts, effected a junction with the remainder of the army.

During the day, the cavalry of General Minon had ascended the elevated plain above Saltillo, and occupied the road from the city to the field of battle, where they intercepted several of our men. Approaching the town, they were fired upon by Captain Webster from the redoubt occupied by his company, and then moved off towards the eastern side of the valley, and obliquely towards Buena Vista. At this time, Captain Shover moved rapidly forward with his piece, supported by a miscellaneous command of mounted volunteers, and fired several shots at the cavalry with great effect. They were driven into the ravines which lead to the lower valley, closely pursued by Captain Shover, who was farther supported by a piece of Captain Webster's battery, under Lieutenant Donaldson, which had advanced from the redoubt, supported by Captain Wheeler's company of Illinois volunteers. The enemy made one or two efforts to charge the artillery, but was finally driven

Official report of General Taylor.

back in a confused mass, and did not again appear upon the plain.

In the mean time, the firing had partially ceased upon the principal field. The enemy seemed to confine his efforts to the protection of his artillery, and I had left the plateau for a moment, when I was recalled thither by a very heavy musketry fire. On regaining that position, I discovered that our infantry (Illinois and 2d Kentucky) had engaged a greatly superior force of the enemy—evidently his reserve—and that they had been overwhelmed by numbers. The moment was most critical. Captain O'Brien, with two pieces, had sustained this heavy charge to the last, and was finally obliged to leave his guns on the field—his infantry support being entirely routed. Captain Bragg, who had just arrived from the left, was ordered at once into battery. Without any infantry to support him, and at the imminent risk of losing his guns, this officer came rapidly into action, the Mexican line being but a few yards from the muzzle of his pieces. The first discharge of canister caused the enemy to hesitate, and the second and third drove him back in disorder, and saved the day. The 2d Kentucky regiment, which had advanced beyond supporting distance in this affair, was driven back and closely pressed by the enemy's cavalry. Taking a ravine which led in the direction of Captain Washington's battery, their pursuers became exposed to his fire, which soon checked and drove them back with loss. In the mean time the rest of our artillery had taken position on the plateau, covered by the Mississippi and 3d Indiana regiments, the former of which had reached the ground in time to pour a fire into the

Battle of Buena Vista.

right flank of the enemy, and thus contribute to his repulse. In this last conflict we had the misfortune to sustain a very heavy loss. Colonel Hardin, 1st Illinois, and Colonel McKee and Lieutenant-Colonel Clay, 2d Kentucky regiment, fell at this time while gallantly leading their commands.

No farther attempt was made by the enemy to force our position, and the approach of night gave an opportunity to pay proper attention to the wounded, and also to refresh the soldiers, who had been exhausted by incessant watchfulness and combat. Though the night was severely cold, the troops were compelled for the most to bivouac without fires, expecting that morning would renew the conflict. During the night the wounded were removed to Saltillo, and every preparation made to receive the enemy, should he again attack our position. Seven fresh companies were drawn from the town, and Brigadier-General Marshall, with a reinforcement of Kentucky cavalry and four heavy guns, under Captain Prentiss, 1st artillery, was near at hand, when it was discovered that the enemy had abandoned his position during the night. Our scouts soon ascertained that he had fallen back upon Agua Nueva. The great disparity of numbers, and the exhaustion of our troops, rendered it inexpedient and hazardous to attempt pursuit. A staff officer was despatched to General Santa Anna to negotiate an exchange of prisoners, which was satisfactorily completed on the following day. Our own dead were collected and buried, and the Mexican wounded, of which a large number had been left upon the field, were removed to Saltillo, and rendered as comfortable as circumstances would permit.

Death of Colonel Clay.

Official report of General Taylor.

On the evening of the 26th, a close reconnoissance was made of the enemy's position, which was found to be occupied only by a small body of cavalry, the infantry and artillery having retreated in the direction of San Luis Potosi. On the 27th, our troops resumed their former camp at Agua Nueva, the enemy's rear-guard evacuating the place as we approached, leaving a considerable number of wounded. It was my purpose to beat up his quarters at Encarnacion early the next morning, but upon examination, the weak condition of the cavalry horses rendered it unadvisable to attempt so long a march without water. A command was finally despatched to Encarnacion, on the 1st of March, under Colonel Belknap. Some two hundred wounded, and about sixty Mexican soldiers were found there, the army having passed on in the direction of Matehuala, with greatly reduced numbers, and suffering much from hunger. The dead and dying were strewed upon the road and crowded the buildings of the hacienda.

The American force engaged in the action of Buena Vista is shown, by the field report, to have been three hundred and thirty-four officers, and four thousand four hundred and twenty-five men, exclusive of the small command left in and near Saltillo. Of this number, two squadrons of cavalry and three batteries of light artillery, making not more than four hundred and fifty-three men, composed the only force of regular troops. The strength of the Mexican army is stated by General Santa Anna, in his summons, to be twenty thousand ; and that estimate is confirmed by all the information since obtained. Our loss is two hundred and sixty-seven killed, four hundred and fifty-six wounded, and twenty-three missing. Of the

Battle of Buena Vista.

numerous wounded, many did not require removal to the hospital, and it is hoped that a comparatively small number will be permanently disabled. The Mexican loss in killed and wounded may be fairly estimated at one thousand five hundred, and will probably reach two thousand. At least five hundred of their killed were left upon the field of battle. We have no means of ascertaining the number of deserters and dispersed men from their ranks, but it is known to be very great."

The nature of the ground at Buena Vista, made the battle a series of detached encounters, in which each side had at times the superiority of force. It was the work of the able commander to give unity to the whole by the proper direction of the several partial efforts. These divided operations gave splendid opportunities for the display of individual gallantry and state pride, which were cheerfully improved, especially by the volunteers, many of whom had never faced an enemy before, and were determined to reap laurels on the first field. It is a fact never before known in the annals of war, that almost every American soldier in the present war, considers himself in some degree its historian. Nearly every one is able to write, many have made engagements with editors at home to furnish accounts of their engagements, and each one is interested in the success of his own company that the account he must give may not be disgraceful. Thus a direct *personal pride* is brought to aid the military pride necessary to the formation of a good soldier, an element which must be of great account in explaining the success of our arms. The future historian of the war, possessed of the immense mass of materials thus furnished, will catch the

Kentucky regiment.

enthusiasm with which the brave soldiers write in the moment of victory, and build up for himself a reputation unsurpassed by that of any of the warrior historians, Xenophon, Cæsar, or Napier.

We give an extract from one of these letters, which illustrates at once the force of the above remark, and the bravery of a particular regiment.

"At a very critical point of the battle when it became necessary to sustain one of our columns, which was staggering under a charge made by the Mexicans, in overwhelming numbers, General Taylor despatched Mr. Crittenden to order Colonel McKee, of the 2d Kentucky regiment, to bring his men into immediate action. Mr. Crittenden found the regiment, men and officers, eager for the fray, delivered the order and rode back to the general, by whose side it was his duty to keep. The Kentuckians moved forward in gallant style, led by McKee and Clay, both of whom, alas! fell in a subsequent part of the day. It so happened that before reaching a position from which they could deliver an effective fire, the regiment had to cross a valley which was broken up by ravines and masses of stone. Whilst crossing this valley the heads only of the men could be seen from the point which General Taylor and Mr. Crittenden occupied—and these were bobbing up and down and crosswise in such confusion as to impress both with the idea that the regiment had fallen into disorder. The Mexicans were annoying them at the same moment by a fire, which helped to confirm the opinion of the general that the Kentuckians were thrown into dismay.

It was one of these decisive crises, which occur in every contested field, when the issue of the day depended, for the time being, upon the gallantry of a particular corps.

General Taylor, who, as before said, could only see the heads of the troops, and misled by their motions in getting across gullies and going around rocks and other obstructions, into the belief that they were about to falter, turned to Mr. Crittenden, who is a Kentuckian, and with a countenance, indicating deep mortification—for the general is a resident in Kentucky too—and an eye fierce with emotion, exclaimed, ' Mr. Crittenden, this will not do —this is not the way for Kentuckians to behave themselves when called upon to make a good battle—it will not answer, sir:' and with this he clenched his hands, and knit his brow, and set his teeth hard together. Mr. Crittenden, who was mistaken by the same indications that deceived the general, could scarcely make a reply from very chagrin and shame. In a few moments, however, the Kentuckians had crossed the uneven places, and were seen ascending the slope of the valley, shoulder to shoulder, and with the firm and regular step of veterans of a hundred fields. On they moved until they reached the crest of the hill, where they met the enemy before the flush of a temporary advantage had subsided. Here they delivered their fires with such regularity and deadly aim that the decimated phalanx of Mexico gave way and retreated precipitately. As the Kentuckians emerged from the valley the countenance of the old general, who was regarding them with the intensest interest, gradually relaxed the bitterness of its expression. A glow of pride supplanted the deep mortification which fixed its muscles, and enthusiasm qualified the fierce glance of his eye. Forward they moved under his riveted gaze, whose feelings became more and more wrought up as they approached the scene of carnage. When they opened their fire the old general could no longer restrain his admiration, but broke forth with a loud huzza,—'Hurrah for old Kentucky!' he exclaimed, talking to himself, and rising in his saddle; 'that's the way to do it; give it to them,' and the tears of exultation rolled down his cheeks as he said it.

Having got rid of this ebullition of state pride, he went about looking after other parts of the field.

The Kentuckians did their duty that day as others did. They paid toll in travelling the high road to glory as the list of killed and wounded shows."

On the 2d of March Mr. Crittenden set out for Washington with the official documents of the battle, escorted by Major Giddings, with two hundred and sixty infantry and two pieces of artillery, and having in charge one hundred and fifty wagons. At a mile distant from Seralvo the escort was attacked by General Urrea with a force of sixteen hundred Mexican cavalry and infantry. The enemy was repulsed with a loss of forty-five killed and wounded. Major Giddings lost seventeen men, fifteen of whom were teamsters. Subsequently General Taylor marched in pursuit of Urrea, who fled over the mountains. General Taylor then returned and fixed his camp at the Walnut Springs, three miles from Monterey, where it remained under the charge of General Wool, to whose care General Taylor committed the army while he himself returned for a little while to visit his family in the United States.

Along the Rio Grande the only warfare urged after the capture of Matamoras was that of the

Order of Canales.

guerillas. The butcheries perpetrated by these bands are appalling, war without pity being their cardinal principle. The following manifesto taken from a captive of the band of Canales, by Lieutenant Bee of Captain Lamar's Rangers. Canales is a graduate of a sanguinary school, a robber chief by profession, and a cut-throat by nature; he is just the man to gloat over the barbarities of such a war. The pretended necessity for retaliation with which his proclamation commences refers to an excess of vengeance perpetrated by a few disorderly soldiers in a moment of excitement, occasioned by the most dastardly murder of one of their comrades by two of the band of Canales, who were found among the party of Mexicans that were slain. Without this outrage, however, the guerilla system would have been adopted, as it has been in the Central States. The Mexicans themselves are not more free from outrage and plunder at the hands of these bands than the Americans; and many instances can be cited where the unfortunate inhabitants welcome the approach of their foes that they may have protection from these their pretended friends.

"I this day send to the adjutant inspector of the National Guards the following instructions:

I learn, with the greatest indignation, that the Americans have committed a most horrible massacre at the rancho of the Guadalupe. They made prisoners, in their own houses and by the side of their families, twenty-five peaceable men, and immediately shot them. To repel this class of warfare, which is not war but atrocity in all its fury, there is no other course left us than retaliation; and in order to pursue this method, rendered imperative by the fatal circumstances above mentioned, you will

Commencement of the Guerilla Warfare.

Order of Canales.

immediately declare martial law, with the understanding that eight days after the publication of the same every individual who has not taken up arms (being capable of so doing) shall be considered a traitor and instantly shot.

Martial law being in force, you are bound to give no quarters to any American whom you may meet, or who may present himself to you, even though he be without arms. You are also directed to publish this to all the towns in this state, forcibly impressing them with the severe punishment that shall be inflicted for the least omission of this order.

We have arrived at that state in which our country requires the greatest sacrifices; her sons should glory in nothing but to become soldiers, and as brave Mexicans to meet the crisis. Therefore, if the army of invasion continues, and our people remain in the towns which they have molested, they deserve not one ray of sympathy; nor should any one ever cease to make war upon them. You will send a copy of this to each of your subordinates, and they are authorized to proceed against the chiefs of their squadrons, or against their colonels or any other, even against me, for any infraction of this order—the only mode of salvation left. The enemy wages war against us, and even against those peaceable citizens who, actuated by improper impulses, desire to remain quiet in their houses. Even these they kill, without quarter; and this is the greatest favour they may expect from them. The only alternative left us, under these circumstances, is retaliation, which is the strong right of the offended against the offending. To carry this into effect, attach yourself to the authorities. Your failing to do this will be considered a crime of the greatest magnitude. All the officers of the troops are directed to assist you in carrying out this order, and it is distinctly understood there shall be no exceptions. Neither the clergy, military, citizens, nor other persons, shall enjoy the privilege of remaining peaceably at their homes. The whole of the corporation shall turn out with the citizens, leaving solely as authority of the town one of the members who is over the age of sixty years; at the same time, if all of the members are capable of bearing arms, then none shall be excepted; leaving to act some one who is incapable of military service. You yourself must be an example to others, by conforming to this requisition. And I send this to you for publication, and charge you to see it executed in every particular, and communicate it also to the commanders of the squadrons in your city, who will aid you in carrying into effect these instructions; and in fact you are directed to do all and every thing which your patriotism may prompt. God and liberty!"

We turn next to the sphere of operations of General Winfield Scott, the commander-in-chief of the armies of the United States. That officer sailed from New York on the 30th of November, and reached the Rio Grande on the 1st of January. His object was to capture the city of Vera Cruz and the castle of San Juan d'Ulloa, the naval forces under Commodore Conner being intended to co-operate in the attack. As we have seen, all the regular force was detached from General Taylor's command, and ordered to the general rendezvous at the island of Lobos, not very distant from Vera Cruz, and the anchorage of the Gulf Squadron at Anton Lizardo. The transports slowly gathered together at

Landing at Vera Cruz.

that place the troops from the Brazos, from New Orleans, and the north, cavalry, infantry, artillery, mortars, bomb-ketches, shells and shot—in short, all the materiel necessary for the successful execution of the brilliant designs of General Scott. At length the army, amounting to about twelve thousand men, thoroughly equipped, re-embarked on board of the transports numbering nearly a hundred sail, and proceeded to effect a landing at Vera Cruz. It became the duty of the navy to co-operate in the landing, and the particulars of the disembarkation are given in the despatch of Commodore Conner, which we subjoin.

"After a joint reconnoissance, made by the general and myself in the steamer Petrita, the beach due west from Sacrificios, one of the points spoken of in my previous letters, was selected as the most suitable for the purpose. The anchorage near this place being extremely contracted, it became necessary, in order to avoid crowding it with an undue number of vessels, to transfer most of the troops to the vessels of war for transportation to Sacrificios. Accordingly, on the morning of the 9th, at daylight, all necessary preparations—such as launching and numbering the boats, detailing officers, &c.—having been previously made, this transfer was commenced. The frigates received on board between twenty-five and twenty-eight hundred men each, with their arms and accoutrements, and the sloops and smaller vessels number in proportion.

This part of the movement was completed very successfully about eleven o'clock, A. M., and a few minutes thereafter the squadron under my command, accompanied by the commanding general, in the steamship

Massachusetts, and such of the transports as had been selected for the purpose, got under way. The weather was very fine—indeed we could not have been more favoured in this particular than we were. We had a fresh, and yet gentle breeze from the south-east, and a perfectly smooth sea. The passage to Sacrificios occupied us between two and three hours. Each ship came in and anchored without the slightest disorder or confusion, in the small space allotted to her—the harbour being still very much crowded, notwithstanding the number of transports we had left behind. The disembarkation commenced on the instant. Whilst we were transferring the troops from the ships to the serf-boats, (sixty-five in number,) I directed the steamers Spitfire and Vixen, and the five gun-boats, to form in a line parallel with and close in to the beach, to cover the landing. This order was promptly executed, and these small vessels, from the lightness of their draught, were enabled to take positions within good grape-range of the shore. As the boats severally received their complements of troops, they assembled, in a line abreast, between the fleet and the gun-boats; and when all were ready, they pulled in, together, under the guidance of a number of the officers of the squadron, who had been detailed for this purpose. General Worth commanded this, the first line of the army, and had the satisfaction of forming his command on the beach and neighbouring heights just before sunset. Four thousand five hundred men were thus thrown on shore, almost simultaneously.

No enemy appeared to offer us the slightest opposition. The first line being landed, the boats, in successive trips, relieved the men of war and transports of

Landing at Vera Cruz.

their remaining troops, by ten o'clock, P. M. The whole army, (save a few straggling companies,) consisting of upwards of ten thousand men, were thus safely deposited on shore, without the slightest accident of any kind. The officers and seamen under my command, vied with each other on this occasion, in a zealous and energetic performance of their duty. I cannot but express to the department the great satisfaction I have derived from witnessing their efforts to contribute all in their power to the success of their more fortunate brethren of the army. The weather still continuing fine, to-day we were engaged in landing the artillery, horses, provisions, and other materiel. The steamer New Orleans, with the Louisiana regiment of volunteers, eight hundred strong, arrived most opportunely at Anton Lizardo, just as we had put ourselves in motion. She joined us, and her troops were landed with the rest."

"The brilliant scene," says the Rev. F. M. Taylor, in his new work, "The Broad Pennant," "the brilliant scene presented by the disembarkation of our army of twelve thousand men from the ships, so successfully and beautifully conducted, might well excite the admiration and claim the interested gaze of the beholders. The scene has never been equalled on the continent of America, and no disembarkation on record can have surpassed it for its successful accomplishment. It has been compared with the landing of the French expedition against Algiers, in 1830, which is said to have been one of the most complete armaments, in every respect, that ever left Europe. That expedition had been prepared with labour, attention, and experience; and nothing had been omitted to insure success, particularly in the means and facilities for landing the troops. Its disembarkation took place in a wide bay, which was more favourable than an open beach directly on the ocean; and, as in the present instance, it was made without any resistance on the part of the enemy. Yet only nine thousand men were landed the first day, and thirty to forty lives were lost by accidents or upsetting of boats; whereas on the present occasion, twelve thousand were landed in one day without the slightest accident or loss of a single life. The great credit of this, of course belongs to the navy, under whose orders and arrangements, and by whose exertions it was effected, and reflects the highest credit on Commodore Conner, and the gallant officers and seamen belonging to the squadron."

It may not be amiss, before proceeding to give an account of the siege, to subjoin a short extract from an article descriptive of Vera Cruz, from the New York Herald, the more especially as they serve to justify in some degree the opinion entertained by the Mexicans that it was impregnable.

" The fortifications consist of nine towers connected together by means of a stone and mortar wall, which, however, is not very thick. The two towers named Santiago and Conception are the most important, as well from their size and strength, as from the fact that by their position they contribute much to the defense of the port. They are situated at that portion of the walls looking toward the castle of San Juan, and are distant from each other one thousand two hundred and seventy varas. The other towers, including the one called San Fernando, are almost equal in shape, size, and strength. All of them can mount one hundred pieces of artillery

Siege of Vera Cruz.

of various sizes; and save those of the middle ones, their fires all cross in front of the guard-houses, the external walls of which form part of the walls which surround the city.

Having completed the investment of the city, General Scott sent a summons to the commander to surrender, that Vera Cruz might be saved "from the imminent hazard of demolition—its gallant defenders from a useless effusion of blood, and its peaceful inhabitants—women and children, inclusive—from the inevitable horrors of a triumphant assault." He offered in case the city and castle had separate commanders, and the former were surrendered, to agree not to fire a shot from the city upon the castle, unless the castle should previously fire upon the city. The answer to this summons was the announcement of the determination of Don Juan Morales to defend both the city and the castle to the last.

Seven ten-inch mortars being in battery, opened upon the city on the receipt of this reply, and the small vessels of the squadron approached to within a mile and an eighth of the city, and opened a fire upon it, which they continued until called off by the commodore on the succeeding day. On the 23d, three other mortars were added to the seven already at work; on the 24th another battery, commanded by officers of the navy, consisting of three thirty-two-pounders and three eight-inch Paixhan guns, all landed from the squadron, was opened with great activity. On the 25th, a new battery, mounting four twenty-four-pounders and two eight-inch Paixhan guns, was opened with great effect, making five batteries in awful activity. Such a terrible effect had now been produced upon the city as to make its early fall inevitable. On the 24th, the consuls of the European powers sent a memorial to General Scott, asking for a truce, in order that neutrals and women and children might withdraw from the city. This request, preferred after they had despised the early warning of General Scott to retire, was of course refused.

On the morning of the 26th, General Landero, on whom General Morales had devolved the command, made overtures which resulted in a capitulation signed on the evening of that day. On the 29th of March, the flag of the United States was raised in triumph over the city and castle of Vera Cruz. There was one drawback to the joy felt on this occasion, regret for the loss of the brave and pious Captain John R. Vinton of the 3d artillery.* General Scott writes on the 23d as follows: "Including the preparation and defense of the batteries, from the beginning — now many days — and

---

* John R. Vinton, who had been brevetted a major at the time he fell, although without his knowledge of the promotion, was one of the most valuable officers in the army. He was educated at West Point, commissioned at seventeen, employed for several years on topographical duty on the Atlantic coast, and in Canada, adjutant under General Eustis, aid to General Brown, and having served with distinction in the Seminole war, and particularly at the battle near Lake Monroe, he finally raised his military reputation to the highest point at the siege of Monterey. Here he was with General Worth's division, and accompanied the troops as they passed so long under fire from the two heights, in the storming of those heights, the capture of the palace, and the subsequent street assault, where the soldiers dug through the walls of houses amid a continual fire of musketry from the house tops.

Vinton was not only highly distinguished as an officer, but he was profoundly learned, skilled in the fine arts, and a man of unquestionable piety.

Siege of Vera Cruz.

notwithstanding the heavy fire of the enemy, from city and castle—we have only had four or five men wounded, and one officer and one man killed, in or near the trenches. That officer was Captain John R. Vinton, of the United States 3d artillery, one of the most talented, accomplished, and effective members of the army, and who was highly distinguished in the brilliant operations at Monterey. He fell, last evening, in the trenches, where he was on duty as field and commanding officer, universally regretted. I have just attended his honoured remains to a soldier's grave—in full view of the enemy and within reach of his guns.

As soon as Commodore Perry perceived the land forces engaged, he ordered Captain Tatnall, with what is called the "Mosquito Fleet," consisting of the steamers Spitfire and Vixen, and five gun-boats, viz: Reefer, Bonita, Tampico, Falconer, and Petrel, to attack. Captain Tatnall inquired at what point he should engage? Commmodore Perry very emphatically replied, "Wherever you can do the most execution, sir." Accordingly the little fleet took position under a point of land known as the "Lime Kiln," about a mile from the city, where they were protected from a point blank shot of the castle. As soon as they got their position in line they opened a fire of round shot and shell at a rapid rate, and threw them "handsomely" into the town and Fort Santiago.

The castle soon paid its respects to Captain Tatnall, and the powerful engines of havoc and destruction were now in full blast from every quarter, hurling their dreadful and deadly missiles into each other's ranks in rapid succession, which they kept up till about dark, when the Mexican batteries comparatively ceased, and the " Mosquito Fleet" also held off for the night.

At eight o'clock the party that were in the trenches were relieved by another detail. The troops who returned from the intrenchments were literally covered with smoke and dust, and so much disfigured that they could not be recognized except by their voices. Shell after shell exploded in their midst, and shot after shot threw barrels of earth from the embankments over their heads as they lay in the trenches.

An incident occurred during the heaviest of the fire, evincing the coolness of the American soldiers in time of the greatest danger. A small party who had been lying in the trenches all day, becoming tired of doing nothing, as they said, were devising some means of passing away the time. At length one of them proposed a game at cards, and hauled out an old greasy pack, and some half dozen of them sat down in the ditch to play, with nothing but tobacco for stakes. They became much interested, and it was not long before they forgot all about cannon, bomb-shells, Mexican batteries, or any thing else but their tobacco and cards. It was not long, however, before a thirteen inch shell fell on the top of the embankment; the explosion completely covered them with the earth; they all scrambled out as quick as they could, and shaking the sand from their clotl - ing, and cleaning it out from their eyes, one of them very coolly remarked, " Well, boys, I'll be darned if that didn't come mighty near being a ten strike !"

At daylight on the 23d, Captain Tatnall's Mosquito

Fleet weighed anchor, and under cover of a moon somewhat clouded, approached within six hundred yards of the castle. As soon as they had got their respective positions, they opened a broadside from the fleet, which was answered by the castle with great spirit, both by round shot and shell. Captain Tatnall continued the engagement for about half an hour, although the signal from the commodore's ship, calling him off, had been hoisted for some time; but was not seen on account of a cloud of smoke which hung around the shipping."

On the 25th, information was received in camp that a body of Mexicans were hanging in our rear, intending to force the lines if possible and make their way into the city with a number of cattle. Colonel Harney, with one hundred and twenty dragoons, was ordered out in search of them, and report his observations. He discovered them, about two thousand in number, intrenched at a bridge, and supported by two pieces of artillery, three miles from General Patterson's head-quarters. Colonel Harney started on his return, intending to prepare properly and attack them the next morning. But the gallant soldier knowing that delays are dangerous, could not bear the idea of leaving the enemy after having come in sight of them without having a brush. Accordingly he returned to the place, took a position where he could watch their movements, and keep his men secure from the enemy's fire. The Mexicans commenced firing at him, and threw a perfect shower of balls all around him, but without injury.

Colonel Harney then despatched a messenger to camp for a small reinforcement, and some artillery to break the breastworks. He was reinforced from General Patterson's division by Lieutenant Judd, with two pieces of artillery, about sixty dragoons, dismounted, and six companies of the 1st and 2d Tennessee volunteers, under the command of Colonel Haskell, accompanied by General Patterson in person, although he did not take the command from Colonel Harney, but merely participated as any other individual who was engaged. Colonel Harney then formed the Tennesseeans on the right, his dragoons on the left, and advanced slowly to draw the fire of the Mexicans, until Lieutenant Judd got his artillery in such a position as he desired.

The movement succeeded admirably: Lieutenant Judd got his ground within one hundred and fifty yards of the Mexicans, and commenced firing—they attempted to return it, but as soon as a slight breach was made in the parapet, Colonel Harney ordered a charge, which was answered by a yell from the dragoons and Tennesseeans. Colonel Haskell, Captain Cheatham, and Captain Foster, were the first men to leap over the breastwork, and as a naval officer remarked, who witnessed the whole affair, the balance went over so much like a "thousand of brick," that there was no telling who was first or last. As might have been expected, the Mexicans were unable to stand a charge from "the boys who stood the fire of the Black Fort at Monterey."

A few of the encumbrances were soon thrown out of the way, and Colonel Harney, with his dragoons, leaped the breastwork and gave chase. He had not proceeded more than a mile before he found the enemy formed in line to receive him. He immedi itely deployed, and from the head of the line ordered a charge. When he approached within about twenty yards of the enemy's line they gave him a fire from their side-arms, but overshot. Then came the test of strength and skill—the dragoon, with sword in hand, met the confiding lancer, with pointed lance, ready to receive him. The contest was but for a short time.

In many instances lances were twisted from their clenched hands; the Mexicans were unsaddled and driven, helter-skelter, in every direction, and pursued by the dragoons in detachments. Colonel Harney and several of his officers met their men in single combat, but none of them received any injury except Lieutenant Neill, adjutant of the regiment, who was wounded severely in two places from his magnanimity in attempting to capture a Mexican instead of killing him. In full run he overtook the retreating Mexican, and placing his sword in front of him commanded him to surrender, whereupon the Mexican drove his lance into his magnanimous adversary. As the lieutenant wheeled his horse to despatch him, another Mexican charged up and struck him with a lance. However, severely wounded as he was in two places, he conquered one of his foes, and a corporal came up in time to 'settle accounts' with the other.

In this affair Colonel Harney had four wounded and one killed; Lieutenant Judd had one killed; and the Tennesseeans had Messrs. Fox, Long, Woodly, and one other of Captain McCown's company, whose name I could not ascertain, wounded. Mr. Young, a Texan ranger, who was acting as guide, was also wounded slightly. Nineteen Mexicans were found dead at the bridge behind the breastwork. Colonel Harney killed fifty and wounded about the same number. The Mexican force near two thousand; Colonel Harney's about five hundred.

American flag saluted.

Colonel Haskell, Captains Cheatham, Foster, Snead, Lieutenant Judd, and all the officers and men in the command, are spoken of in the very highest terms by Colonel Harney for their gallant conduct throughout the whole affair.

On the 27th, Commodore Perry was preparing to land another battery of ten guns from the Ohio, but the necessity was obviated by the ratification by both parties of the stipulations agreed upon by the commissioners.

The Mexicans surrendered the city of Vera Cruz and castle of San Juan de Ulloa, and the armaments and munitions of war, together with their small arms. The officers retained their side arms, and the whole surrendered as prisoners of war, and were allowed to retire into the country on their parole, General Scott furnishing them four days rations.

The surrender of the city took place on the 29th. The Americans were drawn up in two lines facing each other, and extending for more than a mile across the plain. The Mexicans left the city with their national music playing at ten o'clock, passed between the American lines, laid down their colours and arms, and marched for the interior. The Americans then entered the city with their national music, the stars and stripes were saluted by the batteries, the castle, and the fleet, (*see opposite*) as they were flung to the breeze in the Plaza; General Scott established his head-quarters at the place, and General Worth became military governor of the city.

The effect of our shells upon the city was now seen, and proved to have been deplorable.

Hardly a house had escaped, and a large portion of them were ruined. The shells had fallen through the

American fleet saluting the castle at Vera Cruz.

Rations issued to the poor of Vera Cruz.

roofs and exploded inside, tearing every thing into pieces—bursting through the partitions and blowing out the windows.

The killed and wounded among the soldiery was very slight, about sixty in all; but the citizens suffered severely. It is said that between six and seven hundred men, women, and children were killed and wounded, more than three hundred being killed.

A vast quantity of ammunition was found in the work. The Mexicans, says a letter writer, left their national pets behind in the castle, and our troops suffered much annoyance from them last night. I allude, of course, to fleas and other vermin.

Santiago Fort, that spiteful little place which played so warmly upon our intrenchments, is a beautiful work, with nine guns in barbette, most of them fine English pieces. In fact, most of their best ordnance is of English manufacture, though they have some fine pieces made in the United States.

General Scott ordered ten thousand rations to be issued to the suffering poor of Vera Cruz, and it was an affecting scene to witness the crowd of half famished creatures as they gathered timidly around to receive their respective shares.

After some time spent in restoring the city to cleanliness from the disgusting state of filth in which its late possessors had left it, the Americans recruited themselves from their fatigues. Before setting out for the interior General Scott issued a manifesto declaring his principle of non-interference with Mexican religion and customs.

On the 1st of April the army left Vera Cruz, and

Description of Santa Anna's position.

advanced on the road to Mexico in high spirits, and in the expectation of a speedy battle, as Santa Anna was known to be in the neighbourhood with a large force. He had assembled another army after his defeat at Buena Vista, and now retired before the advance of General Scott to Puebla, stripped that city of every thing that could be of service to his army, and finally took up a strong position at Cerro Gordo, awaiting the attack of General Scott.

The following graphic description of the Mexican general's position, and General Scott's arrangements, is by a gentlemen who witnessed the battle.

"The road from Vera Cruz, as it passes the Plan del Rio, which is a wide, rocky bed of a once large stream, is commanded by a series of high cliffs, rising one above the other, and extending several miles, and all well fortified. The road then debouches to the right, and, curving around the ridge, passes over a high cliff, which is completely enfiladed by forts and batteries. This ridge is the commencement of the *Terra Templada*, the upper or mountainous country. The high and rocky ravine of the river protected the right flank of the position, and a series of most abrupt and apparently impassable mountains and ridges covered their left. Between these points, running a distance of two or three miles, a succession of strongly fortified forts bristled at every turn, and seemed to defy all bravery and skill. The Cerro Gordo commanded tne road on a gentle declination, like a glacis, for nearly a mile—an approach in that direction was impossible. A front attack must have terminated in the almost entire annihilation of our army. But the enemy expected such an attack, confiding in the

Battle of Cerro Gordo.

desperate valour of our men, and believing that it was impossible to turn their position to the right or left. General Scott, however, with the eye of a skilful general, perceived the trap set for him, and determined to avoid it. He, therefore, had a road cut to the right, so as to escape the front fire from the Sierra, and turn his position on the left flank. This movement was made known to the enemy by a deserter from our camp, and consequently a large increase of force under General Vega was sent to the forts on their left. General Scott, to cover his flank movements, on the 17th of April, ordered forward General Twiggs against the fort on the steep ascent, in front and a little to the left of the Sierra. Colonel Harney commanded this expedition, and, at the head of the rifles and some detachments of infantry and artillery, carried his position under a heavy fire of grape and musketry. Having secured this position in front and near the enemy's strongest fortification, and having by incredible labour elevated one of our large guns to the top of the fort, General Scott prepared to follow up his advantages. A demonstration was made from this position against another strong fort in the rear, and near the Sierra, but the enemy were considered too strong and the undertaking was abandoned. A like demonstration was made by the enemy."

On the morning of the 18th, the army moved to the attack in columns, and their success was rapid and decisive. General Twiggs's division assaulted the enemy's left, where he had remained during the night, and, after a slight resistance, carried the breastwork at the point of the bayonet, and completely routed its defenders. Meanwhile Pillow's brigade, accompanied by General

Battle of Cerro Gordo.

Shields, moved rapidly along the Jalapa road, and took up a position to intercept the retreat of the Mexicans. At the same time General Worth pushed forward toward the left, to aid the movement of Twiggs. The rout was total. Three thousand men, with field and other officers, surrendered, and an immense amount of small arms, ordnance and batteries, were also captured. About six thousand Mexicans gained the rear of the Americans on the Jalapa road, but were closely pursued. The Americans lost two hundred and fifty in killed and wounded—among the latter, General Shields; the loss of the Mexicans, exclusive of prisoners, was about one hundred more.

The following description of Twiggs's attack upon the Mexican fort, is from the account of an eye-witness:

"On the 18th, General Twiggs was ordered forward from the position he had already captured, against the fort which commanded the Sierra. Simultaneously an attack on the fortifications on the enemy's left was to be made by Generals Shields and Worth's divisions, who moved in separate columns, while General Pillow advanced against the strong forts and difficult ascents on the right of the enemy's position. The enemy, fully acquainted with General Scott's intended movement, had thrown large bodies of men into the various positions to be attacked. The most serious enterprise was that of Twiggs, who advanced against the main fort that commanded the Sierra. Nothing can be conceived more difficult than this undertaking. The steep and rough character of the ground, the constant fire of the enemy in front, and the cross fire of the forts and batteries which enfiladed our lines, made the duty assigned to General Twiggs one of surpassing difficulty.

Battle of Cerro Gordo.

Battle of Cerro Gordo.

Nothing prevented our men from being utterly destroyed but the steepness of the ascent under which they cou'd shelter. But they sought no shelter, and onward rushed against a hailstorm of balls and musket-shot, led by the gallant Harney, whose noble bearing elicited the applause of the whole army. His conspicuous and stalwart frame at the head of his brigade, his long arm waving his men on to the charge, his sturdy voice ringing above the clash of arms and din of conflict, attracted the attention and admiration alike of the enemy and of our own men. On, on, he led the columns, whose front lines melted before the enemy's fire like snow-flakes in a torrent, and stayed not their course until leaping over the rocky barriers, and bayoneting their gunners, they drove the enemy pellmell from the fort, delivering a deadly fire into their ranks, from their own guns, as they hastily retired. This was truly a gallant deed, worthy the Chevalier Bayard of our army, as the intrepid Harney is well styled. General Scott, between whom and Colonel Harney there had existed some coolness, rode up to the colonel after this achievement, and remarked to him— 'Colonel Harney, I cannot now adequately express my admiration of your gallant achievement, but at the proper time I shall take great pleasure in thanking you in proper terms.' Harney, with the modesty of true valour, claimed the praise as due to his officers and men. Thus did the division of the gallant veteran, Twiggs, carry the main position of the enemy, and occupy the front which commanded the road. It was here the enemy received their heaviest loss, and their general, Vasquez, was killed. A little after, General Worth, having, by great exertions, passed the steep and craggy heights on the enemy's left, summoned a strong fort in the rear of the Sierra to surrender. This fort was manned by a large force under General Pinzon, a mulatto officer of considerable ability and courage, who, seeing the Sierra carried, thought it prudent to surrender, which he did with all his force. General Shields was not so fortunate in the battery which he attacked, and which was commanded by General La Vega. A heavy fire was opened on him, under which the fort was carried with some loss by the gallant Illinoisians, under Baker and Bennett, supported by the New Yorkers, under Burnett. Among those who fell under this fire was the gallant general, who received a grape-shot through his lungs, by which he was completely paralyzed, and thrown into a critical and dangerous state. On the enemy's right, General Pillow commenced the attack against the strong forts near the river. The Tennesseeans, under Haskell, led the column, and the other volunteer regiments followed. This column unexpectedly encountered a heavy fire from a masked battery, by which Haskell's regiment was nearly cut to pieces, and the other volunteer regiments were severely handled. General Pillow withdrew his men, and was preparing for another attack, when the operations at the other points having proved successful, the enemy concluded to surrender. Thus the victory was complete, and four generals, and about six thousand men, were taken prisoners by our army. One of their principal generals and a large number of other officers killed. The Mexican force on this occasion certainly exceeded our own.

According to the account of the captured officers, Santa Anna had in his lines at least eight thousand men,

Jalapa.

and without the intrenchments about six thousand, of which a third was cavalry. The army was composed of the best soldiers in Mexico. The infantry who had fought so bravely at Buena Vista, and all the regular artillerists of the republic, including several naval officers, were present. Some of the officers whom General Scott released at the capitulation of Vera Cruz without extorting the parole on account of their gallantry, were found among the killed and wounded. Of the latter was a gallant young officer named Halzinger, a German by birth, who excited the admiration of our army during the bombardment of Vera Cruz, by seizing a flag which had been cut down by our balls, and holding it in his right hand until a staff could be procured. He had been released by General Scott without a parole, and was found on the field of Cerro Gordo dangerously wounded. In addition to the loss of the enemy in killed and taken they lost about thirty pieces of brass cannon, mostly of large calibre, manufactured at the royal foundry of Seville. A large quantity of fixed ammunition, of a very superior quality, together with the private baggage and money-chest of Santa Anna, containing twenty thousand dollars, was also captured."

Leaving the scene of this great victory the army moved forward towards the capital. On the 19th of April, General Twiggs took the city of Jalapa with one detachment, and on the 22d, another under General Worth entered the city of Perote, where, to use the words of a humorous writer, " an officer politely handed over the keys of the well-known castle and prison, bowed, and followed the footsteps of his twice-whipped excellency."

Worth enters Puebla.

"The enemy's forces had all left that place, and our general took possession of the castle, with its armament in perfect order. Colonel Velasques had been left behind to surrender all things in the name of the government. Fifty cannons, three mortars, four stone mortars, and four or five howitzers, together with a large number of round shot and shells, and great quantities of other ammunition, and small arms were delivered up to us. Generals Morales and Landero, who had been imprisoned by Santa Anna for capitulating at Vera Cruz, were released on the appearance of the Americans. Two South Carolina volunteers, and an American sailor, taken near Vera Cruz, were prisoners in the castle, and of course released by our troops. Ampudia was in the vicinity of Perote on the approach of General Worth, but had not the politeness to visit him before taking his departure, which is said to have been hurried. Some two or three thousand infantry and cavalry of the enemy were also in the neighbourhood at the time.

On the road the inhabitants complained bitterly of outrages perpetrated by the retreating soldiers from Cerro Gordo, and many of them had left their homes."

This treatment received from their own countrymen contrasted strongly with that experienced from their generous foe. Pushing on from Perote, General Worth took possession on the 15th of May of the city of Puebla, Santa Anna retiring before him with nothing more than a show of opposition.

When General Worth had reached a point some miles distant from Puebla, General Santa Anna was in the city, engaged in distributing shoes to his soldiers, and a detachment, with which General Worth had a skirmish,

Northern extremity of Puebla de los Angelos.

American army concentrated at Puebla.

was sent out by him to delay the advance. General Worth advanced so rapidly, however, as to enter the city almost directly behind the flying cavalry, and General Santa Anna was obliged to retire in all haste, leaving many of his soldiers to run barefoot. He marched directly to the capital, issuing on the march, at Ayotla, an address, perhaps the most ingenious Mexican document occasioned by the present war, offering to resign all power, but suggesting at the same time a plan by which he hoped to conduct the war to a successful termination. Of course the answer to this letter was an entire acquiescence in the views of Santa Anna by the president substitute, an invitation to the capital, and its consequence, the assumption of supreme power. Santa Anna left the army to follow, and with some officers entered the capital, and commenced making preparations for its defense. In May he left the city and manœuvered about, threatening an attack on Vera Cruz, but returned without effecting any thing.

In the latter part of May, General Scott concentrated his army at Puebla, and prepared to advance upon the capital itself. The history of his operations is given with great perspicacity in his official despatches. We quote them in preference to following the statements made by others, because as the head of the army, all its operations come under his control and knowledge, and the account of them which he gives is naturally more comprehensive than those of other officers or observers, however valuable the latter may be as testimonials of individual gallantry. Writing on the 19th of August, nine miles from Mexico, he states that—

"Leaving a competent garrison in Puebla, the American army advanced upon the capital by divisions, becoming more closely approximated as they descended into the basin of the capital (seventy-five miles from Puebla) about the head of Lake Chalco, with Lake Tescuco a little in front and to the right. On the 12th and 13th we pushed reconnoissances upon the Penon, an isolated mound (eight miles from Mexico) of great height, strongly fortified to the top (three tiers of works) and flooded around the base by the season of rains and sluices from the lakes. This mound, close to the national road, commands the principal approach to the city from the east. No doubt it might have been carried, but at a great and disproportionate loss, and I was anxious to spare the lives of this gallant army for a general battle which I knew we had to win before capturing the city, or obtaining the object of the campaign—a just and honourable peace.

Another reconnoissance was directed (13th) upon Mexicalcingo, to the left of the Penon, a village at a fortified bridge across the outlet or canal, leading from Lake Jochimilco to the capital—five miles from the latter. It might have been easy (masking the Penon) to force the passage; but on the other side of the bridge we should have found ourselves four miles from this road, on a narrow causeway, flanked to the right and left by water or boggy grounds. Those difficulties, closely viewed, threw me back upon the project, long entertained, of turning the strong eastern defenses of the city, by passing around south of Lake Chalco and Jochimilco, at the foot of the hills and mountains, so as to reach this point, and hence to manœuver, on hard ground, though much broken, to the south and south-west of the capital, which has been more or less under our view, since the 10th instant.

Accordingly, Worth's division, with Harney's cavalry brigade leading—we marched on the 15th instant. Pillow's and Quitman's divisions followed closely, and then Twiggs's division, which was left till the next day at Ayotla, in order to threaten the Penon and Mexicalcingo, and to deceive the enemy as long as practicable.

Twiggs, on the 16th, marching from Ayotla towards Chalco, (six miles,) met a corps of more than double his number—cavalry and infantry—under General Valencia. Twiggs halted, deployed into line, and by a few rounds from Captain Taylor's field battery, dispersed the enemy, killing and wounding many men and horses. No other molestation has been experienced except a few random shots from guerilleros, on the height; and the march of twenty-seven miles, over a route deemed impracticable by the enemy, is now accomplished by all the corps—thanks to their indomitable zeal and physical prowess.

Arriving here, the 18th, Worth's division and Harney's cavalry were pushed forward a league, to reconnoiter and to carry or to mask San Antonio, on the direct road to the capital. This village was found strongly defended by field-works, heavy guns, and a numerous garrison. It could only be turned by infantry, to the left, over a field of volcanic rocks and lava; for, to our right, the ground was too boggy. It was soon ascertained, by the daring engineers, Captain Mason, and Lieutenants Stevens and Tower, that the point could only be approached by the front, over a narrow causeway, flanked with wet ditches of great depth. Worth was ordered not to attack, but to threaten and to mask the place.

Death of Captain Thornton.

The first shot fired from San Antonio (the 8th) killed Captain S. Thornton, 2d dragoons, a gallant officer, who was covering the operations with his company.

The same day, a reconnoissance was commenced to the left of San Augustin, first over difficult mounds, and farther on, over the same field of volcanic rocks and lava which extends to the mountains, some five miles from San Antonio, towards Magdalena. This reconnoissance was continued to-day, by Captain Lee, assisted by Lieutenants Beauregard and Tower, all of the engineers; who were joined, in the afternoon, by Major Smith of the same corps. Other divisions coming up, Pillow's was advanced to make a practicable road for heavy artillery, and Twiggs's thrown farther in front, to cover that operation; for, by the partial reconnoissance of yesterday, Captain Lee discovered a large corps of observation in that direction, with a detachment of which his supports of cavalry and foot under Captain Kearney and Lieutenant-Colonel Graham, respectively, had a successful skirmish.

By three o'clock this afternoon, the advanced divisions came to a point where the new road could only be continued under the direct fire of twenty-two pieces of the enemy's artillery, (most of them of large calibre,) placed in a strong intrenched camp to oppose our operations, and surrounded by every advantage of ground, besides immense bodies of cavalry and infantry, hourly reinforced from the city, over an excellent road beyond the volcanic field, and consequently entirely beyond the reach of our cavalry and artillery.

Arriving on the ground, an hour later, I found that Pillow's and Twiggs's divisions had advanced to dis-

Battle of San Augustin.

lodge the enemy, picking their way (all officers on foot) along his front, and extending themselves towards the road, from the city and the enemy's left. Captain Magruder's field battery, of twelve and six-pounders, and Lieutenant Callender's battery of mounted howitzers and rockets, had also, with great difficulty, been advanced within range of the intrenched camp. These batteries, most gallantly served, suffered much, in the course of the afternoon, from the enemy's superior metal.

The battle, though mostly stationary, continued to rage with great violence, until nightfall. Brevet Brigadier-General P. F. Smith's and Brevet Colonel Riley's brigades (Twiggs's division) supported by Brigadier-Generals Pierce's and Cadwalader's brigades (Pillow's division) were more than three hours under a heavy fire of artillery and musketry, along the almost impassable ravine in front and to the left of the intrenched camp. Besides the twenty-two pieces of artillery, the camp and ravine were defended closely by masses of infantry, and these again supported by clouds of cavalry at hand and hovering in view: Consequently no decided impression could be made by daylight, on the enemy's most formidable position, because, independent of the difficulty of the ravine, our infantry, unaccompanied by cavalry and artillery, could not advance in column without being mowed down by the grape and canister of the batteries, nor advance in line without being ridden over by the enemy's numerous cavalry. All our corps, however, including Magruder's and Callender's last batteries, not only maintained the exposed positions early gained, but all attempted charges upon tl ›m, respectively—particularly on Riley, twice closely engaged with cavalry in greatly superior numbers—were repulsed and punished.

From an eminence, soon after arriving near the scene, I observed the church and hamlet of Contreras (or Ansalda) on the road leading up from the capital, through the intrenched camp to Magdalena, and seeing, at the same time, the stream of reinforcements advancing by the road, from the city, I ordered (through Major-General Pillow) Colonel Morgan, with his regiment, the 15th, till then held in reserve by Pillow, to move forward, and to occupy Contreras, or Ansalda,—being persuaded, if occupied, it would arrest the enemy's reinforcements and ultimately decide the battle.

Riley was already on the enemy's left, in advance of the hamlet. A few minutes later, Brigadier-General Shields, with his volunteer brigade, (New York and South Carolina regiments,) coming up under my orders from San Augustin, I directed Shields to follow and sustain Morgan. These corps, over the extreme difficulties of ground—partially covered with a low forest—before described, reached Contreras, and found Cadwalader's brigade, in position, observing the formidable movement from the capital and much needing the timely reinforcement.

It was already dark, and the cold rain had begun to fall in torrents upon our unsheltered troops; for the hamlet, though a strong defensive position, can hold only the wounded men, and, unfortunately, the new regiments have little or nothing to eat in their haversacks. Wet, hungry, and without the possibility of sleep, all our gallant corps, I learn, are full of confidence, and only wait for the last hour of darkness to

Battle of Contreras.

gain the positions whence to storm and carry the enemy's works.

Of the seven officers despatched, since about sundown, from my position, opposite to the enemy's centre, and on this side of the field of rocks and lava—to communicate instructions to the hamlet—not one has succeeded in getting through those difficulties, increased by darkness. They have all returned. But the gallant and indefatigable Captain Lee, of the engineers, who has been constantly with the operating forces, is just in from Shields, Smith, Cadwalader, &c., to report as above, and to ask that a powerful diversion be made against the centre of the intrenched camp towards morning.

Brigadier-General Twiggs, cut off, as above, from the part of his division beyond the impracticable ground, and Captain Lee are gone, under my orders, to collect the forces remaining on this side, with which to make that diversion about five o'clock, in the morning."

"The morning of the 20th opened with one of a series of unsurpassed achievements, all in view of the capital, and to which I shall give the general name—*Battle of Mexico*.

In the night of the 19th, Brigadier-General Shields, P. F. Smith, and Cadwalader, and Colonel Riley, with their brigades, and the 15th regiment, under Colonel Morgan, detached from Brigadier-General Pierce—found themselves in and about the important position—the village, hamlet or hacienda, called, indifferently, Contreras, Ansalda San Geronimo—half a mile nearer to the city than the enemy's intrenched camp on the same road, towards the factory of Magdalena.

Battle of Contreras.

That camp had been, unexpectedly, our formidable point of attack the afternoon before, and we had now to take it, without the aid of cavalry or artillery, or to throw back our advanced corps upon the road from San Augustin to the city, and thence force a passage through San Antonio.

Accordingly to meet contingencies, Major-General Worth was ordered to leave, early in the morning of the 20th, one of his brigades to mask San Antonio, and to march with the other six miles, via San Augustin, upon Contreras. A like destination was given to Major-General Quitman and his remaining brigade in San Augustin —replacing, for the moment, the garrison of that important depot with Harney's brigade of cavalry, as horse could not pass over the intervening rocks, &c., to reach the field of battle.

A diversion for an earlier hour (daylight) had been arranged the night before, according to the suggestion of Brigadier-General Smith, received through the engineer, Captain Lee, who conveyed my orders to our troops remaining on the ground opposite to the enemy's centre—the point for the diversion or a real attack, as circumstances might allow.

Guided by Captain Lee, it proved the latter under the command of Colonel Ransom, of the 9th, having with him that regiment and some companies of three others—the 3d, 12th, and rifles.

Shields, the senior officer at the hamlet, having arrived in the night, after Smith had arranged with Cadwalader and Riley the plan of attack for the morning, delicately waived interference; but reserved to himself the double task of holding the hamlet with his two regiments,

General Butler.

Battle of Contreras.

(South Carolina and New York volunteers,) against ten times his numbers on the side of the city, including the slopes to his left, and, in case the camp in his rear should be carried, to face about and cut off the flying enemy.

At three o'clock, A. M., the great movement commenced on the rear of the enemy's camp, Riley leading, followed successively by Cadwalader's and Smith's brigades, the latter temporarily under the orders of Major Dimick of the 1st artillery—the whole force being commanded by Smith, the senior in the general attack, and whose arrangements, skill, and gallantry, always challenge the highest admiration.

The march was rendered tedious by the darkness, rain, and mud; but about sunrise, Riley, conducted by Lieutenant Tower, engineer, had reached an elevation behind the enemy, whence he precipitated his columns;— stormed the intrenchments, planted his several colours upon them, and carried the work—all in seventeen minutes.

Conducted by Lieutenant Beauregard, engineer, and Lieutenant Brooks, of Twiggs's staff, both of whom, like Lieutenant Tower, had, in the night, twice reconnoitered the ground—Cadwalader brought up to the general assault, two of his regiments—the voltigeurs and the 11th, and at the appointed time, Colonel Ransom, with his temporary brigade, conducted by Captain Lee, engineer, not only made the movement to divert and to distract the enemy; but, after crossing the deep ravine in his front, advanced, and poured into the works and upon the fugitives, many volleys from his destructive musketry.

In the mean time Smith's own brigade, under the

Battle of Contreras.

temporary command of Major Dimick, following the movements of Riley and Cadwalader, discovered, opposite to, and outside of the works, a long line of Mexican cavalry, drawn up as a support. Dimick, having at the head of the brigade the company of sappers and miners, under Lieutenant Smith, engineer, who had conducted the march, was ordered by Brigadier-General Smith, to form line faced to the enemy, and in a charge against a flank, routed the cavalry.

Shields, too, by the wise disposition of his brigade and gallant activity, contributed much to the general results. He held masses of cavalry and infantry, supported by artillery, in check below him, and captured hundreds, with one general, (Mendoza,) of those who fled from above.

I doubt whether a more brilliant or decisive victory—taking into view, ground, artificial defenses, batteries, and the extreme disparity of numbers—without cavalry or artillery on our side—is to be found on record. Including all our corps directed against the intrenched camp, with Shields's brigade at the hamlet, we positively did not number over four thousand five hundred rank and file; and we know, by sight and since, more certainly by many captured documents and letters, that the enemy had actually engaged on the spot seven thousand men, with at least twelve thousand more hovering within sight, and striking distance—both on the 16th and 20th. All, not killed or captured, now fled with precipitation.

Thus was the great victory of Contreras achieved; one road to the capital opened: seven hundred of the enemy killed, eight hundred and forty-three prisoners,

Results of the battle.

including, among eighty-eight officers, four generals; besides many colours and standards; twenty-two pieces of brass ordnance—half of large calibre; thousands of small arms and accoutrements; an immense quantity of shot, shells, powder, and cartridges; seven hundred pack mules, many horses, &c., all in our hands.

It is highly gratifying to find that, by skilful arrangement, and rapidity of execution, our loss in killed and wounded, did not exceed, on the spot, sixty—among the former the brave Captain Charles Hanson, of the 7th infantry—not more distinguished for gallantry, than for modesty, morals, and piety. Lieutenant J. P. Johnstone, 1st artillery, serving with Magruder's battery—a young officer of the highest promise, was killed the evening before.

One of the most pleasing incidents of the victory is the recapture, in the works, by Captain Drum, 4th artillery, under Major Gardner, of the two brass six pounders, taken from another company of the same regiment, though without the loss of honour, at the glorious battle of Buena Vista—about which guns the whole regiment had mourned for so many long months! Coming up, a little later, I had the happiness to join in the protracted cheers of the gallant 4th on the joyous event, and, indeed, the whole army sympathizes in its just pride and exultation.

The battle being won before the advancing brigades of Worth's and Quitman's divisions were in sight, both were ordered back to their late positions—Worth, to attack San Antonio, in front, with his whole force, as soon as approached in the rear, by Pillow's and Twiggs's divisions—moving from Contreras, through San Angel

Battle of Churubusco.

and Coyoacan. By carrying San Antonio we knew that we should open another—a shorter and better road to the capital, for our siege and other trains.

Accordingly, the two advanced divisions and Shields's brigade marched from Contreras, under the immediate orders of Major-General Pillow, who was now joined by the gallant Brigadier-General Pierce of his division, personally thrown out of activity, late the evening before, by a severe hurt received from the fall of his horse.

After giving necessary orders on the field, in the midst of prisoners and trophies, and sending instructions to Harney's brigade of cavalry, left at San Augustin, to join me, I personally followed Pillow's movement.

Arriving at Coyoacan, two miles by a cross road, from the rear of San Antonio, I first detached Captain Lee, engineer, with Captain Kearney's troop, 1st dragoons, supported by the rifle regiment, under Major Loring, to reconnoiter that strong point, and next despatched Major-General Pillow, with one of his brigades (Cadwalader's) to make the attack upon it, in concert with Major-General Worth, on the opposite side.

At the same time, by another road to the left, Lieutenant Stevens, of the engineers, supported by Lieutenant G. W. Smith's company of sappers and miners, of the same corps, was sent to reconnoiter the strongly fortified church or convent of San Pablo, in the hamlet of Churubusco—one mile off. Twiggs with one of the brigades, and Captain Taylor's field battery, were ordered to follow and attack the convent. Major Smith, senior engineer, was despatched to concert with Twiggs the mode and means of attack, and Twiggs's other brigade, I soon ordered up to support him.

Battle of Churubusco.

Next (but all in ten minutes) I sent Pierce (just able to keep the saddle) with his brigade (Pillow's division) conducted by Captain Lee, engineer, by a third road, a little farther to our left, to attack the enemy's right and rear, in order to favour the movement upon the convent and cut off the retreat towards the capital. And finally, Shields, senior brigadier to Pierce, with the New York and South Carolina volunteers, (Quitman's division,) was ordered to follow Pierce, closely, and to take the command of our left wing. All these movements were made with the utmost alacrity by our gallant troops and commanders.

Finding myself at Coyoacan, from which so many roads conveniently branched, without escort or reserve, I had to advance, for safety, close upon Twiggs's rear. The battle now raged from the right to the left of our whole line.

Learning, on the return of Captain Lee, that Shields, in the rear of Churubusco, was hard pressed, and in danger of being outflanked, if not overwhelmed, by greatly superior numbers, I immediately sent, under Major Sumner, 2d dragoons, the rifles, (Twiggs's reserve,) and Captain Sibley's troop, 2d dragoons, then at hand, to support our left, guided by the same engineer.

About an hour earlier, Worth had, by skilful and daring movements upon the front and right, turned and forced San Antonio—its garrison, no doubt, much shaken by our decisive victory at Contreras.

His second brigade, (Colonel Clarke's,) conducted by Captain Mason, engineer, assisted by Lieutenant Hardcastle, topographical engineer, turned the right, and by

Battle of Churubusco.

a wide sweep, came out upon the high road to the capital. At this point, the heavy garrison (three thousand men) in retreat, was, by Clarke cut in the centre: one portion, the rear driven upon Dolores, off to the right; and the other upon Churubusco, in the direct line of our operations. The first brigade, (Colonel Garland's,) same division, consisting of the second artillery, under Major Galt, the 3d artillery, under Lieutenant-Colonel Belton, and the 4th infantry, commanded by Major F. Lee, with Lieutenant-Colonel Duncan's field battery (temporarily) followed in pursuit through the town, taking one general prisoner, the abandoned guns, (five pieces,) much ammunition and other public property.

The forcing of San Antonio was the *second* brilliant event of the day.

Worth's division being soon reunited in hot pursuit, he was joined by Major-General Pillow, who, marching from Coyoacan and discovering that San Antonio had been carried, immediately turned to the left, according to my instruction, and though much impeded by ditches and swamps, hastened to the attack of Churubusco.

The hamlet or scattered houses, bearing this name, presented, besides the fortified convent, a strong fieldwork, (*tete de pont*) with regular bastions and curtains, at the head of a bridge, over which the road passes from San Antonio to the capital.

The whole remaining forces of Mexico—some twenty-seven thousand men—cavalry, artillery, and infantry, collected from every quarter—were now in, on the flanks or within supporting distance of those works, and seemed resolved to make a last and desperate stand; for if beaten here, the feebler defenses at the gates of the

Battle of Churubusco.

city—four miles off—could not, as was well known to both parties, delay the victors an hour. The capital of an ancient empire, now of a great republic; or an early peace, the assailants were resolved to win. Not an American—and we were less than a third of the enemy's numbers—had a doubt as to the result.

The fortified church or convent, hotly pressed by Twiggs, had already held out about an hour, when Worth and Pillow—the latter having with him only Cadwalader's brigade—began to manœuver upon the *tete de pont*, with the convent at half gun-shot, to their left. Garland's brigade, (Worth's division,) to which had been added the light battalion under Lieutenant-Colonel Smith, continued to advance in front, and under the fire of a long line of infantry, off on the left of the brigade; and Clarke, of the same division, directed his brigade along the road or close by its side. Two of Pillow's and Cadwalader's regiments, the 11th and 14th, supported and participated in this direct movement: the other (the voltigeurs) was left in reserve. Most of these corps—particularly Clarke's brigade, advancing perpendicularly—were made to suffer much by the fire of the *tete de pont*, and they would have suffered greatly more by flank attacks from the convent, but for the pressure of Twiggs on the other side of that work.

This well-combined and daring movement, at length reached the principal point of attack, and the formidable *tete de pont*, was, at once, assaulted and carried by the bayonet. Its deep wet ditch was first gallantly crossed by the 8th and 5th infantry, commanded respectively by Major Waite and Lieutenant-Colonel Scott—followed closely, by the 6th infantry, (same brigade) which had

Battle of Churubusco.

been so much exposed in the road—the 11th regiment, under Lieutenant-Colonel Graham, and the 14th, commanded by Colonel Trousdale, both of Cadwalader's brigade, Pillow's division. About the same time, the enemy, in front of Garland, after a hot conflict of an hour and a half, gave way, in a retreat towards the capital.

The immediate result of this *third* signal triumph of the day were three field-pieces, one hundred and ninety-two prisoners, much ammunition and two colours, taken in the *tete de pont*.

As the concurrent attack upon the convent favoured physically and morally, the assault upon the *tete de pont*, so, reciprocally, no doubt, the fall of the latter, contributed to the capture of the former. The two works were only some four hundred and fifty yards apart; and as soon as we were in possession of the *tete de pont*, a captured four-pounder was turned and fired—first by Captain Larkin Smith, and next by Lieutenant Snelling, both of the 8th infantry—several times upon the convent. In the same brief interval, Lieutenant-Colonel Duncan, (also of Worth's division,) gallantly brought two of his guns to bear, at a short range, from the San Antonio road, upon the principal face of the work, and on the tower of the church, which, in the obstinate contest had been often refilled with some of the best sharp-shooters of the enemy.

Finally, twenty minutes after the *tete de pont* had been carried by Worth and Pillow, and at the end of a desperate conflict of two hours and a half, the church or convent—the citadel of the strong line of defense along the rivulet of Churubusco—yielded to Twiggs's division,

Battle of Churubusco.

Battle of Churubusco.

and threw out, on all sides, signals of surrender. The white flags, however, were not exhibited until the moment when the 3d infantry, under Captain Alexander, had cleared the way by fire and bayonet, and had entered the work. Captain J. M. Smith and Lieutenant O. L. Shepherd, both of that regiment with their companies, had the glory of leading the assault. The former received the surrender, and Captain Alexander instantly hung out from a balcony, the colours of the gallant 3d. Major Dimick, with a part of the 1st artillery, serving as infantry, entered nearly abreast with the leading troops.

Lieutenant J. F. Irons, 1st artillery, aid-de-camp to Brigadier-General Cadwalader, a young officer of great merit, and conspicuous in battle, on several previous occasions, received, in front of the work, a mortal wound. (Since dead.)

Captain Taylor's field battery, attached to Twiggs's division, opened its effective fire, at an early moment, upon the out-works of the convent and the tower of its church. Exposed to the severest fire of the enemy, the captain, his officers and men, won universal admiration; but at length much disabled in men and horses, the battery was, by superior orders, withdrawn from the action thirty minutes before the surrender of the convent.

These corps, excepting Taylor's battery, belonged to the brigade of Brigadier-General Smith, who closely directed the whole attack in front, with his habitual coolness and ability; while Riley's brigade—the 2d and 7th infantry, under Captain T. Morris and Lieutenant-Colonel Plympton, respectively, vigorously engaged the right of the work and part of its rear. At the

The fourth victory.

moment, the rifles, belonging to Smith's, were detached in support of Brigadier-General Shields on our extreme left, and the 4th artillery, acting as infantry, under Major Gardner, belonging to Riley's brigade had been left in charge of the camp, trophies, &c., at Contreras. Twiggs's division, at Churubusco, had thus been deprived of the services of two of its most gallant and effective regiments.

The immediate results of this victory were:—the capture of seven field-pieces, some ammunition, one colour, three generals, and one thousand two hundred and sixty-one prisoners, including other officers.

The capture of the enemy's citadel was the *fourth* great achievement of our arms in the same day.

It has been stated that, some two hours and half before, Pierce's, followed closely by the volunteer brigade, both under the command of Brigadier-General Shields, had been detached to our left to turn the enemy's works; —to prevent the escape of the garrisons, and to oppose the extension of the enemy's numerous corps, from the rear, upon and around our left.

Considering the inferior numbers of the two brigades, the objects of the movement were difficult to accomplish. Hence the reinforcement (the rifles, &c.,) sent forward a little later.

In a winding march of a mile around to the right, this temporary division found itself on the edge of an open wet meadow, near the road from San Antonio to the capital, and in the presence of some four thousand of the enemy's infantry, a little in rear of Churubusco, on that road. Establishing the right at a strong building, Shields extended his left, parrallel to the road, to out-

The fifth victory.

flank the enemy towards the capital. But the enemy extending his right, supported by three thousand cavalry, more rapidly, (being favoured with better ground,) in the same direction, Shields concentrated the division about a hamlet, and determined to attack in front. The battle was long, hot, and varied; but ultimately success crowned the zeal and gallantry of our troops, ably directed by their distinguished commander, Brigadier-General Shields. The 9th, 12th, and 15th regiments, under Colonel Ransom, Captain Wood and Colonel Morgan, respectively, of Pierce's brigade, (Pillow's division,) and the New York and South Carolina volunteers, under Colonels Burnett and Butler, respectively, of Shields's own brigade, (Quitman's division,) together with the mountain howitzer battery, now under Lieutenant Reno, of the ordnance corps, all shared in the glory of this action—our *fifth* victory in the same day.

Brigadier-General Pierce, from the hurt of the evening before—under pain and exhaustion—fainted in the action. Several other changes in command, occurred on this field. Thus, Colonel Morgan, being severely wounded, the command of the 15th infantry devolved on Lieutenant-Colonel Howard. Colonel Burnet, receiving a like wound, the command of the New York volunteers fell to Lieutenant-Colonel Baxter; and, on the fall of the lamented Colonel P. M. Butler—earlier badly wounded, but continuing to lead nobly in the hottest part of the battle—the command of the South Carolina volunteers devolved first, on Lieutenant-Colonel Dickinson, who being severely wounded (as before in the seige of Vera Cruz,) the regiment ultimately fell under the orders of Major Gladden.

Pursuit of the enemy.

Lieutenants David Adams and W. R. Williams, of the same corps; Captain Augustus Quarles and Lieutenant J. B. Goodman, of the 15th, and Lieutenant E. Chandler, New York volunteers—all gallant officers, nobly fell in the same action.

Shields took three hundred and eighty prisoners, including officers, and it cannot be doubted that the rage of the conflict between him and the enemy, just in the rear of the *tete de pont* and the convent, had some influence on the surrender of those formidable defenses.

As soon as the *tete de pont* was carried, the greater part of Worth's and Pillow's forces passed that brigade in rapid pursuit of the flying enemy. These distinguished generals, coming up with Brigadier-General Shields, now also victorious, the three continued to press upon the fugitives to within a mile and a half of the capital. Here Colonel Harney, with a small part of his brigade of cavalry, rapidly passed to the front and charged the enemy up to the nearest gate.

The cavalry charge was headed by Captain Kearney, of the first dragoons, having in squadron with his own troop, that of Captain McReynolds, of the 3d—making the usual escort to general head-quarters; but being early in the day, detached for general service, was now under Colonel Harney's orders. The gallant captain not hearing the *recall* that had been sounded, dashed up to the San Antonio gate, sabreing, in his way, all who resisted. Of the seven officers of the squadron, Kearney lost his left arm; McReynolds and Lieutenant Lorimer Graham were both severely wounded, and Lieutenant R. S. Ewell, who succeeded to the command of the escort, had two horses killed under him. Major F. D.

Mills, of the 15th infantry, a volunteer in this charge, was killed at the gate.

So terminated the series of events which I have but feebly presented. My thanks were freely poured out on the different fields—to the abilities and science of generals and other officers—to the gallantry and prowess of all—the rank and file included. But a reward infinitely higher—the applause of a grateful country and government, will, I cannot doubt, be accorded, in due time, to so much merit, of every sort, displayed by this glorious army, which has now overcome all difficulties—distance, climate, ground, fortifications, numbers.

It has in a single day, in many battles, as often defeated thirty-two thousand men; made about three thousand prisoners, including eight generals, (two of them ex-presidents,) and two hundred and sixty-five other officers; killed or wounded four thousand of all ranks—besides entire corps dispersed and dissolved;—captured thirty-seven pieces of ordnance—more than trebling our siege train and field batteries—with a large number of small arms, a full supply of ammunition of every kind, &c., &c.

These great results have overwhelmed the enemy.

Our loss amounts to one thousand and fifty-three;—killed, one hundred and thirty-nine, including sixteen officers; wounded, eight hundred and seventy-six, with sixty officers.

After so many victories, we might, with but little additional loss, have occupied the capital the same evening. But Mr. Trist, commissioner, &c., as well as myself, had been admonished by the best friends of peace—intelligent neutrals and some American residents—against precipitation- lest, by wantonly driving

Armistice.

away the government and others—dishonoured—we might scatter the elements of peace, excite a spirit of national desperation, and thus indefinitely postpone the hope of accommodation. Deeply impressed with this danger, and remembering our mission—to conquer a peace—the army very cheerfully sacrificed to patriotism —to the great wish and want of our country—the *eclat* that would have followed an entrance—sword in hand— into a great capital. Willing to leave something to this republic—of no immediate value to us—on which to rest her pride, and to recover temper—I halted our victorious corps at the gates of the city, (at least for a time,) and have them now cantoned in the neighbouring villages, where they are well sheltered and supplied with all necessaries.

On the morning of the 21st, being about to take up battering or assaulting positions, to authorize me to summon the city to surrender, or to sign an armistice with a pledge to enter at once into negotiations for a peace—a mission came out to propose a truce. Rejecting its forms, I despatched my contemplated note to President Santa Anna—omitting the summons. The 22d, commissioners were appointed by the commanders of the two armies; the armistice was signed the 23d, and ratifications exchanged the 24th.

Negotiations were actively continued with, as was understood, some prospect of a successful result up to the 2d inst., when our commissioner handed in his *ultimatum*, (on boundaries,) and the negotiators adjourned to meet on the 6th.

Some infractions of the truce, in respect to our supplies from the city, were earlier committed, followed by

The city of Mexico.

Violation of the armistice by Santa Anna.

apologies on the part of the enemy. Those vexations I was willing to put down to the imbecility of the government, and waived pointed demands of reparation while any hope remained of a satisfactory termination of the war. But on the 5th, and more fully on the 6th, I learned that as soon as the *ultimatum* had been considered in a grand council of ministers and others, President Santa Anna, on the 4th or 5th, without giving me the slightest notice, actively recommenced strengthening the military defenses of the city, in gross violation of the third article of the armistice.

On that information which has since received the fullest verification, I addressed to him a note on the 6th. His reply dated the same day, received the next morning, was absolutely and notoriously false, both in recrimination and explanation.

Being delayed by the terms of the armistice more than two weeks, we had now, late on the 7th, to begin to reconnoiter the different approaches to the city, within our reach, before I could lay down any definitive plan of attack.

The same afternoon a large body of the enemy was discovered hovering about the *Molinos del Rey* within a mile and a third of this village, where I am quartered with the general staff and Worth's division.

It might have been supposed that an attack upon us was intended; but knowing the great value to the enemy of those mills (*Molinos del Rey*) containing a cannon foundry, with a large deposit of powder in *Casa Mata* near them ; and having heard, two days before, that many church bells had been sent out to be cast into guns—the enemy's movemen' was easily understood, and I resolved, at once, to drive him early the next morning; to seize the powder and to destroy the foundry.

Another motive for this decision—leaving the general plan of attack upon the city for full reconnoissance—was, that we knew our recent captures had left the enemy not a fourth of the guns necessary to arm, all at the same time, the strong works at each of the eight city gates, and we could not cut the communication between the foundry and the capital without first taking the formidable castle on the heights of Chapultepec which overlooked both and stood between. For this difficult operation we were not entirely ready, and moreover we might altogether neglect the castle, if, as we then hoped, our reconnoissances should prove that the distant southern approaches to the city were more eligible than this south-western approach.

Hence the decision promptly taken, the execution of which was assigned to Brevet Major-General Worth, whose division was reinforced with Cadwalader's brigade, of Pillow's division, three squadrons of dragoons, under Major Sumner, and some heavy guns of the siege train under Captain Huger, of the ordnance, and Captain Drum of the 4th artillery—two officers of the highest merit."

For the particulars of this decisive and brilliant result, General Scott refers to General Worth's despatch, and the reader will find them in the life of that officer, in a subsequent part of this book.

The enemy having several times reinforced his line, the action soon becoming much more general than I had expected, I called up from the distance of three

Molinos del Rey.

miles; first, Major-General Pillow, with his remaining brigade, (Pierce's,) and next Riley's brigade of Twiggs's division—leaving his other brigade (Smith's) in observation at San Angel. Those corps approached with zeal and rapidity; but the battle was won just as Brigadier-General Pierce reached the ground and had interposed his corps between Garland's brigade (Worth's division) and the retreating enemy.

General Worth's report mentions, with just commendation, two of my volunteer aids—Major Kirby, paymaster, and Major Gaines of the Kentucky volunteers. I also had the valuable services, on the same field, of several other officers of my staff, general and personal:—Lieutenant-Colonel Hitchcock, acting inspector-general; Captain R. E. Lee, engineer; Captain Irwin, chief quartermaster; Captain Grayson, chief commissary; Captain H. L. Scott, acting assistant adjutant-general; Lieutenant Williams, aid-de-camp, and Lieutenant Lay, military secretary."

"At the end of another series of arduous and brilliant operations, of more than forty-eight hours continuance, this glorious army hoisted, on the morning of the 14th of September, the colours of the United States on the walls of the national palace of Mexico.

The victory of the 8th, at the Molinos del Rey, was followed by daring reconnoissances on the part of our distinguished engineers, Captain Lee, Lieutenants Beauregard, Stevens, and Tower—Major Smith, senior, being sick, and Captain Mason, third in rank, wounded. Their operations were directed principally to the south—toward the gates of the Piedad, San Angel, (Nino Per- dido,) San Antonio, and the Passeo de la Viga.

Survey of the southern gates.

This city stands on a slight swell of ground, near the centre of an irregular basin, and is girdled with a ditch in its greater extent—a navigable canal of great breadth and depth—very difficult to bridge, in the presence of an enemy, and serving at once for drainage, custom-house purposes, and military defense—leaving eight intrenches or gates, over arches—each of which we found defended by a system of strong works that seemed to require nothing but some men and guns to be impregnable.

Outside and within the cross fires of those gates, we found to the south other obstacles but little less formidable. All the approaches near the city are over elevated causeways, cut in many places (to oppose us) and flanked, on both sides, by ditches also of unusual dimensions.—The numerous cross roads are flanked in like manner, having bridges at the intersections, recently broken. The meadows thus checked, are, moreover, in many spots, under water or marshy; for, it will be remembered, we were in the midst of the wet season, though with less rain than usual, and we could not wait for the fall of the neighbouring lakes and the consequent drainage of the wet grounds at the edge of the city—the lowest in the whole basin.

After a close personal survey of the southern gates, covered by Pillow's division and Riley's brigade of Twiggs's—with four times our numbers, concentrated in our immediate front—I determined, on the 11th, to avoid the net work of obstacles, and to seek, by a sudden inversion, to the south-west and west, less unfavourable approaches.

To economize the l'ves of our gallant officers and

Scott's stratagem.

men, as well as to insure success, it became indispensable that this resolution should be long masked from the enemy, and again that the new movement, when discovered, should be mistaken for a feint, and the old as indicating our true and ultimate point of attack.

Accordingly, on the spot, the 11th, I ordered Quitman's division from Coyoacan, to join Pillow *by daylight*, before the southern gates, and then that the two major-generals, with their divisions, should, *by night*, proceed (two miles) to join me, at Tacubaya, where I was quartered with Worth's division. Twiggs, with Riley's brigade and Captains Taylor's and Steptoe's field batteries—the latter twelve-pounders—was left in front of those gates—to manœuver, to threaten, or to make false attacks, in order to occupy and deceive the enemy. Twiggs's other brigade (Smith's,) was left at supporting distance, in the rear, at San Angel, till the morning of the 13th, and also to support our general depot at Miscoaque. The stratagem against the south was admirably executed throughout the 12th and down to the afternoon of the 13th, when it was too late for the enemy to recover from the effects of his delusion.

The first step in the new movement was to carry Chapultepec, a natural and isolated mound, of great elevation, strongly fortified at its base, on its acclivities and heights. Besides a numerous garrison, here was the military college of the republic, with a large number of sub-lieutenants and other students. Those works were within direct gun-shot of the village of Tacubaya, and until carried, we could not approach the city on the west without making a circuit too wide and too hazardous.

In the course of the same night, (that of the 11th,)

Battle of Chapultepec.

heavy batteries, within easy ranges, were established. No. 1, on our right, under the command of Captain Drum, 4th artillery, (relieved late next day, for some hours, by Lieutenant Andrews, of the 3d,) and No. 2, commanded by Lieutenant Hagner, ordnance—both supported by Quitman's division. Nos. 3 and 4, on the opposite side, supported by Pillow's division, were commanded, the former by Captain Brooks and Lieutenant S. S. Anderson, 2d artillery, alternately, and the latter by Lieutenant Stone, ordnance. The batteries were traced by Captain Huger and Captain Lee, engineer, and constructed by them, with the able assistance of the young officers of those corps and the artillery.

To prepare for an assault it was foreseen that the play of the batteries might run into the second day; but recent captures had not only trebled our siege pieces, but also our ammunition, and we knew that we should greatly augment both by carrying the place. I was, therefore, in no haste in ordering an assault before the works were well crippled by our missiles.

The bombardment and cannonade, under the direction of Captain Huger, were commenced early in the morning of the 12th. Before nightfall, which necessarily stopped our batteries, we had perceived that a good impression had been made on the castle and its outworks, and that a large body of the enemy had remained outside towards the city, from an early hour, to avoid our fire, and to be at hand, on its cessation, in order to reinforce the garrison against an assault. The same outside force was discovered the next morning after our batteries had reopened upon the castle, by which we again **reduced its garrison to the minimum needed for the guns.**

Chapultepec.

Battle of Chapultepec.

Pillow and Quitman had been in position since early in the night of the 11th. Major-General Worth was now ordered to hold his division in reserve, near the foundry, to support Pillow; and Brigadier-General Smith, of Twiggs's division, had just arrived with his brigade, from Piedad, (two miles,) to support Quitman. Twiggs's guns, before the southern gates, again reminded us, as the day before, that he, with Riley's brigade, and Taylor's and Steptoe's batteries, was in activity, threatening the southern gates, and there holding a great part of the Mexican army on the defensive.

Worth's division furnished Pillow's attack with an assaulting party of some two hundred volunteer officers and men, under Captain McKenzie, of the 2d artillery, and Twiggs's division supplied a similar one, commanded by Captain Casey, 2d infantry to Quitman. Each of these little columns was furnished with scaling ladders.

The signal I had appointed for the attack, was the momentary cessation of the fire on the part of our heavy batteries. About eight o'clock in the morning of the 13th, judging that the time had arrived, by the effect of the missiles we had thrown, I sent an aid-de-camp to Pillow, and another to Quitman, with notice that the concerted signal was about to be given. Both columns now advanced with an alacrity that gave assurance of prompt success. The batteries, siezing opportunities, threw shots and shells upon the enemy, over the heads of our men, with good effect, particularly at every attempt to reinforce the works from without, to meet our assault.

Major-General Pillow's approach, on the west side, lay through an open grove, filled with sharp-shooters, who were speedily dislodged; when, being up with the front

Battle of Chapultepec.

of the attack, and emerging into the open space, at the foot of a rocky acclivity, that gallant leader was struck down by an agonizing wound. The immediate command devolved on Brigadier-General Cadwalader, in the absence of the senior brigadier (Pierce) of the same division—an invalid since the events of August 19. On a previous call of Pillow, Worth had just sent him a reinforcement—Colonel Clark's brigade.

The broken acclivity was still to be ascended, and a strong redoubt, midway, to be carried, before reaching the castle on the heights. The advance of our brave men, led by brave officers, though necessarily slow, was unwavering, over rocks, chasms, and mines, and under the hottest fire of cannon and musketry. The redoubt now yielded to resistless valour, and the shouts that followed announced to the castle the fate that impended. The enemy were steadily driven from shelter to shelter. The retreat allowed not time to fire a single mine, without the certainty of blowing up friend and foe. Those who at a distance attempted to apply the matches to the long trains, were shot down by our men. There was death below as well as above ground. At length the ditch and wall of the main work were reached; the scaling-ladders were brought up and planted by the storming parties; some of the daring spirits first in the assault were cast down—killed or wounded; but a lodgment was soon made; streams of heroes followed; all opposition was overcome, and several of our regimental colours flung out from the upper walls, amidst long continued shouts and cheers, which sent dismay into the capital. No scene could have been more animating or glorious.

Battle of Chapultepec.

Major-General Quitman, nobly supported by Brigadier Generals Shields and Smith, (P. F.,) his other officers and men, was up with the part assigned him. Simultaneously with the movement on the west, he had gallantly approached the south-east of the same works over a causeway with cuts and batteries, and defended by an army strongly posted outside, to the east of the works. Those formidable obstacles Quitman had to face, with but little shelter for his troops or space for manœuvering. Deep ditches, flanking the causeway, made it difficult to cross on either side into the adjoining meadows, and these again were intersected by other ditches. Smith and his brigade had been early thrown out to make a sweep to the right, in order to present a front against the enemy's line, (outside,) and to turn two intervening batteries near the foot of Chapultepec. This movement was also intended to support Quitman's storming parties, both on the causeway. The first of these furnished by Twiggs's division, was commanded in succession by Captain Casey, 2d infantry, and Captain Paul, 7th infantry, after Casey had been severely wounded; and the second, originally under the gallant Major Twiggs, marine corps, killed, and then Captain Miller, 2d Pennsylvania volunteers. The storming party, now commanded by Captain Paul, seconded by Captain Roberts of the rifles, Lieutenant Stewart, and others of the same regiment, Smith's brigade, carried the two batteries in the road, took some guns, with many prisoners, and drove the enemy posted behind in support. The New York and South Carolina volunteers, (Shields's brigade,) and the 2d Pennsylvania volunteers, all on the left of Quitman's line, together with portions of his storming

Battle of Chapultepec.

parties, crossed the meadows in front, under a heavy fire and entered the outer inclosures of Chapultepec just in time to join in the final assault from the west.

Those operations all occurred on the west, south-east, and heights of Chapultepec. To the north, and at the base of the mound, inaccessible on that side, the 11th infantry, under Lieutenant-Colonel Herbert, the 14th, under Colonel Trousdale, and Captain Magruder's field battery, 1st artillery—one section advanced under Lieutenant Jackson—all of Pillow's division—had, at the same time, some spirited affairs against superior numbers, driving the enemy from a battery in the road, and capturing a gun. In these, the officers and corps named gained merited praise. Colonel Trousdale, the commander, though twice wounded, continued on duty until the heights were carried.

Early in the morning of the thirteenth, I repeated the orders of the night before to Major-General Worth, to be, with his division at hand, to support the movement of Major-General Pillow from our left. The latter seems soon to have called for that entire division, standing, momentarily in reserve, and Worth sent him Colonel Clarke's brigade. The call, if not unnecessary, was at least, from the circumstances, unknown to me at the time; for soon observing that the very large body of the enemy, in the road in front of Major-General Quitman's right, was receiving reinforcements from the city —less than a mile and a half to the east—I sent instructions to Worth, on our opposite flank, to turn Chapultepec with his *division*, and to proceed, cautiously by the road at its northern base, in order, if not met by **very** superior numbers, to threaten or to attack, in **rear,** that body of the enemy. The movement, it was also believed, could not fail to distract and to intimidate the enemy generally.

Worth promptly advanced with his remaining brigade —Colonel Garland's—Lieutenant-Colonel C. F. Smith's light battalion, Lieutenant-Colonel Duncan's field battery —all of his division—and three squadrons of dragoons, under Major Sumner, which I had just ordered up to join in the movement.

Having turned the forest on the west, and arriving opposite to the north centre of Chapultepec, Worth came up with the troops in the road under Colonel Trousdale, and aided by a flank movement of a part of Garland's brigade in taking the one gun breastwork, then under the fire of Lieutenant Jackson's section of Captain Magruder's field battery. Continuing to advance, this division passed Chapultepec, attacking the right of the enemy's line, resting on that road, about the moment of the general retreat consequent upon the capture of the formidable castle and its outposts.

Arriving some minutes later, and mounting to the top of the castle, the whole field to the east lay plainly under my view.

There are two routes from Chapultepec to the capital —the one on the right entering the same gate, Belen, with the road from the south *via* Piedad; and the other obliquing to the left, to intersect the Great Western, or San Cosme road, in a suburb outside of the gate of San Cosme.

Each of these routes (an elevated causeway) presents a double roadway on the sides of an aqueduct of strong masonry, and great height, resting on open arches and massive pillars, which, together, afford fine points both for attack and defense. The sideways of both aqueducts are, moreover, defended by many strong breastworks at the gates, and before reaching them. As we had expected, we found the four tracts unusually dry and solid for the season.

Worth and Quitman were prompt in pursuing the retreating enemy—the former by the San Cosme aqueduct, and the latter along that of Belen. Each had now advanced some hundred yards.

Deeming it all-important to profit by our successes, and the consequent dismay of the enemy, which could not be otherwise than general, I hastened to despatch from Chapultepec—first Clarke's brigade, and then Cadwalader's, to the support of Worth, and gave orders that the necessary heavy guns should follow. Pierce's brigade was, at the same time, sent to Quitman, and, in the course of the afternoon, I caused some additional siege pieces to be added to his train. Then, after designating the 15th infantry, under Lieutenant-Colonel Howard—Morgan, the colonel, had been disabled by a wound at Churubusco—as the garrison of Chapultepec, and giving directions for the care of the prisoners of war, the captured ordnance and ordnance stores, I proceeded to join the advance of Worth, within the suburb, and beyond the turn at the junction of the aqueduct with the great highway from the west to the gate of San Cosme.

At this junction of roads, we first passed one of those formidable systems of city defenses, spoken of above, and it had not a gun!—a strong proof—1, That the enemy had expected us to fail in the attack upon

Street fight in the city of Mexico.

Chapultepec, even if we meant any thing more than a feint; 2, That, in either case, we designed, in his belief, to return and double our forces against the southern gates—a delusion kept up by the active demonstrations of Twiggs and the forces posted on that side; and 3, That advancing rapidly from the reduction of Chapultepec, the enemy had not time to shift guns—our previous captures had left him, comparatively, but few— from the southern gates.

Within those disgarnished works, I found our troops engaged in a street fight against the enemy posted in gardens, at windows, and on house-tops—all flat, with parapets. Worth ordered forward the mountain howitzers of Cadwalader's brigade, preceded by skirmishers and pioneers, with pick-axes and crow-bars, to force windows and doors, or to burrow through walls. The assailants were soon in an equality of position fatal to the enemy. By eight o'clock in the evening, Worth had carried two batteries in this suburb. According to my instructions, he here posted guards and sentinels, and placed his troops under shelter for the night. There was but one more obstacle—the San Cosme gate (customhouse) between him and the great square in front of the cathedral and palace—the heart of the city; and the barrier, it was known, could not by daylight, resist our siege guns thirty minutes.

I had gone back to the foot of Chapultepec, the point from which the two aqueducts begin to diverge, some hours earlier, in order to be near that new depot, and in easy communication with Quitman and Twiggs as well as with Worth.

From this point I ordered all detachments and stragglers to their respective corps then in advance; sent to Quitman additional siege guns, ammunition, intrenching tools; directed Twiggs's remaining brigade (Riley's) from Piedad to support Worth, and Captain Steptoe's field battery, also at Piedad, to rejoin Quitman's division.

I had been, from the first, well aware that the western, or San Cosme, was the less difficult route to the centre and conquest of the capital; and, therefore, intended that Quitman should only manœuver and threaten the Belen or south-western gate, in order to favour the main attack by Worth—knowing that the strong defenses at the Belen were directly under the guns of the much stronger fortress, called the *citadel*, just within. Both of these defenses of the enemy were also within easy supporting distance from the San Angel (or *Nino Perdido*) and San Antonio gates. Hence the greatest support, in numbers, given to Worth's movement as the *main* attack.

Those views I repeatedly, in the course of the day, communicated to Major-General Quitman; but, being in hot pursuit—gallant himself, and supported by Brigadier-Generals Shields and Smith—Shields badly wounded before Chapultepec, and refusing to retire—as well as by all the officers and men of the column—Quitman continued to press forward, under flank and direct fires— carried an intermediate battery of two guns, and then the gate, before two o'clock in the afternoon, but not without proportionate loss, increased by his steady maintenance of that position.

Quitman, within the city—adding several new defenses to the position he had won, and sheltering his corps as well as practicable—now awaited the return of daylight under the guns of the formidable citadel, yet to be subdued.

At about four o'clock next morning, (September 14,) a deputation of the *ayuntamiento* (city council) waited upon me to report that the federal government and the army of Mexico had fled from the capital some three hours before, and to demand terms of capitulation in favour of the church, the citizens, and the municipal authorities. I promptly replied, that I would sign no capitulation; that the city had been virtually in our possession from the time of the lodgments effected by Worth and Quitman the day before; that I regretted the silent escape of the Mexican army; that I should levy upon the city a moderate contribution, for special purposes; and that the American army should come under no terms, not *self*-imposed—such only as its own honour, the dignity of the United States, and the spirit of the age, should, in my opinion, imperiously demand and impose.

At the termination of the interview with the city deputation, I communicated, about daylight, orders to Worth and Quitman to advance slowly and cautiously, (to guard against treachery,) towards the heart of the city, and to occupy its stronger and more commanding points. Quitman proceeded to the great *plaza* or square, planted guards, and hoisted the colours of the United States on the national palace—containing the halls of Congress and executive departments of federal Mexico. In this grateful service, Quitman might have been anticipated by Worth, but for my express orders, halting the latter at the head of the *Alameda*, (a green park,) within three squares of that goal of general ambition. The capital

Firing from the houses.

however, was not taken by any one or two corps, but by the talent, the science, the gallantry, the prowess of this entire army. In the glorious conquest, *all* had contributed—early and powerfully—the killed, the wounded, and *the fit for duty*—at Vera Cruz, Cerro Gordo, Contreras, San Augustin, Churubusco, (three battles,) the Molinos del Rey, and Chapultepec—as much as those who fought at the gates of Belen and San Cosme.

Soon after we had entered, and were in the act of occupying the city, a fire was opened upon us from the flat roofs of the houses, from windows and corners of streets, by some two thousand convicts liberated the night before by the flying government—joined by, perhaps, as many Mexican soldiers, who had disbanded themselves and thrown off their uniforms. This unlawful war lasted more than twenty-four hours, in spite of the exertions of the municipal authorities, and was not put down till we had lost many men, including several officers killed or wounded, and had punished the miscreants. Their objects were to gratify national hatred; and in the general alarm and confusion, to plunder the wealthy inhabitants—particularly the deserted houses. But families are now generally returning; business of every kind has been resumed, and the city is already tranquil and cheerful, under the admirable conduct (with exceptions very few and trifling) of our gallant troops.

I recapitulate our losses since we arrived in the basin of Mexico.

August 19, 20.—Killed, one hundred and thirty-seven, including fourteen officers. Wounded, eight hundred and seventy-seven, including sixty-two officers.

Trophies.

Missing, (probably killed,) thirty-eight rank and file. Total, one thousand and fifty-two.

September 8.—Killed, one hundred and sixteen, including nine officers. Wounded, six hundred and fifty-five, including forty-nine officers. Missing, eighteen rank and file. Total, seven hundred and eighty-nine.

September 12, 13, 14.—Killed, one hundred and thirty, including ten officers. Wounded, seven hundred and three, including sixty-eight officers. Missing, twenty-nine rank and file. Total, eight hundred and sixty-two.

Grand total of losses, two thousand seven hundred and three, including three hundred and eighty-three officers.

On the other hand, this small force has beaten on the same occasions, in view of their capital, the whole Mexican army, of (at the beginning) thirty odd thousand men—posted always in chosen positions, behind intrenchments, or more formidable defenses of nature and art; killed or wounded, of that number, more than seven thousand officers and men ; taking three thousand seven hundred and thirty prisoners ; including thirteen generals, of whom three had been presidents of this republic ; captured more than twenty colours and standards, seventy-five pieces of ordnance, besides fifty-seven wall-pieces, twenty thousand small arms, an immense quantity of shot, shells, powder, &c., &c.

Of that enemy once so formidable in numbers, appointments, artillery, &c., twenty odd thousand have disbanded themselves in despair, leaving, as is known, not more than three fragments—the largest about two thousand five hundred—now wandering in different directions, without magazines, or a military chest, and living *at free quarters* upon their own people.

Scheme of the priesthood.

In the national palace of Mexico opposite the entrance of the great reception room, there hung a portrait of the celebrated Mexican, Iturbide. Rumaging about the palace, some of the officers found, in a neglected room, a portrait of Washington. Amid the greatest enthusiasm, the frowning representative of Mexican greatness gave place to the mild benevolent countenance of the great American hero; the proper sequel to the overthrow of the forces of the Mexican nation by the army of the North American republic. From the taking of the capital to the present, all has remained quiet and tranquil. The priesthood attempted to carry out a plan for the annoyance of the American army, refusing to open the churches, and in other modes cherishing the popular ill will. But the prompt and energetic orders of General Scott brought a sudden termination upon their plans. Signor Pena y Pena, who had been called to the administration of the government of Mexico, issued an address marked by the moderation of its views, and his secretary of state followed with one similar in tenor.

In October, Senor Rosa, the secretary of state, in the name of the president called a meeting of the Mexican Congress, to assemble at Queretaro in November, the results of whose deliberations have as yet been unimportant. During the same month, the attention of the government was directed towards General Paredes, who had effected an entrance into the country in disguise, and issued a very florid address to his countrymen. The government refused his proffered services, and directed harsh measures to be taken against him.

Santa Anna, though driven from the capital, continued his indefatigable efforts in behalf of his ungrateful

Death of Walker.

country. With nearly eight thousand men he advanced upon and took Puebla, and on the 25th of September, laid siege to the American works near that city, commanded by Colonel Childs. A siege of twenty-eight days failed to induce the gallant colonel and his starved troops to depart from their intention to make a successful defense. A cannonading was briskly maintained on both sides for three days. On the 1st of October, Santa Anna sallied out from the city with a large force, in order to attack General Lane, who was on his way up from Vera Cruz with a large train, and a force of about three thousand men. On the evening of the 8th of October, information was received that Santa Anna, with four thousand men and several pieces of artillery, was prepared to dispute their passage at the pass of Pinal Venta del Final. The army prepared for a battle, when it was learned that Santa Anna himself was at the town of Huamantla, some ten miles distant, and General Lane determined to advance upon that town with a portion of his forces, Captain Walker leading the van with a force of two hundred cavalry. Santa Anna had left that morning for the pass with four thousand men, leaving his artillery with a detachment of five hundred to follow. Captain Walker dashed into the town, defeated this detachment, captured four guns, and supposing the fight to be ended, suffered his men to disperse through the town in search of guns and ammunition. With some fifty men he remained in the plaza, where he suddenly found himself fiercely attacked by the enemy's cavalry, who had seen his advance and returned to save their artillery. In the struggle which followed, the gallant captain was slain. The arrival of the infantry soon put an end to the battle; the enemy withdrawing from the town. The Mexicans lost two of the four cannon, and some thirty wagon loads of ammunition. Santa Anna thus out-generaled, abandoned his intention of contesting the pass of Pinal. But for this manœuver the Americans must have suffered severely in this narrow and difficult pass.

After relieving the garrison at Puebla, which city was evacuated by General Rea, General Lane advanced upon Atlisco, which he captured after gaining a victory over General Rea, who contested the field with unusual spirit, having suffered a loss of more than five hundred killed and wounded.

General Santa Anna, after these reverses, fled with a small band to Tehuacan, where even these troops became mutinous for want of pay, and soon deserted him. The president then deposed him from the head of the army and appointed General Rincon to succeed him. In grief and indignation at this treatment from the executive whom he himself had just called to power, Santa Anna issued an address on the 16th of October to the army, and another on the 22d of October to the people of Mexico, both more remarkable than any of his papers for its lofty tone, for the appeal to his enemies to testify concerning his conduct, and the assertion that his enemies are in favour of peace.

We now turn our attention to the operations of the navy, which had been engaged under Commodores Conner and Perry in the difficult service of blockading the rocky coast of Mexico. On the 8th of August, and on the 15th of October, 1846, two unsuccessful attempts were made by Commodore Conner to capture the town

Capture of Tuspan.

of Alvarado, the high seas and strong currents rendering it unadvisable to land troops on the rocky coast, and the bar preventing some of the vessels from entering the river. The people made a considerable show of defense, for which the government rewarded them in a peculiarly Mexican manner *by brevetting their town a city!*

During the summer, almost the only events that occurred to break the monotony of a blockade were the accidents that arose from the dangerous character of the coast. On the 15th of August, 1846, the brig Truxtun ran aground on the bar off Tuspan, while standing in shore to cover her boats on an expedition for fresh water and provisions. Every effort was made to lighten her without success. A boat was sent off to the squadron for aid, and a Mexican vessel was captured in the hope that the crew might be taken off, but the sea ran so high as to render this impossible, and the small boat's crew and the crew of the prize reached the squadron after several days of danger and privation. The Princeton was sent to the relief of the stranded brig, but the crew had gone on shore and surrendered as prisoners before her arrival, and they could only burn and blow her up. Every thing of value was gone except an iron cable attached to an anchor overboard. In April, 1847, the town of Tuspan was, by an expedition under Commodore Perry, so well planned that failure was impossible. Three forts, the guns of which raked the river and defended the approach to the town, were silenced in succession, and each of them was taken possession of by the seamen and marines under their immediate officers who landed in boats along the shores of the river, and

Expedition against Tobasco.

planted the soul-stirring flag of our Union upon the battlements. On reaching the town, Commodore Perry proceeded to the shore with his staff and took possession of the city without opposition, Senor General Don Martin P. de Cos, commandant of the place, "having," to use the words of a humorous letter writer, " struck out for country quarters some time before the fight with the forts was done. A disembarkation of the marines was made, and the stars and stripes saluted by a stalwart band of sea soldiers with two brass field-pieces in the plaza. Commodore Perry established his head-quarters in the city. From the forts and one of the public stores were taken guns, sails, rigging, &c., that had belonged to the unfortunate brig Truxtun, and an expedition sent up the river returned with her boats, besides schooners, launches, and boats captured from the enemy.

On the 16th of October, 1846, Commodore Perry sailed from the squadron to attack the town of Tobasco. On the 24th the bar was crossed, and Frontera, the town at the mouth of the river, captured with all the vessels in port. The expedition then moved up the river to Tobasco, which Commodore Perry consented to spare from the horrors of a bombardment on the representation of foreigners, that the military had no interest in the place. But while the flag of truce was flying from the mastheads, in agreement with the arrangements made, and by which the commodore was to retire unmolested, one of the prize schooners got aground below the town, and a brisk fire of musketry was immediately opened upon her from the shore. Lieutenant Morris being sent from the flag ship to the assistance of Lieutenant Parker, who commanded the stranded vessel, was also fired upon

Capture of Panuco.

and mortally wounded. The vessel however was got off, and a severe vengeance taken upon the town before the fleet departed. At the close of the summer of 1847, Commodore Perry found it necessary to pay another visit to Tobasco, to show the people there that they were not forgotten.

On the 12th of November, 1846, Commodore Conner sailed for Tampico, which surrendered on the 14th without resistance. The guns belonging to the enemy at Tampico had been carried to Panuco, a town of some five thousand inhabitants, eighty miles inland, on the Panuco river. Commander Tatnall was sent thither with the steamer Spitfire and the schooner Petrel, landed a hundred men, and demanded the surrender of the town which was complied with; the inhabitants being extremely polite and communicative, informing the commander where all the military stores were placed. The result of the expedition was the capture of eleven guns, which were on their way to San Luis Potosi for the use of the Mexican forces, and the destruction by burning and sinking in the river, of army equipments to the amount of thirty thousand dollars.

After the capture of Vera Cruz, Commodore Perry and General Scott planned an attack upon Alvarado, which had twice repulsed the forces of the navy. While the formidable array which was to accomplish this object was preparing, Lieutenant Hunter was despatched in the little steamer Scourge to blockade the town. He sailed thither, opened a fire upon the place with round shot and shell, stood off and on during the night, and in the morning received the surrender of the town, the garrison frightened out of their propriety, having run away in the night. The city-by-brevet being captured, the American flag was hoisted and saluted with twenty-one guns, and the little steamer proceeded up the river in pursuit of several vessels which were hastening up the river laden with arms, ammunition, and public property. Four schooners were captured, one of which was burned, another abandoned as worthless, and the two others carried away as prizes. The city of Tlacotalpam, containing seven thousand inhabitants, was summoned to surrender within half an hour, and the demand was complied with. The higher authorities of the navy put a grave face upon this comical achievement, and Lieutenant Hunter was court-martialed, found guilty of disobedience of orders, and sentenced to be publicly reprimanded.

The reprimand was worded with much severity; but the conduct of the lieutenant seems to have been generally approved by his countrymen, and the government gave him the command of the United States schooner Taney, destined for a cruise in the Mediterranean.

One of the most daring achievements of the war, which was followed closely by one of its most lamentable occurrences we have omitted to notice. We close our account of the naval operation with a notice of these incidents.

On the 20th of November, 1846, Lieutenant Parker, with Midshipmen Rodgers and Hynson, and a crew of six men, rowed into the harbour of Vera Cruz in a small boat, and burned the Mexican barque Creole, anchored under the guns of the castle of San Juan de Ulloa. These officers belonged to the beautiful brig Somers, and had performed this skilful and daring feat to sig-

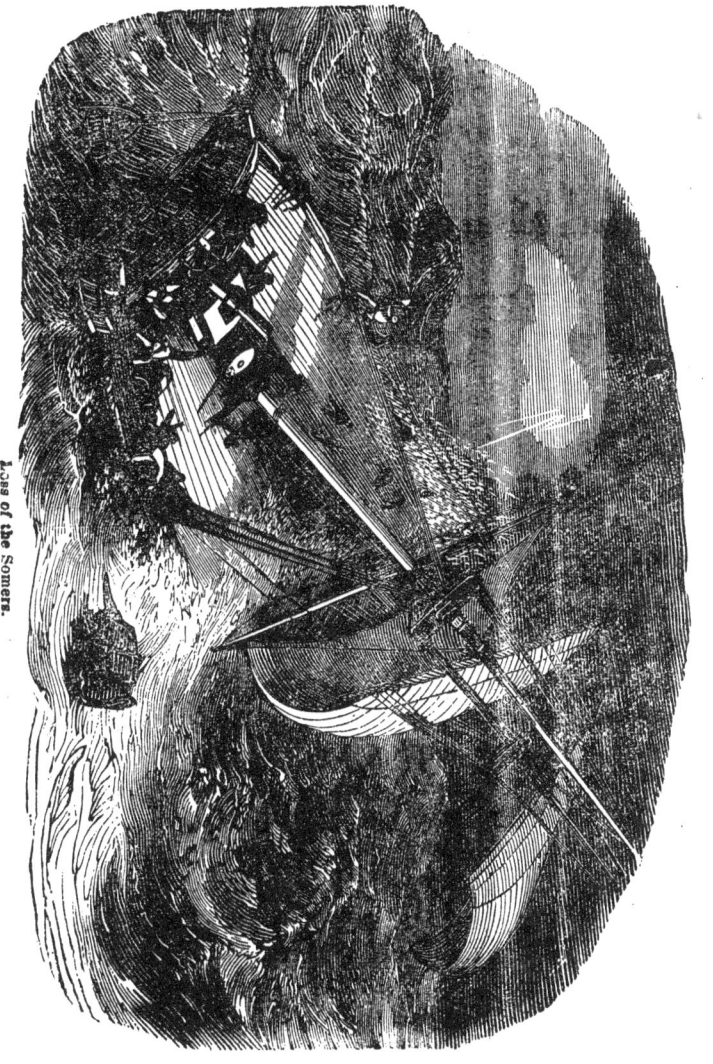

Loss of the Somers.

nalize themselves whilst the other vessels of the squadron were on the expedition to Tampico. The gallantry of the crew of the Somers was more fully exemplified, however, on the occasion of the loss by shipwreck of that vessel. While endeavouring to intercept a sail that had hove in sight, a squall from the north struck her and threw her on her beam ends, and in a few minutes she filled and sunk. Midshipmen Clemson and Hynson, with thirty-nine of the crew, lost their lives; the others were picked up by the crews of the English, French, and Spanish men-of-war lying near by

We now turn our attention to the conquest of New Mexico.

In June, 1846, a military force of three hundred United States dragoons, and three thousand Missouri volunteers, was concentrated at Fort Leavenworth, on the Missouri river, under General Stephen W. Kearny, destined for the subjugation of New Mexico. General Kearny took up the line of march for Santa Fe, eight hundred and forty miles distant, on the 22d of June, and on the 18th of August took possession of the city with the principal division of his forces. He issued, on the 22d, a proclamation calling on the people who had left their houses to return, and promising to protect all who should remain quiet and peaceable. Five days afterwards he completed the organization of a free government, appointed Charles Bent governor, and fixed a code of municipal laws. On the 25th of September he set out from Santa Fe, upon the route for Upper California, with the dragoons under Major Sumner, and two mountain howitzers. Colonel Doniphan was left in

Murder of Governor Bent and others.

command at Santa Fe, Colonel Price with the second division of the forces having not yet arrived.

At Albuquerque, General Kearny received such information from California, as induced him to send back two hundred of the dragoons, leaving orders for the Mormon battalion which formed part of his forces, to follow in his trail. From La Joya, two hundred miles below Santa Fe, on the Rio Grande, he sent an order to Colonel Doniphan to make a campaign against the Narajo Indians, who inhabited the country between the Rio Grande and the Colorado of the West. Colonel Doniphan was employed on this successful expedition until the 14th of December.

Leaving Colonel Price in command at Santa Fe, Colonel Doniphan again took up the line of march, on the 17th of December, with his own regiment and a command under Lieutenant-Colonel Mitchell. The departure of this force, and the Mormon battalion, left Colonel Price about fifteen hundred men. About the time of Colonel Doniphan's departure a revolution was concocted by several of the citizens of the province, which, however, was discovered and apparently suppressed. Nearly all the most influential persons in the vicinity of Santa Fe were concerned in it. On the nineteenth of January, Governor Bent, with five others, was murdered at Hernando de Taos, seven more at the Arroya Honda, and two at the Rio Colorado. It appeared to be the object of the insurrectionists to put to death every American, and every Mexican, who had taken office under the new government. The insurgents having gathered in considerable force, a battle was fought on the 24th of January, at Canada, which

Battle of Pueblo de Taos.

they commenced by an attack on Colonel Price, who repulsed them.

On the 29th, the enemy were discovered to the number of six or seven hundred, occupying a very strong position on the mountains at either side of the pass which leads to Embudo, and which was only wide enough to admit of the passage of three men marching abreast. Captain Burgwin with one hundred and eighty men, rank and file, attacked them, ascended the hills and forced them to fly with a heavy loss. They retreated over the steep and rugged sides of the mountains with a speed that defied pursuit. Embudo was then surrendered. Marching through snow, and beating it down into a road for artillery, on the 3d, the army reached the city of Pueblo de Taos, which was found to be admirably fortified. On the 4th, it was attacked by our gallant little army at nine o'clock in the morning, and the battle raged with great fierceness until night. The Americans at that time had made themselves masters of a part of the town, and at daybreak next morning the enemy sued for peace. It was granted on condition of the delivery of Tomas, one of the principal conspirators, who was shot. The other leaders met a similar fate.

Having defeated the enemy wherever they were to be found and thereby crushed the revolution, Colonel Price found himself again quietly established in the government of New Mexico. He had in the three battles, killed two hundred and six of the enemy, and wounded a much larger number, with the loss of only eight killed, and fifty-two wounded on his own side, and had exhibited a degree of vigilance and gallantry calculated to inspire the people with awe and respect.

Battle of Sacramento.

Colonel Doniphan, on the march for El Paso del Norte, was attacked on Christmas day, at Brazito, by a Mexican force of eleven hundred men. The American force engaged numbered four hundred and fifty. The battle was decided in forty minutes, by the flight of the enemy, leaving sixty-three killed, one hundred and fifty wounded, and one howitzer. On the 29th, the city of El Paso was taken without opposition. Leaving El Paso on the 8th of February, the army marched on the city of Chihuahua. At the pass of the Sacramento, the enemy was discovered in great force: twelve hundred cavalry and two thousand seven hundred and twenty infantry, artillerists, and rancheros, with ten pieces of artillery. Colonel Doniphan commanded nine hundred and twenty-four effective men, who were obliged to protect a train of three hundred and fifteen traders' wagons, besides the regular army train. The enemy's infantry were securely posted behind a series of twenty-seven redoubts. While the two twelve-pound howitzers unlimbered within fifty yards of the enemy, and supported by the cavalry, poured destruction into his ranks, the infantry and riflemen charged the intrenchments with the utmost coolness and rapidity, delivering a deadly fire, and then clearing the redoubts with their sabres. The enemy fled over the mountains in great confusion, losing his entire artillery, ten wagons, masses of provisions, three hundred killed, and as many wounded. The Americans lost the incredibly small number of one man killed, and eight wounded, one of whom afterwards died. This victory was gained on the 28th of February. On the 1st of March formal possession was taken of Chihuahua. On the 23d of April, Colonel

Doniphan's return to the United States.

Doniphan received orders from General Wool to march to Saltillo with his command. He reached that place on the 23d of May, having taken eight or ten Mexican cities on the route. On the 27th, he reached Monterey, where his command was reviewed by General Taylor. The account of the battle of Sacramento given by Colonel Doniphan to General Taylor is very amusing. We extract it from Frank Edwards's new work, "A Campaign with Colonel Doniphan."

"While we were at Walnut Springs, General Taylor addressed Colonel Doniphan thus:—By-the-by, Colonel, every one is talking of your charge at Sacramento. I understand it was a brilliant affair. I wish you would give me a description of it, and of your manœuvres." "Manœuvers be hanged," returned Doniphan, and added, "I don't know any thing about the charge, except that my boys kept coming to me to let them charge, but I would not permit them; for I was afraid they would be all cut to pieces. At last I saw a favourable moment and told them they might go—they were off like a shot—and that's all I know about it."

From Monterey Colonel Doniphan marched to the Brazos, and there took passage to New Orleans, the term of service of his troops having expired.

In the spring of 1846, Captain, now Lieutenant-Colonel John C. Fremont was sent with sixty-one men in the service of the United States topographical corps to make an exploration of Upper California. He found soon after his entrance into that territory, that its governor, General Castro, was preparing to attack him. He promptly assumed the initiative, captured thirteen men and two hundred horses on the 11th of June, and

Kearny reconquers the City of the Angels.

on the 15th took possession of the Sanoma Pass, containing nine cannon, two hundred and fifty muskets, and a small garrison. Having marched toward the Sacramento river, he learned that General Castro was about to attack the garrison he had left at Sanoma, and hurried back with ninety riflemen raised among the American settlers in California, and dispersed the advance guard of General Castro, who thereupon retired to Santa Clara. Meanwhile Commodore Sloat had taken the sea-port of Monterey, on the Pacific, and was prepared to act in conjunction with Fremont against Castro. On the 12th of August, a body of riflemen under Fremont and Stockton, Sloat's successor, took possession of the City of Angels, and Stockton appointed Fremont governor.

On the 11th of December, General Kearny reached the city of San Diego, in California, having gained a victory five days previously at San Pasqual, after a severe conflict, in which the general himself, with many of his officers and men were wounded, and two captains, one lieutenant, and fourteen others killed. On the 8th of January, he fought another battle with the enemy, on his march to regain possession of the City of the Angels, which had been retaken by the Mexicans. He was victorious, and the city was taken, while Fremont on the march thither with four hundred volunteers from the Sacramento, met the retreating enemy, who capitulated, laying down their arms. These operations comp'eted the conquest of California.

Major-General Taylor.

GENERAL ZACHARY TAYLOR.

OMITTING genealogical details, we come at once to the fact that Major-General Zachary Taylor, the third son of Colonel Richard Taylor, was born in Orange county, Virginia, on the 24th of November, 1784. In the succeeding summer Colonel Taylor emigrated to Kentucky, then just beginning to be settled, and his children from their earliest years were inured to the hardships and perils of frontier life. His first military lessons are said to have been from a man named Whetsel, who loaded

Commands Fort Harrison.

his rifle while running and successively killed four Indians, who were pursuing him. Zachary Taylor was enrolled as a volunteer in one of the companies formed to oppose any scheme that might be concocted by Aaron Burr, during his suspicious sojourn in the west. In May, 1808, he received a commission as first lieutenant in the 7th regiment of United States infantry, the vacancy he was appointed to fill having been made by the death of his brother. He was ordered to report himself to General Wilkinson at New Orleans, where he was taken with the yellow fever, and recovered with a constitution so much shattered as to compel his temporary retirement from active service.

General Harrison having been ordered to march into the Indian country, erected a block-house and stockade on the Wabash, which afterwards was called Fort Harrison. Lieutenant Taylor was employed in the perilous duty of watching the movements of the hostile savages at this post, and performed it in such a manner as to be promoted to a captaincy in the beginning of 1812. He was then placed in command of Fort Harrison, and in September, 1812, made his memorable successful defense of that post, with a sickly garrison of fifty men, against a large body of Indians of Tecumseh's party. The attack was begun at midnight and the lower building was set on fire by the enemy. The flames soon reached the store-room where a quantity of whisky took fire, and spread the conflagration rapidly. By great perseverance and presence of mind, however, the fire was stopped in the building where it commenced, and the garrison kept up a steady discharge of musketry upon the enemy, who continued the assault for seven

Defense of Fort Harrison.

hours. They then retired, carrying off the horses and cattle. The danger to which the whisky thus exposed the gallant captain, of death by flames on one side, or savage arms on the other, was probably remembered when he issued stringent orders against those who dealt in that article on the Rio Grande.

General Hopkins said of this achievement, in a letter to the governor of Kentucky, "the firm and almost unparalleled defense of Fort Harrison by Captain Zachary Taylor, has raised for him a fabric of character not to be effaced by eulogy." The government acknowledged it by conferring upon Taylor the rank of major by brevet.

In October and November, Major Taylor, in command of the Kentucky volunteers, and accompanied by General Hopkins, made two expeditions into the Indian country; one against the Kickapoo villages on the Illinois river, the other against the settlements in the neighbourhood of Tippecanoe. No general engagement was fought, but they were attended with many hardships and privations, and proved of incalculable benefits to the territories of Indiana and Illinois. Several of the enemy's towns, and large quantities of provisions were destroyed. This demonstration of our strength inspired them with awe. In the winter of 1813 Major Taylor was appointed to superintend the recruiting service in Indiana and Illinois, in which he continued with industry and success until July. In that month he proceeded with a force of Rangers and Kentucky volunteers against the Massassinawa town near the source of the Wabash. The town was found abandoned, and meeting with no supply of provisions, the detachment was exposed during its return to the severest privations.

Ordered to erect a fort on Rock river.

In the spring of 1814 he was ordered to St. Louis, to take command of the troops in the Missouri territory, and was actively employed on its frontiers until August. It was then ascertained that the British had taken Fort Shelby at Prairie du Chien, and were in great force on the Mississippi, with regulars and Indian allies. General Howard was furnished with ten companies of badly organized rangers, and about one hundred and twenty efficient regulars, to protect the frontier of Indiana, Illinois, and Missouri, and restrain the depredations of the various savage tribes. With these slender resources he had to protect the interior settlements, and furnish detachments to invade the Indian territory. Of these, that which ascended the Mississippi, under Major Taylor, was the most important in its objects and the most beneficial in its results.

On the 22d of August, 1814, Major Taylor received orders to take command of three hundred and twenty men, principally militia, provided with boats and a few pieces of artillery, to ascend the Mississippi as high as the Indian village at the mouth of Rock river, to destroy the villages and corn, to disperse the Indians, and erect a fort on the most eligible site to command the river. The leading objects of the expedition were to restrain the Indians by the establishment of a military post in the heart of their country, and to arrest the descent of the British forces on St. Louis. The general closes his orders to the commanding officer thus: "should this command succeed in effecting all the objects for which it is intended the beneficial consequences to our country will be great. On the other hand, should this movement be stamped with disaster, no longer can even a hope be indulged of the frontiers maintaining their ground. But from the officer who commands and those commanded by him, the most flattering expectations may be indulged." Thus was the fate of the frontier a second time staked on the fortunes of the defender of Fort Harrison.

In pursuance of his orders, Major Taylor proceeded to the mouth of Rock river, against a rapid current and amid the dangers of a lurking enemy, five hundred miles above the highest settlement or post on the Mississippi. Contrary to his expectations, and those of the general, he found a detachment of British troops, well supplied with artillery, and an immense body of Indians in possession of the place. After skirmishing with the Indians, and being sometime cannonaded by the British, without a possibility of returning their fire with effect, he dropped down to the rapid Desmoines, and having landed his forces, secured his boats, and fortified his camp, and commenced a fort so situated as to command the Mississippi and the mouth of the Desmoines. The erection of this fort in the face of the enemy, and at so great a distance from the source of supply, was attended with peculiar hazard, and almost incredible privation and toil. But the judgment, resolution, and skill of the commander, seconded by his animating example, surmounted every obstacle, enabled him to complete his important labour and to realize the most sanguine expectations of his superior.

The death of General Howard in October, called Major Taylor to St. Louis. In November he accompanied Colonel Russell several hundred miles up the Missouri, to secure a small settlement on that river, left much exposed to Indian depredations. In December

His personal appearance and character.

he was again ordered to Vincennes to take command of the troops in Indiana, where he remained until the conclusion of peace.

"When we look back," says Mr. Breckenridge, in a biographical sketch of General Taylor, written thirty years since ; " when we look back on the many important services rendered by this officer to his country during the late war ; when we reflect on the peculiar perils and hardships to which those services must have perpetually exposed him, performing as he did, in one year, marches in the territories of Indiana, Illinois, and Missouri, amounting to more than three thousand miles, and find no solitary instance in which the extent of his achievements did not exceed the scanty measure of his means, we cannot restrain the expression of our regret at his detention from those glorious fields of civilized combat, where his genius might have borne him to nobler enterprise, and his valour displayed itself on a more conspicuous theatre. * * * * *

"With a frame fitted for the most active and hardy enterprise, an ardent spirit, a sanguine temper, and an invincible courage, gifted with a rapid discernment, a discriminating judgment, and a deep knowledge of mankind, and possessing a heart susceptible of the most generous impulses of humanity, we regard Major Taylor as an officer of peculiar promise, and hazard, we think, but little in the prediction that, in the event of a war at no distant period, between the United States and England or Spain, riding on the tide of military glory, he will find his true level at the head of the army."

The reduction of the army list on the conclusion of the war, led to the change of Major Taylor's rank to that

Anecdote.

of a captain. He resigned in consequence, but in a year he was restored to the service and his former rank by President Madison. He was employed in the monotonous life of a soldier in time of peace until he became engaged in the Black Hawk war in 1832. He then held the rank of colonel, and was detached by General Atkinson to pursue the Indians after they had fled over the Wisconsin. He met them at a place called the Bad Axe, and, though they fought with the energy of despair, totally defeated them. The betrayal of Black Hawk shortly afterwards put an end to this war. An anecdote related of his conduct during this war by a writer in the "Literary World," gives an amusing example of his decision of character. He states that "while pursuing Black Hawk with a mixed force of volunteers and regulars, he found himself approaching Rock river, then said to be the north-western boundary of Illinois. The volunteers, as Taylor was informed, would refuse to cross the stream. They were militia, they said, called out for the defense of the state, and it was unconstitutional to order them to march beyond its frontier into the Indian country. Taylor thereupon halted his command and encamped within the acknowledged boundaries of Illinois. He would not, as the relator of the story said, budge an inch farther without orders. He had already driven Black Hawk out of the state, but the question of crossing Rock river seemed hugely to trouble his ideas of integrity to the constitution on one side, and military expediency on the other. During the night, however, orders came, either from General Scott or General Atkinson, for him to follow up Black Hawk to the last. The quietness of the regular colonel had rather

Anecdote.

encouraged the mutinous militia to bring their proceedings to a head. A sort of town meeting was called upon the prairie, and Taylor invited to attend. After listening some time quietly to the proceedings, it became Rough and Ready's turn to address the chair. 'He had heard,' he said, ' with much pleasure the views which several speakers had expressed of the independence and dignity of each private American citizen. He felt that all gentlemen there present were his equals—in reality, he was persuaded that many of them would in a few years be his superiors, and perhaps in the capacity of members of Congress, arbiters of the fortunes and reputation of humble servants of the republic like himself. He expected then to obey them as the interpreters of the will of the people; and the best proof he could give that he would obey them was now to observe the orders of those whom the people had already put in the places of authority, to which many gentlemen around him justly aspired. In plain English, gentlemen and fellow-citizens, the word has been passed on to me from Washington to follow Black Hawk, and to take you with me as soldiers. I mean to do both. There are the flat boats drawn up on the shore, and here are Uncle Sam's men drawn up behind you on the prairie.' " No answer could be made to such an argument. Instant obedience followed.

When the command of Major Dade had been massacred in Florida, the government determined to prosecute hostilities against the enemy with vigour, and Colonel Taylor was ordered to the seat of war. In December, 1837, he received orders to seek out any portion of the enemy, wherever to be found, and to destroy or capture his forces. He soon displayed his skill

Battle of Okee-Chobee.

in finding an Indian enemy, and his ability in defeating him. He was informed that the Micasukies had determined to fight him, and he was determined to indulge them, and accordingly the conflict took place on the 25th of December, on the shore of lake Okee-Chobee. The Indians, after a severe conflict, were beaten, and driven at all points. They had several hundred warriors engaged in an admirable position, which they defended for two hours and a half with the greatest gallantry, killing and wounding one-fifth of Taylor's whole command. After the victory, Colonel Taylor turned his whole attention to the care of the wounded, who were most tenderly treated. For his services in this affair, Colonel Taylor received the thanks of the president, and promotion to the rank of brigadier-general by brevet.

General Taylor continued to prosecute hostilities against the savages until April, 1840, when he was relieved by General Armistead.

He was then appointed to the command of the first department of the army in the south-west, and continued in the service there until, as we have already seen, he was ordered to Corpus Christi. We have already given detailed accounts of the four brilliant achievements which have made his name so universally popular throughout our country, and we will not now repeat them. We pass on to narrate such anecdotes of him as will serve to give the best idea of the man and his character.

When his reply to the communication of Ampudia respecting the blockading of the Rio Grande was published, it received the universal approbation of the

Anecdotes.

soldiers and their patriotic countrymen, and all felt assured that the honour of the country was safe in his hands. The troops felt that the man who could talk in such a manner was able to make good his words, and his order issued when about to march from Matamoras to Point Isabel, on the 7th of May, assured them of a speedy victory. He spoke to his inferior force of raw troops as to veterans, and in the confident tone of one who knows his own power, assured them of victory, and reminded them to place *their main dependence on the bayonet*, and as if his words had not been sufficient, his demeanour on the battle-field was such as to make the veriest coward dare a hundred deaths in his cause. When one of his officers saw him sitting on his horse in the thickest of the fight, with his sword drawn, while the balls were rattling around him, and desired him to retire a short distance, where his person would not be so much exposed, he smiled good-humouredly, and anwered, "*let us ride a little nearer, the balls will fall behind us.*"

When the Mexican lancers made a charge upon the American right at Palo Alto, and the 5th infantry stood ready to receive it, General Taylor rode up and said, "Men, I place myself in your square." How could a man falter after such a mark of confidence?

Somewhat in the style of his speech to the militia men, is the remark made to General Ricardo, who exculpated his troops from the charge of stripping and mutilating the American dead, by saying that the women and rancheros did it; that they could not control them. General Taylor replied, "I am coming over to Matamoras, and I'll control them for you."

Anecdotes.

On the 30th of May, President Polk wrote to him, forwarding a commission as brevet major-general, and complimenting him on "the bright page he had added to American history." The legislature of Louisiana passed a vote of thanks, and ordered a sword to be presented to him. By an act of Congress he was promoted to be a full major-general.

At Monterey, he was in the town with his staff on foot, walking about perfectly regardless of danger, where the shot flew about as "if bushels of hickory nuts were hurled at us." Captain Henry says that seeing him crossing a street in a walk, while such a terrible crossfire swept it that it seemed impossible for him to escape, he ran across and reminded him how much he was exposing himself. The answer the gallant captain received was, "Take an axe and knock in that door." Another officer, noticing his conduct in the streets of Monterey, says, "He was as cool as a cucumber, and ordered us to pass into the city and break open the houses. God knows how many of us got out."

Speaking of the battle of Buena Vista, Captain Henry says in his Campaign Sketches, "Our rear was in danger; the tide of battle was decidedly against us; the fortunes of the day seemed cast upon a die, when, at this critical juncture, General Taylor arrived upon the field, and occupied a commanding position upon an elevated plateau. *His presence restored confidence.* * * * General Taylor stood calm and unmoved upon the plateau—all eyes were turned upon him. The leaden messengers of death swept harmlessly by his person, while hundreds were passing to futurity. Bragg, with his battery had arrived at the point of fearful struggle. Alone

Anecdote.

and unsupported was that battery and that brave old chief. Confident to the last of victory, he ordered his trusty captain to unlimber—to load with grape, and await the arrival of their masses until they nearly reached the muzzles of his pieces. On came the enemy like legions of fiends, certain of victory. When almost within grasp of the battery, Bragg opened his fire. The first volley staggered them, the second opened streets through their ranks, and the third put them in full retreat and saved the day."

"It was not," says Colonel Davis, "alone on the battle field that we learned to love General Taylor. The excitement of the carnage over, the same soul that could remain unmoved when his friends were falling like leaves about him, who could look unblanched upon the front of the thundering artillery, became the poor soldier's most sympathizing friend; and the eye so stern in battle was as mild as the tenderhearted matron's."

When the gallant Mississippi regiment was about to leave him, overpowered by the recollection of the high deeds which had endeared them to him, and with their demonstrations of respect and affection, he attempted in vain to address them. With tears streaming down his furrowed cheeks, all he could say was, "Go on, boys—go on—I can't speak." Such is the character of General Taylor, as a man.

General Worth.

Worth at Monterey.

GENERAL WILLIAM J. WORTH.

N his youth, Worth was engaged in a mercantile business in Albany; but just before the commencement of the war of 1812, he left his employment, and entered the service of his country.

The first signal opportunity which occurred for displaying the military talent for which he is now so celebrated, occurred at the battle of Chippewa, July 5th, 1814. In his official account of that battle, General Brown says, "the family of General Scott were conspicuous in the field, Lieutenant Smith, of the 6th infantry, the major of the brigade, and Lieutenants Worth and Watts, his aids."

A captain's commission, dated August 19th, 1814, was the result of this notice. At the battle of Niagara, or Lundy's Lane, Captain Worth again distinguished himself, and was rewarded by promotion to the rank of a major, but a severe wound received in the battle, compelled him to remain for a time inactive. After the peace, he was some time, military instructor of the West Point Military Academy. He gradually rose in the army, but found no active service until he was employed against the Indians, in the Florida war. In April, 1842, he gained a brilliant victory at Palaklaklaha, which brought the war to a close for a time. He was made brigadier-general by brevet, March 1st, 1842, but some point of military etiquette caused him to resign, when the army of occupation was lying before Matamoras, by which he was deprived, greatly to his regret, of all participation in the glorious conflicts of the 8th and 9th of May. Hearing of these battles, he withdrew his resignation, hastened to join the standard of General Taylor, and gained imperishable renown at Monterey.

General Taylor employed the other divisions of the army in making a diversion on the east side of the city, in order to favour the operations of General Worth, who was directed to gain the Saltillo road at its junction with those leading from the city, and then when the enemy's supplies and retreat should be cut off, to storm the heights overlooking it and the south-western angle of the city. The fortifications were on one height, a large unfinished structure designed for the Bishop's Palace, and known by that name, and opposite the Bishop's Palace, and across the San Juan, (Federation Hill,) two others, one called from the name of the battery on its crest, Federation Hill, the other **Soledad, or Soldada.**

Storming of Federation Hill.

Storming of Federation Hill.

At daylight, on the morning of the 21st, General Worth put his division in motion, so formed as to present the readiest order of battle at any point at which it might be assailed. As he advanced, he found a large body of lancers drawn up to oppose him, and a spirited engagement ensued between them and McCulloch's Texan rangers, aided by Captains C. F. Smith and Scott, and Duncan's battery. The Mexicans were defeated with heavy loss, and driven beyond the gorge where all the roads from Monterey united, and thereby shut out from the city. When his preparations were completed, at noon, General Worth rode up to the men he had designed for the storming of Federation Hill, and pointing up the hill, said to them as they moved off, "Men, you are to take that hill—and I know you will do it." With one shout they replied, "we will;" and they did. The words of their general had nerved their arms and inspirited their hearts, and they crossed the river amid a shower of grape and musket balls, and advanced up the hill, supported by reinforcements sent in good season by the general, and beating back, inch by inch, the gallant forces who opposed them. At the top of this hill a cannon was captured, remounted, and turned upon the foe. The enemy had retreated to the other peak of the ridge, Fort Soldada, and a perfect race now ensued between the 5th and 7th regiments of infantry, and the Texas rangers, as to which should first enter that fortress. Captain Gillespie, of the rangers, was the first to mount the works, but he was so closely followed by Lieutenant Pitcher, of the 5th, that the two regiments shared equally the honour of having captured a gun, abandoned by the enemy as he was driven from the fort. The

Capture of the Bishop's Palace.

cannon captured in these two places, were immediately turned upon the Bishop's Palace. The generalship exhibited by General Worth in this affair, is deserving of the highest praise. The completion of his labours is not less so. Before day on the morning of the 22d, a detachment moved to assault the fortifications on Independence Hill, an almost inaccessible height, nearly perpendicular, between seven and eight hundred feet high. The party which captured this formidable position, was led by Colonel Childs and Captain John R. Vinton. His loss was few in numbers, but among the slain was the gallant Captain R. A. Gillespie, who had so distinguished himself on the preceding day. The height gained, Lieutenants Roland, McPhail, and Deas succeeded in two hours, in raising a twelve-pound howitzer to the top of this steep and rugged acclivity, and opened a terrible fire upon the Bishop's Palace, not four hundred yards distant. By a brilliant manœuver, Captain Vinton enticed a party of the defenders to come out of the palace, then defeated them, drove them down the hill beyond it, entered the palace, and overpowered its remaining defenders. Thus, says Mr. Kendall, by a series of brilliant, well-planned, and successful movements, General Worth found himself in full possession of three of the enemy's batteries, the stronghold known as the Bishop's Palace, seven pieces of artillery, and a large quantity of ammunition and intrenching tools, two of their standards, and what was of still greater importance, the entire occupation of the Saltillo road, and a complete command of all the western portion of the city of Monterey.

The street fight in which General Worth participated

largely, will be more particularly described among the achievements of General Quitman. General Worth was soon summoned away from this scene of his triumphs to the siege of Vera Cruz, where, under General Scott, he bore a conspicuous part, and was present at the surrender. He was made commander of the city of Vera Cruz, but was not long employed on garrison duty. Leaving Colonel Wilson to look after the city, he took up his line of march for the city of Mexico, and was so fortunate as to obtain a share with his division in the brilliant victory of Cerro Gordo. With increased reputation he marched onward with Scott to Churubusco, where his brilliant feat, the capture of the *tete du pont*, contributed largely to the success of the day.

For an account of the taking of the Molino del Rey and Chapultepec, we have drawn largely upon the official report of General Worth himself.

"On a reconnoissance of the formidable dispositions of the enemy, near and around the castle of Chapultepec, they were found to exhibit an extended line of cavalry and infantry, sustained by a field battery of four guns—occupying directly, or sustaining, a system of defenses collateral to the castle and summit. This examination gave fair observation of the configuration of the grounds, and the extent of the enemy's lines, but, as appeared in the sequel, an inadequte idea of the nature of his defenses—they being skilfully masked.

The general-in-chief ordered that General Worth should attack and carry those lines and defenses, capture the enemy's artillery, destroy the machinery and material supposed to be in the foundry, (El Molino del Rey;) but limiting the operations to that extent. After which his command was to be immediately withdrawn to its position in the village of Tucubaya.

A close and daring reconnoissance, by Captain Mason, of the engineers, made on the morning of the 7th, represented the enemy's lines collateral to Chapultepec, to be as follows: His left rested upon and occupied a group of strong stone buildings, called El Molino del Rey, adjoining the grove at the foot of the hill of Chapultepec, and directly under the guns of the castle which crowns the summit. The right of his line rested upon another stone building, called Casa Mata, situated at the foot of the ridge that slopes gradually from the heights above the village of Tacubaya to the plain below. Midway between these buildings was the enemy's field battery, and his infantry forces were disposed on either side to support it. This reconnoissance was verified by Captain Mason and Colonel Duncan, on the afternoon of the same day. The result indicated that the centre was the weak point of the enemy's position; and that his flanks were the strong points, his left flank being the stronger.

Having made the necessary directions, at three o'clock on the morning of the 8th, the several columns were put in motion, on as many different routes; and, when the gray of the morning enabled them to be seen, they were as accurately in position as if posted in midday for review. The early dawn was the moment appointed for the attack, which was announced to our troops by the opening of Huger's guns on El Molino del Rey, upon which they continued to play actively until this point of the enemy's line became sensibly shaken, when the assaulting party, commanded by Captain Wright,

View from Tacubaya.

and guided by that accomplished officer, Captain Mason, of the engineers, assisted by Lieutenant Foster, dashed gallantly forward to the assault. Unshaken by the galling fire of musketry and canister that was showered upon them, on they rushed, driving infantry and artillerymen at the point of the bayonet. The enemy's field battery was taken, and his own guns were trailed upon his retreating masses; before, however, they could be discharged, perceiving that he had been dispossessed of this strong position by comparatively a handful of men, he made a desperate effort to regain it. Accordingly his retiring forces rallied and formed with this object. Aided by the infantry, which covered the house-tops, (within reach of which the battery had been moved during the night,) the enemy's whole line opened upon the assaulting party a terrific fire of musketry which struck down *eleven* out of the *fourteen* officers that composed the command, and non-commissioned officers and men in proportion. This severe shock staggered, for a moment, that gallant band. The light battalion, held to cover Huger's battery, under Captain E. Kirby Smith, (Lieutenant-Colonel Smith being sick,) and the right wing of Cadwalader's brigade, were promptly ordered forward to support, which order was executed in the most gallant style; the enemy was again routed, and this point of his line carried, and fully possessed by our troops. In the mean time Garland's (1st) brigade, ably sustained by Captain Drum's artillery, assaulted the enemy's left, and, after an obstinate and very severe contest, drove him from this apparently impregnable position, immediately under the guns of the castle of Chapultepec. Drum's section, and the battering

Assault on Casa Mata.

guns under Captain Huger, advanced to the enemy's position, and the captured guns of the enemy were now opened on his retreating forces, on which they continued to fire until beyond their reach. While this work was in progress of accomplishment, by our centre and right, our troops on the left were not idle. Duncan's battery opened on the right of the enemy's line, up to this time engaged; and the 2d brigade, under Colonel McIntosh, was now ordered to assault the extreme right of the enemy's line. The direction of this brigade soon caused it to mask Duncan's battery—the fire of which, for the moment, was discontinued—and the brigade moved steadily on to the assault of Casa Mata, which, instead of an ordinary field intrenchment, as was supposed, proved to be a strong stone citadel, surrounded with bastioned intrenchments and impassable ditches—an old Spanish work, recently repaired and enlarged. When within easy musket range, the enemy opened a most deadly fire upon our advancing troops, which was kept up, without intermission, until our gallant men reached the very slope of the parapet of the work that surrounded the citadel. By this time, a large proportion of the command was either killed or wounded, amongst whom were the three senior officers present—Brevet-Colonel McIntosh, Brevet-Lieutenant-Colonel Scott, of the 5th infantry, and Major Waite, 8th infantry; the second killed, and the first and last desperately wounded. Still the fire from the citadel was unabated. In this crisis of the attack, the command was, momentarily, thrown into disorder, and fell back on the left of Duncan's battery, where they rallied. As the 2d brigade moved to the assault, a very large cavalry and infantry force was discovered approaching rapidly upon our left flank, to reinforce the enemy's right. As soon as Duncan's battery was masked, as before mentioned, supported by Andrews's voltigeurs, of Cadwalader's brigade, it moved promptly to the extreme left of our line, to check the threatened assault on this point. The enemy's cavalry came rapidly within canister range, when the whole battery opened a most effective fire, which soon broke the squadrons, and drove them back in disorder. During this fire upon the enemy's cavalry, Major Sumner's command moved to the front, and changed direction in admirable order, under a most appalling fire from the Casa Mata. This movement enabled his command to cross the ravine immediately on the left of Duncan's battery, where it remained, doing noble service until the close of the action. At the very moment the cavalry were driven beyond reach, our own troops drew back from before the Casa Mata, and enabled the guns of Duncan's battery to reopen upon this position; which, after a short and well-directed fire, the enemy abandoned. The guns of the battery were now turned upon his retreating columns, and continued to play upon them until beyond reach.

He was now driven from every point of the field, and his strong lines, which had certainly been defended well, were in our possession. In fulfilment of the instructions of the commander-in-chief, the *Casa Mata* was blown up, and such of the captured ammunition as was useless to us, as well as the cannon mou s found in El Molino del Rey, were destroyed. After which my command, under the reiterated orders of the general-in-chief, returned to quarters at Tacubaya, with three of the enemy's

Mexican loss in killed, wounded, and prisoners.

four guns, (the fourth, having been spiked, was rendered unserviceable;) as also a large quantity of small arms, with gun and musket ammunition, and exceeding eight hundred prisoners, including fifty-two commissioned officers.

By concurrent testimony of prisoners the enemy's force exceeded fourteen thousand men commanded by General Santa Anna in person. His total loss killed, (including the second and third in command, Generals Valdarez and Leon,) wounded and prisoners, amounts to three thousand, exclusive of some two thousand who deserted after the rout.

My command, reinforced as before stated, only reached three thousand one hundred men of all arms. The contest continued two hours, and its severity is painfully attested by our heavy loss of officers, non-commissioned officers, and privates, including in the first two classes some of the brightest ornaments in the service.

It will be seen that subordinate commanders speak in the warmest terms of the conduct of their officers and men, to which I beg leave to add my cordial testimony. There can be no higher exhibition of courage, constancy, and devotion to duty and to country.

These operations occurring under the observation of the general-in-chief, gives assurance that justice will be done to the noble officers and soldiers whose valour achieved this glorious but dear-bought victory. Commending the gallant dead, the wounded, and the few unscathed to the respectful memory of their countrymen, and the rewards due to valour and conduct, I present the names of those especially noticed by the subordinate commanders, uniting in all they have said, and extending the same testimony to those not named."

The history of the terrible conflict at Chapultepec, where none but the invincible were fit to fight, we have already given in the words of General Scott. The general's whole account is a tribute to the skill and bravery of General Worth.

We cannot better close this sketch of General Worth's achievements, than by the following extract from the eloquent work of Samuel C. Reid, Esq., "Scouting Expeditions with McCulloch's Texas Rangers." Speaking of General Worth and his position at Monterey, after the cavalry fight on the 21st, by which the gorge of the Saltillo road was taken, he says, "the position General Worth then occupied might have been considered as critical as it was dangerous. Separated from the main body of the army—his communication cut off, and no possible route less than eight miles to regain it—with but scanty supplies of provision for only four days—surrounded by gorges and passes of the mountains from whose summits belched forth the destructive shot, shell, and grape; he was liable at any moment to be attacked by an overwhelming force in the direction of Saltillo, which had been reported to be daily expected, and which would have placed his command in the very jaws of the enemy. For although holding the passes and gorges of the Saltillo road, yet a superior force from the advance would certainly have forced him back to, and have turned upon him, the very passes which he then held. It was feared, too, from his impetuous nature that he would rush his command into unnecessary danger by some rash and desperate attempt. But it was not so.

He was collected, calm, and cool, and bore himself with that proud, resolute and commanding mien, giving his orders with promptness and decision which inspired men and officer alike with confidence. He never appeared better than on that day; and all felt that with **WORTH** they were sure of *victory*."

GENERAL JOHN E. WOOL.

JOHN E. WOOL was born in Orange county, New York, and resided at the commencement of the war of 1812 at Troy, New York, where he assisted in organizing a volunteer corps. He was, soon after, appointed to a captaincy in the 13th infantry. At the battle of Queenstown he bore a conspicuous part. The destruction of the American officers by the terrible fire of the enemy, caused the duty of charging their battery to devolve upon Captain Wool, and it could not have been committed to better hands. Rallied by General Brock, the defeated British advanced to retake the battery, but Captain Wool tearing down with his own hands a white flag raised by one of his men, charged them a second time, and defeated them again, with the loss of their brave commander, General Brock. His gallantry won for him the rank of Major, conferred during the campaign of 1813. In this capacity he participated in the battle of Plattsburg, the official account of which, given by General Macomb, contains the following.

"The column on the Beekmantown road proceeded most rapidly; the militia skirmished with his advanced parties, and, except a few brave men, fell back most precipitately in the greatest disorder, notwithstanding the British troops did not deign to fire on them, except by their flankers and advanced patroles. The night previous I ordered Major Wool to advance with a detachment of two hundred and fifty men to support the militia, and set them an example of firmness. Also Captain Leonard, of the light artillery, was directed to proceed with two pieces to be on the ground before day, yet he did not make his appearance until eight o'clock, when the enemy had approached within two miles of the village. With his conduct, therefore, I am not well pleased. Major Wool, with his party, disputed the road with great obstinacy, but the militia could not be prevailed upon to stand, notwithstanding the exertions of their general and staff officers; although the fields were divided by strong stone walls, and they were told that the enemy could not possibly cut them off. The state dragoons of New York wear red coats, and they being on the heights to watch the enemy, gave constant alarm to the militia, who mistook them for the enemy, and feared his getting in their rear. Finding the enemy's columns had penetrated within a mile of Plattsburg, I despatched my aid-de-camp, Lieutenant Root, to bring off the detachment at Dead Creek, and to inform Lieutenant Appling that I wished him to fall on the enemy's right flank. The colonel fortunately arrived just in time to save his retreat, and to fall in with the head of a column debouching from the woods. Here he poured in a destructive fire from his riflemen at rest, and continued to annoy the column until he formed a junction with Major Wool. The field-pieces did considerable execution among the enemy's columns. So undaunted, however, was the enemy, that he never deployed in his whole march, always pressing on in column. Finding that every road was full of troops crowding on us on all sides, I ordered the field-pieces to retire across the bridge and form a battery for its protection, and to cover the retreat of the infantry, which was accordingly done, and the parties of Appling and Wool, as well as that of Sproul, retired alternately, keeping up a brisk fire until they got under cover of the works. The enemy's light troops occupied the houses near the bridge, and kept up a constant firing from the windows and balconies, and annoyed us much. I ordered them to be driven out with hot shot, which soon put the houses in flames, and obliged these sharp-shooters to retire. The whole day, until it was too late to see, the enemy's light troops endeavoured to drive our guards from the bridge, but they suffered dearly for their perseverance. An attempt was also made to cross the upper bridge, where the militia handsomely drove them back."

The conclusion of the official despatch contains a handsome notice of the most distinguished officers, Appling, Wool, Totten, and others. President Madison conferred on Major Wool the rank of Lieutenant-Colonel

Marches to Monclova.

by brevet; the letter by which he was apprized of the honour stating in complimentary terms that it was for his bravery at Plattsburg. After the close of the war he served in various capacities, gradually rising in his profession, until June, 1841, when he received his commission as brigadier-general. At the beginning of the Mexican war, it was determined to direct an expedition against the provinces of Mexico, and General Wool was selected to command it. The mass of this army was composed of volunteers, mostly commanded by regular officers.

He led his command over a long and toilsome march to the city of Monclova, where the governor came out to meet him as a friend, and surrendered the city without a word. Reports of the movement made upon Chihuahua by Colonel Doniphan under the orders of General Kearny, determined General Wool not to advance against that city, and he soon after received orders from General Taylor to capture the city of Parras. He arrived there on the 6th of December, 1846, where the people became so much attached to him that when he left the city to march to Saltillo, the ladies besought him to commit his sick to their care. He did so, and they proved their sincerity by the most anxious and tender nursing. His movements after joining General Taylor have already been recorded. At Buena Vista, the details of the battle were committed to him by General Taylor, and the whole account of the victory shows how fully he justified the confidence of his commander.

GENERAL DAVID E. TWIGGS.

 AVID E. TWIGGS was born in Richmond county, Georgia, in 1790, and bred to the bar, but the war of 1812 brought about a change in his profession. He obtained a captain's commission, conducted himself every where well, and was rewarded for his gallantry by being raised to the rank of major by brevet. He served with distinction under General Jackson in the Indian campaigns, and under Generals Gaines and Scott, in Florida. Under Scott he held the rank of colonel of the 2d regiment of dragoons. His regiment was attached to the "Army of Occupation," and he has borne a part with the utmost honour to himself in every

His discipline and goodness of heart.

great battle, save that of Buena Vista. He commanded the right wing of the army in the battles on the Rio Grande, and contributed greatly to the capture of Monterey. He was complimented by General Taylor for his bravery and valuable services. He has participated in all the glorious triumphs on the road to Mexico, winning honour at every step. He is still at the head of his division, and in case of an opportunity will give a good account of it.

Like his fellow-soldier Wool, he is one of the most rigid disciplinarians in the army. An instance of that perfection of discipline to which he had brought his men, as well as of his goodness of heart may be seen from the following:—On the road from Palo Alto, when the army was advancing to meet the enemy a second time, a wounded Mexican was seen lying in the long grass beside the road. He raised himself up, and showed by signs that he was dying for water. The sight impressed all who witnessed it, and all desired to rush to his relief, but such a breach of discipline they dared not commit under the command of Colonel Twiggs. At length the eye of the colonel fell upon the sufferer. His discipline was forgotten. "Men, the poor fellow wants water!" he exclaimed, and in an instant a dozen canteens were flung at his feet. Twiggs then directed them to give him food, and he ate and died, surrounded by marks of the generosity and kindness of the American colonel and his men. After the taking of Matamoras, Colonel Twiggs was appointed governor of the town, and to his especial care was intrusted the taking possession of the military stores left by the Mexican army. Don Jesus Cardenas, the prefect of Matamoras at the time General Taylor took possession, was distinguished among his fellow-citizens for his oppression, and for his hatred to foreigners. In surrendering the city, the prefect's only care was to know if he could retain his office. He never stipulated for any privileges for the citizens, or seemed in any way to think of their interests. Immediately on Colonel Twiggs taking command, he sent for this notable Cardenas, and asked him for an inventory of the public property. He stated, positively, that he knew of none, and persisted in declaring that none was left by the Mexican forces when they evacuated the city. Colonel Twiggs dismissed him, and entering the city with information obtained from other quarters, soon began to find vast quantities of military stores, in almost all the out-of-the-way places about the plaza.

This outrageous trifling on the part of the prefect Colonel Twiggs was determined to notice. Accordingly he waited upon him the following morning at his office, to give the gentleman what is denominated a "plain talk." The colonel laboured under one difficulty— eloquent himself, it was a great drawback to have it marred by an indifferent translator. Fortunately, an American citizen by the name of Dugden, a v~ y intelligent gentleman of Matamoras. ẓnd an object of the prefect's special oppression, offered his services as an interpreter. "I wish to give this falsifying prefect a proper notion of his conduct," said the colonel, with a variety of expletives. "Can you, Mr. Dugden, do justice to what I say?" Mr. Dugden assented, and the governor laid down the first paragraph of his lecture in English. Dugden did justice to what was said, and, it was thought, added a little on his own responsibility, much to the gratification of the governor.

The prefect, bearded in his own den, began to turn a variety of colours: his consternation increased as the citizens of the town crowded into his office, and, by the wildest expressions of delight, testified their pleasure at what was going on. The prefect literally trembled in his shoes, and promised to act better, and honestly point out the hidden treasures. But he prevaricated so constantly, that he was finally dismissed, and ejected from the shadow of the office he still held, and he left the city, it was supposed, to join Arista or some other general in the interior.*

Captain Henry, in his Campaign Sketches, gives an amusing account of the manner in which General Twiggs crossed the Sierra Madre, on his expedition against Victoria, December 16th, 1846. We make an extract from his narrative. He says, " We passed over a lovely country; it was a succession of stony ridges, and basins of the richest kind of soil. We marched along rapidly, and before noon had passed over twelve miles, when we reached a hill which forbade any chance of our wagons ascending without the assistance of the men. I christened it Disappointment Hill; for we were very anxious to reach Montemorelos, and we saw our march delayed for some time, within sight of the place. We ascended, stacked arms, and marched down again to assist the teams. The artillery got along admirably by hitching twelve horses to a piece; but when the mule teams came, it was entirely another thing. The ascent must

---

* Our Army on the Rio Grande.

have been at least forty-five degrees; certainly one of the steepest hills I ever saw wagons ascend.

General Twiggs assumed the management of the passage in person. Those who know the general cannot but recollect his peculiarities and his faculty of getting more work out of men in a given time than any other officer in the army. A quartermaster stood no chance; his stentorian lungs drowned every one's voice and his tone of command did not admit of any question 'Bring on that team, there!' Along comes the team with a company of men hold of its wheels, and every available point. Quartermaster—'Drive slowly, a little way at a time, and let your mules blow.' Team commences the ascent; all steam is cracked on and the quartermaster cries 'stop.' 'Stop! the devil!' cries the general, 'who *ever* heard of such a thing? Crack ahead! speak to your mules, sir, and keep them going as long as they will.' And away goes the team amid cracking of whips and cheering of men. The men would file on about six feet deep behind, pushing each other along. 'General, those men are certainly doing no good.' 'You are mistaken, sir; they are keeping the man next the wagon from holding on going up hill.' The last to cross was the quartermaster's forge. 'Well,' exclaimed the general, 'do you think you can get up, lasty, asty, without any men?' 'O yes, general.' 'Well, on with you.' By the time 'lasty' had ascended twenty feet, the mules commenced backing. 'Great God! teamster, which way *are* you going? That's not the way up the hill.' And amid peals of laughter, a company went to the assistance of 'lasty.' With any number of jokes, the general succeeded in crossing the train in an hour and a half."

In the estimation of General Scott, General Twiggs evidently holds a very exalted position. The tributes paid to his valour and conduct in the despatches of the general-in-chief, are of the most warm and decisive, as well as respectful character.

General Twiggs's family has long been famous in the military history of the country. His father, General John Twiggs, rendered services in the revolutionary war, of such importance as to gain him the title of "Saviour of Georgia." His brother, Major Twiggs, and his nephew, Lieutenant Twiggs, son of the major, both fell in the recent operations before the city of Mexico.

GENERAL JOHN A. QUITMAN.

No officer has deserved a higher character for all the qualities which constitute a good soldier than General Quitman. He has carved his name in bold characters upon the military records of our country; connected it indissolubly with the victories of Monterey, Cerro Gordo, and the battles of Mexico. At Monterey he was particularly distinguished, and there and in the city of Mexico, his bravery in penetrating the town contributed greatly to secure and hasten victory. The following description of the taking of Fort Teneria at Monterey by his command, will give an idea of the nature of the services he is called on to perform, services only asked of those who know not how to fail.

Taking of Fort Teneria.

"The battle now became furious—the incessant roar of cannon, and the rattling of musketry, told how desperate was the conflict. The cross fire was indeed *terrible*. On marched Quitman's brigade, led by four companies of the 4th infantry, about four hundred yards in the advance, breasting the dreadful storm which made them stagger, and at once struck down one-third of the officers and men, rendering it necessary for the remainder to retire and effect a junction with the two other companies then advancing. Lieutenant Hoskins, the adjutant, and Lieutenant J. S. Woods, of the 2d, but serving with the 4th, were killed; and Lieutenant R. H. Graham fell mortally wounded. Thus the 3d and 4th both lost their adjutants, who were two of the most noble and accomplished officers in the army. The Mississippians and Tennesseeans steadily advanced, braving the galling fire of copper grape, which swept through their ranks, until the centre of the Mississippi rifle regiment rested about three hundred yards in front of the fort, with the Tennessee regiment formed on the left. It was the crisis, and the storm of battle was now at its height. The order was given to "*advance and fire.*" For thirty minutes their fire was kept up, while the men continued to push forward. The long lines moved until within about one hundred yards of the fort, when they became lost in the volume of smoke that enveloped them. The Mexicans had run up a new flag in exultation, and in defiance of the assault, which was now being made in front and rear, while the deafening fire of their artillery, and the rattling of musketry, seemed more deadly than ever. The brave and chivalric Lieutenant-Colonel McClung then ordered a charge; and calling on the "Tom-

Taking of Fort Teneria.

bigbee volunteers," a company he formerly commanded, and the "Vicksburg Southrons," of Captain Willis, to follow him, he rushed forward to the attack. Colonel Davis also gave the order to ch rge nearly at the same time, or shortly after, anticipating General Quitman, who was just on the point himself of issuing the same order. With desperation the lines came down upon the fort, and the escalade was made with the fury of a tempest. Burning for revenge, the men faced the terrible fire, and marched up to the very mouths of the enemy's cannon, while their daring recklessness made the Mexicans quail, and fall back terror-stricken from their guns. Forward sprang the gallant McClung and leaped the ditch; with sword in hand, and brandishing it over his head, he mounted the ramparts and entered the fort, while the regiment rushed after him, cheered on by the gallant Colonel Davis, and followed by the brave Tennesseeans of the noble Campbell. Lieutenant W. H. Patterson, of Captain Rogers's "Tombigbee volunteers," was the second man in the fort, to whom a Mexican officer surrendered and gave up his sword, and but an instant passed before the undaunted Captain D. H. Cooper with his high-souled corps of "Wilkinson county volunteers," and the whole brigade had entered, when a yell and shout of triumph rose above the din of battle, and a wild hurrah rang over the scene of strife, which sent forth the "harbinger of victory."

The Mexicans fled in dismay, and ran to the strong fortified building, called the distillery, about seventy-five yards in the rear, whence they opened a heavy fire of musketry. Without pausing, the heroic McClung, followed by the brigade, rushed on in pursuit, charged

Taking of Fort Teneria.

and entered the work, which immediately surrendered. While a Mexican officer was praying for quarters, and calling out to McClung that he had surrendered, the gallant colonel received two severe wounds, being shot through the hand and body, and was caught by Lieutenant W. P. Townsend, of the Mississippi regiment, who supported him from falling. As the men rushed in, they beheld McClung and the Mexican officer, and thinking that the latter had shot him, the Mexican was immediately slain. On the arrival of Colonel Davis, who reached the distillery at the same time with McClung, by another entrance, he received the sword of another Mexican officer, who surrendered his command to him. Five pieces of artillery, a considerable quantity of ammunition, and thirty prisoners, including three officers, here fell into our hands; the prisoners were placed in charge of Lieutenant Armstrong. The brigade did not halt here, but moving on with rapidity, led by Colonel Davis, they prepared to charge the second fort, called El Diablo, about three hundred yards in the rear of the last work, when General Quitman ordered them to fall back, and they retired.

Thus, after a most desperate and bloody conflict, of more than two hours, was one of the enemy's strong works carried by storm, notwithstanding the obstinate resistance they maintained. Considering that it was the first time that the troops of General Butler's division were ever brought into action—sustaining, as they did, a desperate struggle against a sheltered and inaccessible foe—unprotected and bared to the storm of the murderous artillery of the enemy, which, although it swept one-fifth of their number from the ranks, caused them not to shrink for an instant from a steady advance, proves to the world the undaunted gallantry of our citizen soldiers, who have won for themselves the reputation of veteran troops—the charge led by the Mississippi rifle regiment upon Fort Teneria, without bayonets, has gained for the state a triumph which stands unparalleled.

The spirit of the general was infused into the hearts of his men, and so devoted were they to their duty, that when once they had entered upon an achievement its accomplishment was certain. One of his men, a private, was wounded by a cannon ball. An orderly passing by him complied with his request for water, and asked if he could do any thing more for him. "Yes, my friend," said the poor fellow, "you can take my musket back to the 3d. I am a dead man, but I would like my piece to go back to my old regiment." The musket was delivered, and the soldier died contented.

It was General Quitman's glory to enter the city of Mexico by the most difficult pass, that of the gate of Belen, and to raise the star-spangled banner, for the first time, over the "Halls of the Montezumas." General Scott says,

"I had been, from the first, well aware that the western, or San Cosme, was the less difficult route to the centre and conquest of the capital; and, therefore, intended that Quitman should only manœuver and threaten the Belen or south-western gate, in order to favour the main attack by Worth—knowing that the strong defenses at the Belen were directly under the guns of the much stronger fortress, called the citadel, just within. Both of these defenses of the enemy were also within easy supporting distance from the San Angel (or *Nino Perdido*) and San Antonio gates. Hence the greatest support, in numbers, given to Worth's movement as the main attack.

Those views I repeatedly, in the course of the day, communicated to Major-General Quitman; but, being in hot pursuit—gallant himself, and supported by Brigadier-Generals Shields and Smith—Shields badly wounded before Chapultepec, and refusing to retire—as well as by all the officers and men of the column—Quitman continued to press forward, under flank and direct fires —carried an intermediate battery of two guns, and then the gate, before two o'clock in the afternoon, but not without proportionate loss, increased by his steady maintenance of that position.

Quitman, within the city—adding several new defenses to the position he had won, and sheltering his corps as well as practicable—now awaited the return of daylight under the guns of the formidable citadel, yet to be subdued.

In the night the Mexican army fled from the city, and I communicated, about daylight, orders to Worth and Quitman to advance slowly and cautiously, (to guard against treachery,) towards the heart of the city, and to occupy its stronger and more commanding points. Quitman proceeded to the great *plaza*, or square, planted guards, and hoisted the colours of the United States on the national palace—containing the halls of Congress and executive departments of federal Mexico."

GENERAL PERSIFER F. SMITH.

GENERAL PERSIFER F. SMITH, "of Louisiana," as he is generally designated, is a native of Philadelphia, and one of the bravest men and best soldiers in the army. He served in command of the Louisiana troops in the Florida war, and on the formation of the volunteer division was appointed colonel of the rifles. In six months he was promoted to the rank of brigadier-general by brevet. This was for his services at Monterey. He led the right wing of Worth's division at the entering of that city, and fought his way through one street while Worth was engaged in the next with the other part of his division. This terrible warfare is thus described by S. C. Reid, Esq., in his work on the Scouting Expeditions of McCulloch's Texas Rangers.

"Every street was barricaded with heavy works of masonry, the walls being some three or four feet thick,

Street fight in Monterey.

with embrasures for one or more guns which raked the streets; the walls of gardens and sides of houses were all loop-holed for musketry; the tops of the houses were covered with troops, who were sheltered behind parapets, some four feet high, upon which were piled sand bags for their better protection, and from which they showered down a hurricane of balls.

Between three and four o'clock, from the cessation of the fire in the opposite direction, it was evident that the enemy had become disengaged, which enabled them to draw off men and guns to our side, as their fire had now become almost doubly increased. The street-fight became appalling—both columns were now closely engaged with the enemy, and steadily advanced inch by inch—our artillery was heard rumbling over the paved streets, galloping here and there, as the emergency required, and pouring forth a blazing fire of grape and ball—volley after volley of musketry, and the continued peals of artillery became almost deafening—the artillery of both sides raked the streets, the balls striking the houses with a terrible crash, while amid the roar of battle were heard the battering instruments used by the Texans. Doors were forced open, walls were battered down—entrances made through the longitudinal walls, and the enemy driven from room to room, and from house to house, followed by the shrieks of women, and the sharp crack of the Texan rifles. Cheer after cheer was heard in proud and exulting defiance, as the Texans or regulars gained the house-tops by means of ladders, while they poured in a rain of bullets upon the enemy on the opposite houses. It was indeed a most strange and novel scene of warfare."

Street Fight, on General Worth's side

Battle of Contreras.

In history General Smith will be best known as the hero of Contreras. An article in the New York Courier and Inquirer, giving an account of this battle, contains the following passages. "About two P. M., as we had crawled to the top of a hill, whither we had been ourselves pulling Magruder's battery and the mountain howitzers, we suddenly espied Valencia fortified on a hill two hundred yards off, and strongly reinforced by a column which had just come out of the city. We lay down close to avoid drawing their fire, while the battery moved past at a full gallop. Just then General Smith's manly voice rung out, '*Forward the rifles—to support the battery.*' On they went, till we got about eight hundred yards from the work, when the enemy opened upon them with his long guns, which were afterwards found to be sixteens and eight-inch howitzers. The ground was the worst possible for artillery, covered with rocks large and small, prickly pears and cactus, intersected by ditches filled with water and lined with maguey plant, itself impervious to cavalry, and with patches of corn which concealed the enemy's skirmishers, while it impeded our own passage. The artillery advanced but slowly, under a most tremendous fire, which greatly injured it before it could be got in range, and the thickness of the undergrowth caused the skirmishers thrown forward to lose their relative position, as well as the column. About four the battery got in position under a most murderous fire of grape, canister, and round shot. Here the superiority of the enemy's pieces rendered our fire nugatory. We could get but *three* pieces in battery, while they had *twenty-seven*, all of them three times the calibre of ours. For two hours

Battle of Contreras.

our troops stood the storm of iron and lead they hailed upon them, unmoved. At every discharge they laid flat down to avoid the storm, and then sprang up to serve the guns. At the end of that time, two of the guns were dismounted and we badly hurt; thirteen of the horses were killed and disabled, and fifteen of the cannoneers killed and wounded. The regiment was then recalled. The lancers had been repelled in three successive charges. The 3d infantry and 1st artillery had also engaged and successfully repelled the enemy's skirmishers without loss of either officers or men. The greatest loss has been at the batteries. Officers looked gloomy for the first day's fight, but the brigade was formed, and General Smith in person took command. All felt revived, and followed him with a yell, as creeping low to avoid the grape, which was coming very fast, we made a circuit in rear of the batteries, and passing off to the right we were soon lost to view in the chaparral and cactus. Passing over the path that we scrambled through, behold us, at almost six o'clock in the evening, tired, hungry, and sorrowful, emerging from the chaparral and crossing the road between it and Valencia. Here we found Cadwalader and his brigade already formed, and discovered Riley's brigade skirmishing in rear of the enemy's works. Valencia was ignorant of our approach, and we were as yet safe. In front of us was Valencia strongly intrenched on a hill-side and surrounded by a regular field-work concealed from us by an orchard in our rear. Mendoza with a column of six thousand was in the road, but thinking us to be friends. On our right was a large range of hills, whose continued crest was parallel to the road, and in which were formed

Battle of Contreras.

in line of battle five thousand of the best Mexican cavalry. On our left we were separated from our own forces by an almost impassable wilderness, and it was now twilight. Even Smith looked round for help. Suddenly a thousand *vivas* came across the hill-side, like the yells of prairie wolves in the dead of night, and the squadrons on our right formed for charging. Smith's himself again! 'Face to the rear!' 'Wait till you see their red caps, and then give it to them!' Furiously they came on a few yards, then changed their minds, and, disgusted at our cool reception, retired to their couches.

* * * * * *

At last, just at daylight, General Smith, slowly walking up, asked if all was ready. A look answered him. '*Men, forward.*' And we *did* 'forward.' Springing up at once, Riley's brigade opened, when the crack of a hundred rifles started the Mexicans from their astonishment, and they opened their fire. Useless fire, for we were so close that they overshot us, and before they could turn their pieces on us we were on them. Then such cheers arose as you never heard. The men rushed forward like demons, yelling and firing the while. The carnage was frightful, and though they fired sharply it was of no use. The earthen parapet was cleared in an instant, and the blows of the stocks could be plainly heard, mingled with the yells and groans around. Just before the charge was made, a large body of lancers came winding up the road, looking most splendidly in their brilliant uniforms. They never got to the work, but turned and fled. In an instant all was one mass of confusion, each trying to be foremost in the flight. The road was literally blocked up, and while many perished by their own guns, it was almost impossible to fire on the mass, from the danger of killing our own men. Some fled up the ravine on the left, or on the right, and many of these were slain by turning their own guns on them. Toward the city the rifles and 2d infantry led off the pursuit. Seeing that a large crowd of the fugitives were jammed up in a pass in the road, some of our men ran through the corn-field, and by thus heading them off and firing down upon them, about thirty men took over five hundred prisoners, nearly a hundred of them officers.

After disarming the prisoners, as the pursuit had ceased, we went back to the fort, where we found our troops in full possession, and the rout complete.

Thus ended the glorious battle of Contreras, in which two thousand men, under General P. F. Smith, completely routed and destroyed an army of eight thousand men, under General Valencia, with Santa Anna and a force of twenty thousand men within five miles. Their army was so completely routed that not fifteen hundred men rejoined Santa Anna, and participated in the second battle.

General Kearny.

GENERAL STEPHEN W. KEARNY.

TEPHEN WATTS KEARNY was born at Newark, New Jersey, and educated at Princeton college, where he was a student at the age of eighteen, when the war of 1812 commenced. Having determined to go into the army, he was appointed first lieutenant in the 13th regiment of infantry, and attached to the company of the then Captain John E. Wool. He was engaged in the desperate fight of Scott at Queenstown, and was surrendered a prisoner at the end of it. After he was exchanged he served with honour through the war, and acquired such distinction as to retain his rank as captain during the army reductions of 1815 and 1821. Afterwards he was stationed at Jefferson Barracks, near

Anecdote.

St. Louis. While there, he acquired as wide spread a reputation for his tactics and severe discipline, as he had previously borne for coolness and composure under all circumstances. An anecdote related by Fayette Robinson, Esq., in his extremely valuable new work on the Army of the United States, illustrates these qualities in the best manner. It is as follows :—" While stationed at Jefferson Barracks, General Kearny was drilling a brigade on one of the open fields near the post. The manœuver was the simple exercise of marching in line to the front. An admirable horseman, he sat with his face towards the troops, while the horse he rode, perfectly trained, was backed in the same direction, along which the command was marched. At once the animal fell, fastening the rider to the ground by his whole weight. His brigade had been drilled to such a state of insensibility, that not one of them came to his assistance, nor was it necessary. The line advanced to within about ten feet of him, when, in a loud distinct voice, calmly as if he had been in the saddle under no unusual circumstance, General Kearny gave the command, *'Fourth company—obstacle—march.'* The fourth company which was immediately in front of him was flanked by its captain in the rear of the other half of the grand division. The line passed on, and when he was thus left in rear of his men, he gave the command, *'Fourth company into line—march.'* He was not seriously injured, extricated himself from his horse, mounted again, passed to the front of the regiment, and executed the next manœuver in the series he had marked out for the day's drill."

He was soon afterwards (1833) made lieutenant-

Wounded at San Pasqual.

colonel of dragoons, and had to perform the onerous duty of forming a new arm of the service. The efficiency of his training is exhibited in the bearing of the dragoon regiments and the mounted rifles in the Mexican war. General Gaines has said that the first dragoons drilled by General Kearny were the best troops he ever saw. He served many years in the north-west, continually acquiring valuable information for the government by his expeditions, which at the same time impressed the Indians with a respect for the United States government. In June, 1846, he received the rank of brigadier-general, and was sent out from Fort Leavenworth on the expedition to New Mexico and California, the particulars of which we have before given. He exposed himself very much at the battle of San Pasqual, as he always does when there is danger near. He was severely wounded with a lance, and would have been killed had not Lieutenant Emory of the topographical corps, rode up in time to shoot the enemy as he was about to make a second thrust.

A dispute as to rank and authority occurred between himself and Commodore Stockton in California, by which the interests of the country in some hands might have been compromised. As it was, however, private disagreements produced no public wrongs, and the question was eventually settled by the trial of Lieutenant-Colonel Fremont by a court martial, he having preferred to obey the commands of Commodore Stockton rather than those of General Kearny.

COLONEL JOHN C. FREMONT.

He services of Colonel Fremont in his celebrated expedition to Oregon, are too well known to require recapitulation here, and his exploits in California have already been narrated. We propose merely to give in this connection some illustrations of his character, and to express a hope that the result of a court-martial, before which he is now being tried, at Washington, for alleged offences, growing out of the dispute between Commodore Stockton and General Kearny, may not change his pursuit in life.*

Pico, the brother of the governor of California, had been dismissed by the Americans on parole, and was recaptured in the act of breaking it. He was condemned by court-martial to death, and twelve o'clock was the hour fixed for his execution. The soldiers were clamorous for his death as a traitor, but the gallant colonel could not bear the thought of killing an enemy in any

* 1848.

Humanity triumphant over discipline.

other way than on the battle-field, and he was meditating upon the matter with a heavy heart, when a company of ladies and children was led into the room, and on their knees begged the life of a husband and a father. The question was settled. Humanity triumphed over discipline and the laws of war. He raised the mother and exclaimed, "he is pardoned," and sent for the prisoner that he might learn his fate from the happy faces of his friends. He was overpowered with emotion. He had learned his fate with all the pride and dignity of a Spaniard, but he could not bear the news of pardon. He threw himself at the colonel's feet, swore eternal fidelity, and begged the privilege of fighting and dying for him. How firm a friend he has since been may be apparent from the subjoined account of Colonel Fremont's ride, taken from the National Intelligencer. They passed over eight hundred miles in eight days, including two days detention and all stoppages. Don Pico is called by his Christian name Jesus, pronounced *Haisoos*.

"It was daybreak on the morning of the 22d of March, that the party set out from la Ciudad de los Angelos (the city of the Angels,) in the southern part of Upper California, to proceed in the shortest time to Monterey, on the Pacific ocean, distant full four hundred miles. The way is over a mountainous country, much of it uninhabited, with no other road than a trace, and many defiles to pass, particularly the maritime defile of El Rincon, or Punto Gordo, fifteen miles in extent, made by the jutting of a precipitous mountain into the sea, which can only be passed when the tide is out, and the sea calm, and even then in many places through the waves

Extraordinary travelling.

The towns of Santa Barbara and San Luis Obispo and occasional ranchos, are the principal inhabited places on the route. Each of the party had three horses, nine in all, to take their turns under the saddle. The six loose horses ran ahead without bridle or halter, and required some attention to keep to the track.

When wanted for a change, say at distances of twenty miles, they were caught by the *lasso*, thrown either by Don Jesus or the servant Jacob, who, though born and raised in Washington, in his long expeditions with Colonel Fremont had become as expert as a Mexican with the lasso, as sure as a mountaineer with the rifle, equal to either on horse or foot, and always a lad of courage and fidelity. None of the horses were shod, that being a practice unknown to the Californians. The most usual gait was a sweeping gallop. The first day they rode one hundred and twenty-five miles, passing the San Fernando mountain, the defile of the Rincon, several other mountains, and slept at the hospitable rancho of Don Tomas Robberis, beyond the town of Santa Barbara. The only fatigue complained of in this day's ride was in Jacob's right arm, made tired by throwing the lasso and using it as a whip to keep the loose horses to the track.

The next day they made another one hundred and twenty-five miles, passing the formidable mountain of Santa Barbara, and counting upon it the skeletons of some fifty horses, part of near double that number which perished in the crossing of that terrible mountain by the California battalion on Christmas day, 1846, amidst a raging tempest, and a deluge of rain and cold more killing than that of the Sierra Nevada—the day of severest suffering, say Fremont and his men, that they have ever passed. At sunset the party stopped to sup with the friendly Captain Dana, and at nine San Luis Obispo was reached, the home of Don Jesus, where an affecting reception awaited Lieutenant-Colonel Fremont, in consequence of an incident which occurred there, that history will one day record;* and he was detained till eleven o'clock in the morning receiving the visits of the inhabitants, (mothers and children included,) taking a breakfast of honour, and waiting for a relief of fresh horses to be brought in from the surrounding country.

Here the nine horses from los Angelos were left and eight others taken in their places, and a Spanish boy added to the party to assist in managing the loose horses. Proceeding at the usual gait till eight at night, and having made some seventy miles, Don Jesus, who had spent the night before with his family and friends, and probably with but little sleep, became fatigued, and proposed a halt for a few hours. It was in the valley of the Salinas, (Salt river, called *Buena Ventura* in the old maps,) and the haunt of marauding Indians. For safety during their repose, the party turned off the trace issued through a *canada* into a thick wood, and lay down, the horses being put to grass at a short distance with the Spanish boy in the saddle to watch. Sleep, when commenced, was too sweet to be easily given up, and it was half way between midnight and day when the sleepers were aroused by an *estampedo* among the horses and the calls of the boy.

The cause of the alarm was soon found, not Indians, out white bears—this valley being their great resort,

---

* The pardon narrated before.

Extraordinary travelling.

having encountered them in great numbers the preceding year. The character of these bears is well known, and the bravest hunters do not like to meet them without the advantage of numbers. On discovering the enemy, Colonel Fremont felt for his pistols, but Don Jesus desired him to lie still, saying that "people could scare bears," and immediately he halloed at them in Spanish, and they went off. Sleep went off also, and the recovery of the horses frightened by the bears, building a rousing fire, making a breakfast from the hospitable supplies of San Luis Obispo, occupied the party till daybreak, when the journey was resumed. Eighty miles, and the afternoon brought the party to Monterey.

The next day, in the afternoon, the party set out on their return, and the two horses ridden by Colonel Fremont from San Luis Obispo, being a present to him from Don Jesus, he (Don Jesus) desired to make an experiment of what one of them could do. They were brothers, one a grass younger than the other, both of the same colour, (cinnamon,) and hence called *el canal* or *los canalos*, (the cinnamon, or the cinnamons.) The elder brother was taken for the trial, and the journey commenced upon him at leaving Monterey, the afternoon well advanced. Thirty miles under the saddle done that evening, and the party stopped for the night. In the morning the elder *canalo* was again under the saddle for Colonel Fremont, and for ninety miles he carried him without a change, and without apparent fatigue. It was still thirty miles to San Luis Obispo, where the night was to be passed, and Don Jesus insisted that *canalo* could easily do it, and so said the horse by his looks and action. But Colonel Fremont would not put him to the trial, and, shifting the saddle to the younger brother, the elder was turned loose to run the remaining thirty miles without a rider.

He did so, immediately taking the lead and keeping it all the way, and entering San Luis in a sweeping gallop, nostrils distended, snuffing the air and neighing with exultation of his return to his native pastures, his younger brother all the while running at the head of the horses under the saddle, bearing on his bit, and held in by his rider. The whole eight horses made their one hundred and twenty miles each that day, (after thirty the evening before,) the elder cinnamon making ninety of his under the saddle that day, besides thirty under the saddle the evening before; nor was there the least doubt that he would have done the whole distance in the same time if he had continued under the saddle.

After a hospitable detention of another half day at San Luis Obispo, the party set out for Los Angelos on the same nine horses which they had ridden from that place, and made the ride back in about the same time they had made it up, namely at the rate of one hundred and twenty-five miles a day."

Major McCulloch.

MAJOR BENJAMIN McCULLOCH.

 AJOR McCULLOCH was born in Rutherford county, Tennessee, in the year 1814. His father had seen service under General Jackson in the Creek war. He removed for a time to Alabama, but Benjamin remained in Tennessee at school for some years, when his father returned to the western part of that state, and Benjamin lived with him employed in hunting until he was twenty-one.

In the campaign on the Rio Grande, he told an anecdote of this portion of his life, which we give as we find it in Reid's Scouting Expeditions. "While speaking about the course we had travelled, and referring to our compass, Captain McCulloch related the following anecdote:

Anecdote.

"An old woodman," said he, "seldom wants a compass so long as he can see the sun, and even when it is cloudy you can always tell where the sun is, by a slight shadow from objects, be it ever so obscured. I recollect once I went a hunting with a gentleman and my father, and crossing the river in a boat, we hauled it up on the shore, and put out into the woods. Well, we did not meet with much luck, and so we put back for the boat. It was a cloudy day and the gentleman carried a pocket compass with him, and pointed out our course back. We followed the direction for some time, but could see no river. That we were lost was now beyond a doubt. And father becoming tired of following the course of the gentleman's compass, determined to be guided by it no longer.

"'Well, it *is* strange,' said the gentleman, 'the compass *can't* be wrong!'

"'D—n the compass,' said father, ' my boy Ben is worth all the compasses I ever saw;' and, turning to me, said, 'if you don't take us right straight to that boat, Ben, you shall never go on another hunt.'

"So I took a straight shoot, just by guessing the way the woods ran, and brought them to the boat, sure enough! As we were stepping in the boat, the gentleman said, with a laugh—

"Well, that boy Ben of yours, Mr. McCulloch, is a perfect magnetic needle. He will make as great a geographer as his celebrated namesake.'"

He would kill eighty bears in a winter. When he became of age, he set out for St. Louis, in order to join in an expedition for the Rocky mountains. In 1835, he wished to join Colonel David Crockett, in an expe-

His personal appearance.

dition that was about to take part in the Texas revolution, but the colonel went sooner than McCulloch had supposed, and he set out to follow him. At the river Brazos, he was taken very ill and did not recover until after the fall of the Alamo. He went on, however, and was made captain of a gun in the army of Texas under General Houston, which he served with effect in the memorable battle of San Jacinto. He served in all the border warfare of the day, and was present at the taking of Mier, though he returned home directly afterwards, and thus escaped the fate of his comrades.

In the Mexican war he has been as useful as any man in the American army; his scouting expeditions being among the boldest achievements of the war. "He is a man of delicate frame, five feet ten inches in height, with light hair and complexion. His features are rather regular and pleasing, though from long exposure on the frontier they have a weather-beaten cast. His quick and bright blue eye, with a mouth of thin compressed lips, indicate the cool, calculating, as well as the brave and daring energy of the man." This is the description given of him by S. C. Reid, Esq., in his account of the gallant captain's scouting expeditions.

We quote Mr. Reid's account of some incidents in the cavalry fight with which General Worth commenced the battle at Monterey, as it illustrates the Rangers' desperate yet chivalric method of fighting. "Armstrong, one of our company, was unhorsed by a lancer, having received two wounds; yet on foot, with sword in hand he defended himself against two of the enemy. He killed one, when an Irishman from the artillery battalion discovered his situation, and saying that he did not know whether he had *buck or ball in*, as he drew up his musket, but that he had better kill them both, than to miss the Mexican, fired and saved the Ranger! Fielding Alston, and J. F Minter, also of our company, while fighting gallantly received two lance wounds. Young Musson of New Orleans, who had joined our corps, was engaged at the same time, with a captain of cavalry, hand to hand in a sword fight, and at one time became very nearly overpowered; when asked why he did not shoot his foe, replied, with true southern chivalry, that "the Mexican had no pistol, and it would have been taking an *advantage* over him!" As another of our men was being overcome by a Mexican, the gallant Captain Cheshire, a private in the Rangers, dashed up to his rescue, and having no fire, seized a holster pistol, and with the butt end of it, felled the Mexican to the ground.

Captain Walker.

CAPTAIN SAMUEL H. WALKER.

 APTAIN WALKER entered the American service with a reputation early established by his services in the cause of the gallant state of Texas. A native of Maryland, he left his residence in Washington city to serve in the Creek war, after which he passed a campaign against the Indians in Florida, and was for awhile superintendent of a railroad. In 1842 he emigrated to Texas and served in her operations against Mexico with honour. He was one of Colonel Fisher's company of three hundred men in the famous Mier expedition. He was captured while on a scout before the Texan army reached that place, and after his comrades were defeated, they were all marched together to Matamoras, thence to Perote castle, on their way to the capital. As they proceeded, their

Escapes from Perote.

treatment became daily more and more cruel, and at Salado they determined to revolt and escape. Headed by Walker and Cameron, a Scotchman, each of whom seized and overpowered one of the sentinels, at the inner door of the prison yard, they rushed into the outer court where a hundred and fifty Mexican infantry were guarding the arms and cartridge boxes. These were soon driven out, and the Texans armed themselves while the Mexican cavalry and infantry formed at the gate. The brave band of prisoners charged through them, killing ten, wounding more of them, losing ten of their own men, five killed and five wounded. They escaped but lost their way, became involved in the mountains by false information, starved almost to death, and were finally recaptured. They were taken to Salado, where Santa Anna ordered every tenth man to be shot. Among those thus murdered was the gallant Scotchman, Cameron. Walker afterwards made his escape from Tacubaya, Santa Anna's residence, and after suffering hardships enough to have killed almost any one else, he arrived safe at New Orleans. In one month he returned to Texas, and served in Hays's command, until General Taylor went to the Rio Grande, when he went thither to offer the services of Captain Gillespie's company in which he was a private. He found there some thirty of the old Rangers who had followed the army from Corpus Christi, in hopes to see a little 'fun,' and they urged him to form a company. General Taylor gave him permission to do so, after the murder of Colonel Cross, and the company of Texas Rangers was speedily organized. The services of this brave band are too well known and appreciated to require recounting here. There are

His death.

few officers in the army who possess a greater share of popular affection than Captain Walker enjoyed, and his recent death at Huamantla cast a feeling of sorrow over the whole country. General Lane says in his official account of the battle :—" This victory is saddened by the loss of one of the most chivalric, noble-hearted men that graced the profession of arms—Captain Samuel H. Walker of the mounted riflemen. Foremost in the advance, he had routed the enemy when he fell mortally wounded. In his death the service has met with a loss which cannot be repaired."

In the same battle, Surgeon Lamar was at the side of Captain Walker when the charge was made, and was saved by the devoted act of Walker's slave David, who caught at the lance aimed at him and received it himself. He died in a few minutes, as he probably would have wished, after the death of his master. In death as in life, they were together.

Colonel Hays.

COLONEL JOHN COFFEE HAYS.

OLONEL Hays is twenty-nine years of age, about five feet eight inches in height, with a complexion once fair, but now weatherbeaten and dark, dark brown hair, a hazel eye, broad forehead, Roman nose, large mouth, and a thoughtful, careworn expression, amounting to a frown, always upon his face, which as a whole expresses the utmost firmness and determination on the part of its possessor. His adventures would fill a large volume. He was born in Wilson county, Tennessee, emigrated to Texas, as a surveyor, at the age of nineteen, and soon became distinguished as a successful Indian fighter, as

well among the Indians themselves as among the Texans.
He was made commander of the frontier with the rank
of major in 1840. A story is told of his having defended
himself alone, for three hours against a large party of
Indians on the top of the Enchanted Rock, a hill on
the frontier of Texas. He had his rifle and "five shooter,"
and the Indians knew their man so well, that for a long
time he had only to raise his rifle when they approached
and they would drop back. At length becoming exas-
perated, they determined on taking this "devil Jack,"
as they called him, and he laid several of them low.
As two or three of them would rush up to the spot where
he had intrenched himself, he would shoot them, reload
in the pause that would follow, and give the next cus-
tomer a similar reception. At last, just as they were
determined to take him at any cost, his men having
learned his danger by the report of his rifle, came to
his relief. A battle ensued, the Indians were routed,
and Captain Jack was more firmly believed to bear a
charmed life than ever.

One day talking with some chiefs at San Antonio, one
of them asked him why he so often went out alone, in-
curring danger without a chance of aid. Another Indian
answered for him. "Blue Wing and I," pointing to
his companion, "no fraid to go to hell together—Captain
Jack, great brave—no fraid to go to hell by himself."
By which handsome compliment he meant to imply that
Hays was not afraid to face any danger or death alone.

The following anecdote of a ranger will show to what
an extent he carries his discipline, and perhaps develop
the secret of his success as a partisan soldier. At the
time the advance of General Worth's division had

Anecdote.

reached the foot of the hill, on which stood the Bishop's Palace, before his attempt to capture the heights around, and while the enemy were raining grapeshot among his command from Federation hill and Independence hill. One of the rangers was ordered by Colonel Hays to ascend a large tree, in the corn-field, and reconnoiter the Mexican infantry. The ranger reported, that the enemy kept their position, without any seeming intention of advancing; and receiving no order to descend, being within direct range of the enemy battery, and the shot flying high, he asked the colonel if he should come down.

"No, sir," said Hays, "wait for orders."

Soon after, the Texans were directed to return, when they moved rapidly off, leaving the ranger up the tree; and Hays's attention being called to the fact, he ran back, and cried out,

"Holloa, there—where are the Mexicans?"

"Going back up the hill," replied the ranger, without knowing who it was that addressed him.

"Well, hadn't you better come down from there?" said Hays.

"I don't know," said the ranger, "I am waiting for orders."

"Well, then, I *order* you down," said Hays.

The ranger discovering it to be his colonel, without waiting for a second call, like Martin Scott's coon, forthwith descended from the tree.

COLONEL W. H. WATSON.

IN the prime of life, Colonel William H. Watson left his home and his profession as a lawyer, in Baltimore city, and enrolled his name among the patriots who were defending by arms his country's rights. He performed well his duty: he fulfilled all that the most sanguine of his friends expected of him, and when he fell, there was a calm triumphant smile upon his face that spoke a double victory—one over his country's enemies, and the other over the great destroyer himself. So much was he esteemed in his native city, that when the news of his fall was received, the flags of the shipping were lowered halfmast, the different military and civic societies were convened to pay tributes to his memory and worth. At the meeting of the members of the bar, J. V. L. McMahon, Esq., offered a number of resolutions, among which was the following testimonial of the excellence of his private character.

His gallantry.

"*Resolved*, That while we deplore the loss of a youthful warrior, whose patriotism, courage, and untiring energy, gave the brightest promise to his country, we most deeply mourn the death of one who, as a member of this bar, was respected by all for his professional bearing, and loved by those who best knew him, for the warmth and steadfastness of his friendship."

The gallantry with which he led his beloved Baltimore battalion to victory, has been well described by one of its officers whose letter we quote.

"I saw Colonel Watson shouting, but as to hearing a command, that was an impossibility, owing to the deafening roar of the cannon and musketry. I saw the head of our line changing its direction, and I knew at once that the point of attack was changed, and ran to the head of my company to intercept the head of the column. I reached it just as Colonel Watson was dismounting from his horse, which the next moment fell from a shot. The colonel cried out to his men, 'Shelter yourselves, men, the best way you can.' At this time, the battalion was scattered over a space of about an acre, and the men were lying down, the shot in most instances flying over our heads; but the guns were soon depressed and the shot began to take effect.

I was lying close to Colonel Watson, alongside of a hedge, when he jumped up and cried out, 'Now's the time, boys, follow me.' We were now in a street or lane, with a few houses on either side, and within a hundred yards of three batteries which completely raked it, in addition to which, two twelve-pound guns were planted in the castle on the right, and completely enfiladed the whole distance we had to make. Add to this, the thousand musketeers on the house-tops, and in the barricades at the head of the street up which we advanced, and at every cross street, and you may form some idea of the deluge of balls poured upon us. (Bear in mind that the four companies of regulars were now with us, the one intermingled with the other.) Onward we went, men and horses falling at every step. Cheers, shrieks, groans, and words of command added to the din, whilst the roar of the guns was absolutely deafening.

We had advanced up the street under this awful and fatal fire, nearly two hundred yards, when we reached a cross street, at the corner of which all who had succeeded in getting this far alive, halted, as if by mutual consent. I was shaking Colonel Watson by the hand, while he was complimenting me, when a shower of grape, round, and canister shot came from the corner above, and five officers fell, and I do not know how many privates. Each man sought some place of apparent shelter.

I sat down on the ground, with my back to the wall of a house. On my left were two men torn nearly to pieces. One of them was lying flat on his back, with his legs extending farther into the street than mine. Crash came another shower of grape, which tore one of his wounded legs off. He reared up, shrieked, and fell back a corpse. I never moved, for I was satisfied that one place was as safe as another. Directly opposite to me was my brevet 2d Lieutenant Aisquith; on the right hand corner was Lieutenant Bowie, also of my company; and close to me sat Colonel Watson and Adjutant Schæler. In a few minutes, I saw our colour-sergeant, old Hart, come past with his right arm shattered, (it has

The Baltimore battalion.

since been amputated,) and in a few minutes, there came our battalion flag, borne by one of the colour-guards, our glorious stars and stripes; and, note this, that it was the first American flag in the city of Monterey—an honour which we know belongs to our battalion. * * * * Above, below, alongside, between legs and arms, every where the balls whistled and howled. The air seemed cut to pieces by the quantity that the artillery hurled at us, and it would be childish to tell *how close* they came to me, and what and how many escapes I had. I was exposed to shot in that fight for nine hours. * * * * Colonel Watson met with a gallant soldier's death—his face to the foe. H.. 'oss is deplored by all who know his generosity of heart and chivalry of character. To me, individually, it is great, but to the battalion it is irreparable."

General Scott.

GENERAL WINFIELD SCOTT.

THE genial soil of the Old Dominion, noble, brave, patriotic Virginia, which has given to the republic a host of illustrious names, in the senate, the army, and on the ocean, was the birthplace also of the gallant soldier whose life forms the subject of the present sketch.

Winfield Scott was born June 13th, 1786, at the family seat, near Petersburg. His parents were of Scottish descent.

Of his earlier years but little is known out of the circle of his family. He chose the legal profession, and finished his studies at about his twenty-first year. His disposition for military pursuits manifested itself about the same time. The proclamation of the president, issued after the dastardly attack on the Chesapeake,

Taken prisoner at Queenstown.

having induced the formation of volunteer corps in various parts of the country, Scott enrolled himself in the troop of horse raised in Petersburg. This was in 1807.

Early in the succeeding year he obtained a commission as captain in the light artillery corps of the United States army. During the four years intervening before the declaration of war, he continued in this rank, but nothing occurred to break the monotony of a soldier's life in time of peace.

On the breaking out of hostilities with England, he was promoted to the rank of lieutenant-colonel in the 2d regiment of artillery, and ordered to Black Rock, where lieutenant, afterwards Commodore, Elliott, and himself co-operated in cutting out two British armed brigs, anchored under the guns of Fort Erie.

On the 13th of October, 1812, he was taken prisoner in the battle of Queenstown, after resisting with three hundred, an army of enemies numbering thirteen hundred.

During the battle he had been conspicuous for daring courage and perfect coolness and self-possession. His tall and commanding form made him a constant mark for the Indian sharp shooters, who vainly tried to hit him. So great was their exasperation at their want of success, that after the battle they could with difficulty be restrained from committing violence to his person, and it was found necessary to place him under a close guard.

Having been exchanged, he rejoined the army in May, 1813, and shortly afterwards won the battle of Fort George. He was the first to enter the fort and pull down the British flag, closely followed by Colonel

In the battles of Chippewa and Niagara.

Porter, who exclaimed, "Confound your long legs, Scott, you have got in before me."

On the 9th of March, 1814, he was promoted to the rank of brigadier-general. In that capacity he fought in the battle of Chippewa. He was ever where the balls flew thickest. During the battle, he called out to a battalion, "The enemy say we are good at longshot, but cannot stand the cold iron. I call on the 11th instantly to give the lie to that slander. Charge!" The charge thus ordered decided the day. In the battle of Niagara, which soon followed, General Scott had two horses killed under him, received a wound in the side in the midst of the action, and was afterwards dangerously wounded in the shoulder. For many weeks he suffered from the wounds received on this day. Congress passed a vote of thanks for his skill and gallantry at Chippewa and Niagara, and for his uniform good conduct throughout the war, a compliment paid by Congress to no other officer. A gold medal was also voted to him by Congress. This medal General Scott afterwards deposited in the City Bank of New York for safe keeping. The bank was entered and robbed of two hundred and fifty thousand dollars, but the gold medal was left. The robber afterwards said, when arrested, that in taking the gold beside it, he saw the medal, and knew its value, but scorned to rob a man of the reward given by the gratitude of his country for distinguished services. The states of New York and Virginia each voted him thanks and a sword. After the close of the war, General Scott visited Europe.

He took part in the Black Hawk war, the part of a nurse in the hospitals, where he watched with the utmost

Removes the Cherokee Indians.

solicitude, while sick himself, the bedsides of the many unfortunate soldiers who were sick with the cholera.

In the days of the nullification question he prepared to stand by General Jackson in the preservation of the Union, but took care by his bearing to conciliate rather than exasperate the people of South Carolina. In the Florida war he was unfortunate, devastating diseases and the lateness of the season preventing his meeting the enemy, though his plan of campaign was well devised, and prosecuted with zeal, energy, steadiness, and ability.

During the winter of 1838-9, he was occupied on the Canada frontier, every where by turns, without an army, travelling principally by night, with the thermometer ranging from ten to forty degrees below the freezing point. He made speeches to excited sympathizing Americans with arms in their hands, scattered along a line of eight hundred miles, and with the happiest effect. To the firmness of President Van Buren, and the signal ability of General Scott the country owed its exemption from what appeared to be the inevitable war with Great Britain.

By his masterly skill and energy he also saved the country from difficulties with the Cherokees, whom he removed to the west. By obtaining the esteem and confidence of the poor Cherokees themselves, his noble generosity and humanity effected what all supposed could not be done without the most heartrending scenes of butchery and bloodshed. The Indians, who a few months before were ready to yield their lives rather than leave their homes, looked upon the very man who had

His military genius.

executed the obnoxious measure, as a benefactor and friend who had saved them from entire destruction.

His country found his services invaluable in the settlement of the Maine boundary question. When he was ordered to command the invading army in Mexico, he obeyed the call with his usual promptness, notwithstanding a coolness that had existed for some time between him and the government. From his landing at Vera Cruz till the capture of the capital, his history has been detailed in the preceding pages. Where the danger is greatest he is always to be found, regardless of his life, and only anxious for the safety of his men. Walking along the trenches at Vera Cruz, in full range of the enemy's guns, he noticed the soldiers rise frequently and look over the parapet. "Down, down, men," he exclaimed, "don't expose yourselves." "But, general, *you* are exposed." "Oh," he replied, "generals now-a-days can be made out of any body, *men* cannot be had."

His military genius and foresight has shown out conspicuously during his last campaign. With signal tact he planned the details of all his battles, and prepared with prophetic eye to follow up his victories even before they were gained. In a few short weeks, in the face of gloomy apprehensions and predictions, he seizes the impregnable key to the high road to the capital, storms the Thermopylæ of the country, and consummates the work by an achievement, that it is impossible to overrate, the taking of the capital. All honour to Scott, his officers, and his men.

General Shields.

BRIGADIER-GENERAL JAMES SHIELDS.

ENERAL SHIELDS, one of the most distinguished of all our officers in the Mexican war, is a native of Ireland, but emigrated to this country in early life. Like many of his countrymen, he took a warm interest in our struggle with Great Britain, and entered the army as second lieutenant, 11th infantry, September 1st, 1814. He appears to have served with credit during the war, but left the service soon after its close. The history of his life from this time until the opening of the Mexican war, is lost in the

Shot through the Lungs.

obscurity of retirement. But his merit as a soldier seems to have been known to a large circle of friends; so that on the 1st of July, 1846, soon after the opening of hostilities on the Rio Grande, he received the appointment of brigadier-general. Leaving his residence in Illinois, he joined the Central Division of General Wool, and accompanied that able officer in his famous march through the provinces of Chihuahua and New Mexico, to Monclova. Here, in common with a number of other officers, he was detached as a reinforcement to the army of General Scott. At Vera Cruz he was distinguished for his undaunted bravery, and indefatigable exertions, being in the field during the whole time that the siege lasted, and often exposed to the castle's heaviest fire.

But the military talents of General Shields were first fully developed at Cerro Gordo. In the general orders of April 17th, he was intrusted with the care of the Jalapa road, in order to keep the enemy in that quarter engaged during the main attack, and to cut off retreat. In both these objects he was successful. By his activity he contributed largely to the victory of that memorable day, and elicited the admiration of both General Scott and his brother officers. In the pursuit he received a musket ball through the lungs, by which he was immediately prostrated, the command devolving on Colonel Baker. His life was for a while despaired of, but eventually, to the astonishment of all, he recovered.

During the long stay of the army at Puebla we hear little of General Shields; but he again appears amid the toils and dangers of the march toward the capital. Late on the 19th of August, while the storming of Contreras was in progress, he was sent to a village near that fort

His Magnanimity.

in order to afford assistance to General Smith. A deep rugged ravine, along whose bed rolled a rapid stream, was passed with great difficulty, in consequence of the increasing darkness; after which the general ordered his weary troops to lie upon their arms until midnight, in order to prepare for further duty. In the mean while he threw out two strong pickets, who, perceiving a body of Mexican infantry moving through the fields toward the city, opened a sharp fire, and succeeded in driving them back. At midnight Shields' troops resumed their march, and soon joined Smith's brigade, at the place appointed.

At this time General Shields performed an action so delicate and magnanimous, as to deserve record with the more dazzling ones which were soon to follow. Previous to his arrival, Smith had completed those judicious arrangements for turning and surprising the Mexican position, which were afterwards so brilliantly successful. As Shields was the senior officer, he could have assumed the command, as well as the execution of General Smith's plans, thus debarring that officer from the fruit of his labour. But this he nobly refused to do, and withdrew his men to the position formerly occupied by his brother veteran. About daybreak the Mexicans opened a brisk fire of grape and round shot upon the church and village where the general was stationed, as also upon a part of the troops displayed to divert him on his right and front. This continued until Colonel Riley's brigade opened its fire from the rear, which was delivered with such terrible effect, that the whole Mexican force was thrown into consternation.

At this juncture Shields ordered the two regiments of

his command to throw themselves on the main road by which the enemy must retire, so as to intercept and cut off their retreat. Although officers and men had suffered severely during the night's march, as well as from exposure without shelter or cover, to the incessant rain until daybreak, this movement was executed in good order and with rapidity. Crossing a deep ravine, the Palmetto regiment deployed on both sides of the road, and opened a most destructive fire upon the mingled masses of infantry and cavalry; and the New York regiment, brought into line lower down, and on the roadside, delivered its fire with a like effect. At this point many of the enemy were killed and wounded, some three hundred and sixty-five captured, including twenty-five officers.

Meanwhile the enemy's cavalry, about three thousand strong, which had been threatening the village during the morning, moved down toward it in good order as if to attack. General Shields immediately recalled the infantry so as to place them in a position for meeting the threatened movement; but the cavalry soon changed its position, and retreated toward the capital. Orders now arrived from General Twiggs for the troops to advance by the main road toward Mexico; and accordingly having posted Captain Marshall's company of South Carolina volunteers, and Captain Taylor's New York volunteers in charge of the wounded and prisoners, Shields moved off with the remainder of his force, and reached the positions of those divisions already moving on the main road.

After turning the village of Coyoacan, Shields moved with his command toward the right, through a heavy

Wounded in the Arm.

corn-field, and gained an open and swampy plain, in which is situated the hacienda de los Partales. On arriving there he established his right upon a point recommended by Captain Lee, an engineer officer of great skill and judgment, at the same time commencing a movement to the left so as to flank the enemy's right and throw his troops between them and the city. Finding, however, their right supported by a body of cavalry, three thousand strong, and perceiving that the enemy answered to his own movements by a corresponding one toward the American right flank, and owing to the advantages of the ground, gaining rapidly on him, he withdrew his men to the hacienda for the purpose of attacking the enemy in front. The conflict was close and stubborn, until General Shields, taking advantage of a slight wavering in the Mexican ranks, ordered a charge. This was obeyed with alacrity and success, the enemy breaking and flying on all sides. Shields continued to press upon the fugitives, until passed by Colonel Harney with his cavalry who followed the routed foe into the very gates of the city.

On the 10th of September, General Shields, with the New York and South Carolina regiments, was ordered first to Piedad, and subsequently to Tacubaya, preparatory to the assault upon Chapultepec. Here he continued a heavy cannonade upon the enemy's lines until early on the morning of the 13th, when his command moved to the assault. While directing the advance Shields was severely wounded in the arm; yet no persuasion could induce him to leave his command or quit the field. In company with the remainder of Quitman's division, he pushed rapidly forward along the Belen

Returns to the United States.

road, exposed to the most tremendous fires, overthrowing one after another of the Mexican strongholds, until, finally his victorious banners were planted over the principal gateway. When night fell he was carried from the field sick, exhausted, and writhing with pain. His wound, although severe, was, happily, not mortal; and rest, together with careful attention, united with a strong constitution, speedily restored him to health.

After remaining some time with the army in Mexico, General Shields, in company with several other officers, visited the United States, where he still remains.

SUPPLEMENT.

CONCLUSION OF THE WAR.

Although the attempts of Mr. Trist to conclude a treaty of peace immediately after the battle of Churubusco had not been successful, yet, in concert with the commander-in-chief, he lost no opportunity to repeat his overtures for so desirable an object. It was not, however, until the beginning of the following year, that the Mexicans would listen to such proposals. Their army was then reduced to a few insignificant parties, scattered here and there, more for safety than any hope of opposition to the invaders. Even the guerillas manifested symptoms of weariness. Accordingly, when in January, 1848, General Scott laid before the Mexican congress articles of a treaty, based upon those formerly rejected, that body immediately appointed Luis G. Cuevas, Bernardo Conto, and Miguel Atristain, as commissioners. These gentlemen, with Mr. Trist, acting on behalf of the United States, assembled at Guadalupe Hidalgo, and concluded a treaty of "peace, friendship, limits, and settlement" between the two republics.

The only thing still necessary to the conclusion of the war, was the ratification of the new treaty by the legislature of each country. In February the attested copy was received at Washington by President Polk, and transmitted to the United States senate. After being slightly amended, it was passed in that body, on the

Ratification of the Treaty.

10th of March, by a large majority. Mr. Sevier was appointed envoy extraordinary and minister plenipotentiary to present it for ratification to the Mexican congress. In company with Mr. Clifford, he soon arrived at Queretaro, where the national legislature was sitting, and laid before that body the corrected copy for their final action. It passed through both houses by a large majority, and was received with marked satisfaction by the Mexican people.

By this instrument the boundary line between the two republics was made to begin at the mouth of the Rio Grande, ascending the middle of that river to the southern boundary of New Mexico, thence westwardly, along the whole southern boundary of New Mexico, to its western termination; thence northward along the western line of New Mexico, to the first branch of the river Gila; thence down the middle of this branch and river to its junction with the Colorado; thence between Upper and Lower California to the Pacific. It secured to the United States the vast territories of New Mexico, California, Western Texas, and the Pacific coast, together with the fine harbour of San Francisco, and the internal navigation of the Colorado, Gila, and other rivers. Fifteen millions of dollars were to be paid to Mexico by the United States as compensation for part of this grant.

By an article of the treaty, arrangements had been made, for withdrawing all the United States troops from the Mexican territory within three months after the final ratifications, provided it could be effected before the commencement of the sickly season. In furtherance of this provision, the most active preparations immediately commenced for marching different portions of the army

Return of the United States Troops,

from the capital and interior town to Vera Cruz, whither they were to embark for New Orleans. Previous to this General Scott had left Mexico to attend a court of inquiry appointed by government to investigate reciprocal charges between himself and Generals Worth and Pillow. The duty of superintending the evacuation of the capital, and subsequent embarkation from Vera Cruz, devolved upon the temporary general-in-chief, Major-General Butler. In the early part of June the greater part of the soldiers in the city of Mexico marched for Vera Cruz, under the supervision of Mr. Sevier. They left the latter city by detachments, reached New Orleans about the middle of June, and thence proceeded by steamboat or railway, towards their respective homes. Nothing can exceed the enthusiasm with which these toil-worn veterans were hailed, as they entered, regiment by regiment, into the cities, from which, two years before, they had marched to the scene of strife. Business was suspended, the population rushed to meet them, military and civic processions attended their march, banquets were spread, addresses delivered, and presents bestowed on them throughout their route.

Thus closed, after a duration of two years, the "Mexican War." It gave to the United States an immense tract of fine territory, secured one of the finest harbours in the world, and opened the road to a lucrative trade with those marts of oriental wealth, China and the East Indies. But the mere question of gain and loss is the least important of those developed during the struggle. Europe has long contemplated us as a mere commercial and business-loving nation, smothering our former military abilities, in inordinate love of wealth. The Seminole wars have been sneeringly alluded to as proofs of this degeneracy; and the "wasp-waisted lieutenants" of West Point has been a mock word of contempt, used to deride that cradle of military science, the national academy. The war in Mexico has dissolved this vain dream, and taught astonished Europe a lesson, whose precepts will be remembered in every one of her belligerent assemblies for ages. As an evidence of military skill, Spartan valour, and patient endurance—let us add magnanimity to a humiliated foe—the Mexican war is an episode of history, having but few parallels. The tactics displayed in the great campaign against the capital, has far surpassed even the boasted military perfection of the French schools. How far it surpasses English ability may be inferred from the fact that while General Scott was making his preparations for assaulting Vera Cruz, most of the British prints scouted at the idea of his being successful, and with delusive complacency awaited the gratifying intelligence that the aspiring invaders had been completely foiled. When the astounding truth announced to them how immeasurably superior was American skill to English bravery, they could account for it only by asserting that the castle had been betrayed by its commandant. Yet great as was that achievement, it is now spoken of only as an ordinary event amid the splendid deeds wrought in the valley of Mexico.

It is, therefore, as an evidence of superior skill, as well as bravery that the Mexican war will in future be principally regarded, and in that light it will no doubt convey a wholesome warning to any nation which might hereafter, on frivolous pretences, undertake to interrupt the peace which happily now pervades our midst.

TREATY

OF PEACE, FRIENDSHIP, LIMITS, AND SETTLEMENT,

BETWEEN

THE UNITED STATES OF AMERICA

AND

THE MEXICAN REPUBLIC.

Concluded at Guadalupe Hidalgo, Febraury 2, and Ratified, with the Amendments by the American Senate, March 10, 1848 ; also Ratified by the Mexican Congress, May 25, 1848.

THE TREATY.

IN THE NAME OF ALMIGHTY GOD:

The United States of America and the United Mexican States, animated by a sincere desire to put an end to the calamities of the war which unhappily exists between the two Republics, and to establish on a solid basis relations of peace and friendship, which shall confer reciprocal benefits on the citizens of both, and assure the concord, harmony and mutual confidence wherein the two people should live as good neighbors, have, for the purpose, appointed their respective Plenipotentiaries ; that is to say, the President of the United States has appointed N. P. TRIST, a citizen of the United States, and the President of the Mexican Republic has appointed Don LOUIS GONZAGA CUEVAS, Don BERNARDO CONTO, and Don MIGUEL ATRISTAIN, citizens of the said Republic, who, after a reciprocal communication of their respective powers, have, under the protection of Almighty God, the Author of Peace, arranged, agreed upon and signed the following Treaty of Peace, Friendship, Limits and Settlement, between the United States of America and the Mexican Republic.

ARTICLE I.

There shall be a firm and universal peace between the United States of America and the Mexican Republic, and between their respective countries, territories, cities, towns and people, without exception of places or persons.

THE TREATY.

ARTICLE II.

Immediately on the signature of this Treaty, a Convention shall be entered into between a Commissioner or Commissioners appointed by the General-in-Chief of the forces of the United States, and such as may be appointed by the Mexican Government, to the end that a provisional suspension of hostilities shall take place; and that in the places occupied by the said forces, constitutional order may be re-established, as regards the political, administrative and judicial branches, so far as this shall be permitted by the circumstances of military occupation.

ARTICLE III.

Immediately upon the ratification of the present Treaty, by the Government of the United States, orders shall be transmitted to the commanders of their land and naval forces, requiring the latter (provided this Treaty shall then have been ratified by the Government of the Mexican Republic) immediately to desist from blockading the Mexican ports: and requiring the former (under the same condition) to commence, at the earliest moment practicable, withdrawing all troops of the United States then in the interior of the Mexican Republic, to points that shall be selected by common agreement, at a distance from the sea-ports not exceeding thirty leagues; and such evacuation of the interior of the Republic shall be completed with the least possible delay; the Mexican Government hereby binding itself to afford every facility in its power for rendering the same convenient to the troops, on their march, and in their new positions, and for promoting a good understanding between them and the inhabitants. In like manner, orders shall be dispatched to the persons in charge of the Custom Houses at all ports occupied by the forces of the United States, requiring them (under the same condition) immediately to deliver possession of the same to the person authorized by the Mexican Government to receive it, together with all bonds and evidences of debts for duties on importations and exportations, not yet fallen due. Moreover, a faithful and exact account shall be made out, showing the entire amount of all duties on imports and on exports, collected at such Custom Houses, or elsewhere in Mexico, by authority of the United States, from and after the day of the ratification of this Treaty by the Government of the Mexican Republic; and also an account of the cost of collection; and such entire amount, deducting only the cost of collection, shall be delivered to the Mexican Government, at the City of Mexico, within three months after the exchange of ratifications.

The evacuation of the Capital of the Mexican Republic by the troops of the United States, in virtue of the above stipulation, shall be completed in one month after the orders there stipulated for shall have been received by the Commander of the said troops, or sooner if possible.

ARTICLE IV

Immediately after the exchange of ratifications of the present Treaty, all castles, forts, territories, places and possessions, which have been taken and occupied by the forces of the United States during the present war, within the limits of the Mexican Republic, as about to be established by the following article, shall be definitely restored to the said Republic, together with all the artillery, arms, apparatus of war, munitions and other public property, which were in the said castles and forts when captured, and which shall remain there at the time when this Treaty shall be duly ratified by the Government of the Mexican Republic. To this end, immediately upon the signature of this Treaty, orders shall be dispatched to the American officer commanding such castles and ports, securing against the removal or destruction of any such artillery, arms, apparatus of war, munitions, or other public property. The City of Mexico, within the inner line of intrenchments surrounding the said city, is comprehended in the above stipulations, as regards the restoration of artillery, apparatus of war, &c.

The final evacuation of the territory of the Mexican Republic by the forces of the United States shall be completed within three months from the said exchange of ratifications, or sooner if possible; the Mexican Republic hereby engages, as in the foregoing Article, to use all means in its power for facilitating such evacuation, and rendering it convenient to the troops, and for promoting a good understanding between them and the inhabitants.

If, however, the ratification of this Treaty by both parties should not take place in time to allow the embarkation of the troops of the United States to be completed before the commencement of the sickly season, at the Mexican ports on the Gulf of Mexico, in such case a friendly arrangement shall be entered into between the General-in-Chief of the said troops and the Mexican Government, whereby healthy and otherwise suitable places, at a distance from the ports not exceeding thirty leagues, shall be designated for the residence of such troops as may not yet have embarked, until the return of the healthy season. And the space of time here referred to as comprehending the sickly season, shall be understood to extend from the first day of May to the first day of November.

All prisoners of war taken on either side, on land or on sea, shall be restored as soon as practicable after the exchange of the ratifications of the Treaty. It is also agreed that if any Mexicans should now be held as captives by any savage tribe within the limits of the United States, as about to be established by the following article, the Government of the said United States will exact the release of such captives, and cause them to be restored to their country.

ARTICLE V.

The boundary line between the two Republics shall commence in the Gulf of Mexico, three leagues from land, opposite the mouth of the Rio Grande, otherwise called the Rio Bravo del Norte, or opposite the mouth of its deepest branch, if it should have more than one branch emptying directly into the sea; thence up the middle of that river, following the deepest channel, where it has more than one, to the point where it strikes the southern boundary of New Mexico, which runs north of the town called *Paso*, to its western termination; thence northward along the western line of New Mexico, until it intersects the first branch of the River Gila; or if it should not intersect any branch of that river, then to the point on the said line nearest to such branch, and thence in a direct line to the same, thence down the middle of the said branch and of the said river, until it empties into the Rio Colorado; thence across the Rio Colorado, following the division line between Upper and Lower California, to the Pacific Ocean.

The southern and western limits of New Mexico, mentioned in this article, are those laid down in the map entitled "Map of the United Mexican States, as organized and defined by various acts of the Congress of said Republic and constructed according to the best authorities. Revised edition. Published at New York in 1847, by J. Disturnell."

Of which map a copy is added to this treaty, bearing the signatures and seals of the undersigned Plenipotentaries. And in order to preclude all difficulty in tracing upon the ground the limit separating Upper from Lower California, it is agreed that the said limits shall consist of a straight line, drawn from the middle of the Rio Gila, where it unites with the Colorado, to a point on the coast of the Pacific Ocean—distant one marine league due south of the southernmost point of the port of San Diego, according to the plan of said port, made in the year 1782, by Don Juan Pantojer, second sailing master of the Spanish fleet, and published at Madrid in the year 1802, in the Atlas to the voyage of the schooner Sutil and Mexicana, of which plan a copy is hereunto added, signed and sealed by the respective Plenipotentiaries.

In order to designate the boundary line with due precision, upon authoritative maps, and to establish on the ground landmarks which shall show the limits of both Republics, as described in the present article, the Governments shall each appoint a Commissioner and Surveyor, who, before the expiration of one year from the date of the exchange of ratification of this Treaty, shall meet at the port of San Diego, and proceed to run and mark the said boundary in its whole course to the mouth of the Rio Bravo del Norte. They shall keep journals and make out plans of their operations; and the result agreed upon by them shall be deemed a part of this Treaty, and shall have the same force as if it were inserted therein. The two Governments will amicably agree regarding what may be necessary to these persons, also as to their respective escorts, should such be necessary.

The boundary line established by this article shall be religiously respected by each of the two Republics, and no change shall be made therein, except by the express and free consent of both Nations, lawfully given by the General Government of each, in conformity with its own Constitution.

ARTICLE VI.

The vessels and citizens of the United States shall, in all time, have a free and uninterrupted passage by the Gulf of California, and by the river Colorado; and not by land, without the express consent of the Mexican Government.

If, by the examinations that may be made, it should be ascertained to be practicable and advantageous to construct a Road, Canal, or Railway, which should, in whole or in part, run upon the river Gila, or upon its right or its left bank, within the space of one marine league from either margin of the river, the Governments of both Republics will form an agreement regarding its construction, in order that it may serve equally for the use and advantage of both countries.

ARTICLE VII.

The river Gila, and the part of the Rio del Norte lying below the southern boundary of New Mexico, being agreeably to the Fifth Article, divided in the middle between the two Republics, the navigation of the Gila and the Bravo, below said boundary shall be free and common to the vessels and citizens of both countries; and neither shall, without the consent of the other construct any work that may impede or interrupt in whole or in part, the exercise of this right—not even for the purpose of favoring new methods of navigation. Nor shall any tax or contribution, under any denomination or title be levied upon vessels or persons navigating the same, or upon merchandize, or effects transported thereon, except in the case of landing upon one of their shores. If, for the purpose of making said rivers navigable, or for maintaining them in such a state, it should be necessary or advantageous to establish any tax or contribution, this shall not be done without the consent of both Governments.

The stipulations contained in the present article shall not impair the territorial rights of either Republic, within its established limits.

ARTICLE VIII.

Mexicans now established in territories previously belonging to Mexico, and which remain for the future, within the limits of the United States, as defined by the present Treaty, shall be free to continue where they now reside, or to remove, at any time, to the Mexican Republic, retaining the property which they possess in the said territories, or disposing thereof, and removing the proceeds wherever they please, without their being subjected on this account, to any contribution, or tax whatever.

Those who shall prefer to remain in said territories, may either retain the title and rights of Mexican citizens, or acquire those of citizens of the United States. But they shall be under the obligation to make their selection within one year from the date of the exchange of ratifications of this Treaty; and those who shall remain in the said territories, after the expiration of that year, without having declared their intention to retain the character of Mexicans shall be considered to have elected to become citizens of the United States.

In the said territories, property of any kind, now belonging to Mexicans not established there shall be inviolably respected. The present owners, the heirs of these, and all Mexicans who may hereafter acquire said property by contract, shall enjoy, with respect to it, guaranties equally ample as if the same belonged to citizens of the United States.

[In place of the following Article, the Senate has inserted the third Article of the Treaty between France and the United States, for the cession of Louisiana, which provides that the inhabitants of the ceded territory shall be admitted to all the rights and privileges of citizenship, in accordance with the principles of the Constitution, as soon as Congress shall determine; and that in the meantime, they shall be protected in the enjoyment of all their liberty, property and religious belief.]

ARTICLE IX.

The Mexicans who in the territories aforesaid, shall not preserve the character of citizens of the Mexican Republic, conformably with what is stipulated in the preceding article, shall be incorporated into the Union of the United States, and admitted as soon as possible, according to the principles of the Federal Constitution, to the enjoyment of all the rights of citizens of the United States. In the meantime they shall be maintained and protected in the enjoyment of their liberty, their property, and the civil rights now vested in them, according to the Mexican laws. With respect to political rights, their condition shall be on an equality with that of the inhabitants of other territories of the United States, and at least equally good as that of the inhabitants of Louisiana and the Floridas, when these provinces, by transfer from the French Republic, and the Crown of Spain, became territories of the United States.

The most ample guaranty shall be enjoyed by all ecclesiastics and religious corporations, or communities, as well in the discharge of the offices of their ministry, as in the enjoyment of their property of every kind whether individual or corporate. This guaranty shall embrace all temples, houses and edifices dedicated to the Roman Catholic worship; as well as all property destined to its support, or to that of schools, hospitals or other foundations for charitable or beneficent purposes. No property of this nature shall be considered as having become the property of the American Government, or as subject to be by it disposed of, or diverted to other causes.

Finally, the relations and communications between Catholics living in the territories aforesaid, and their respective ecclesiastic authorities, shall be open, free and exempt from all hindrance whatever, even although such authorities should reside within the limits of the Mexican Republic, as defined by this Treaty; and this freedom shall continue so long as a new debarcation of ecclesiastical districts shall not have been made, conformably with the laws of the Roman Catholic Church.

ARTICLE X.
[EXPUNGED.]

All grants of land made by the Mexican Government, or by the competent authorities, in territories previously appertaining to Mexico, and remaining for the future within the limits of the United States, shall be respected as valid, to the same extent that the same grants would be valid if the territories had remained within the limits of Mexico. But the grantees of land in Texas put in possession thereof, who by reason of the circumstances of the country, since the beginning of the troubles between Texas and the Mexican Government, may have been prevented from fulfilling all the conditions of their grants, shall be under the obligation to fulfill the said conditions within the periods limited in the same respectively, such periods to be now counted from the date of the exchange of ratifications of this Treaty; in default of which, said grants shall not be obligatory on the State of Texas, in virtue of the stipulations contained in this Article.

The foregoing stipulation in regard to grantees of land in Texas, is extended to all grantees of land in the territories aforesaid, elsewhere than in Texas, put in possession under such grants; and in default of the fulfillment of the conditions of any such grants, within the new period which, as is above stipulated, begins with the day of the exchange of ratifications of this treaty, the same shall be null and void.

The Mexican Government declares that no grant whatever of lands in Texas has been made since the second day of March, one thousand eight hundred and thirty-six; and that no grant whatever of lands in any of the territories aforesaid, has been made since the thirteenth day of May, one thousand eight hundred and forty-six.

ARTICLE XI.

Considering that a great part of the territories which, by the present Treaty, are to be comprehended for the future within the limits of the United States, is now occupied by savage tribes, who will hereafter be under the control of the Government of the United States, and whose incursions within the territory of Mexico would be prejudicial in the extreme, it is solemnly agreed that all such incursions shall be forcibly restrained by the Government of the United States, whensoever this may be necessary; and that when they cannot be prevented, they shall be punished by the said Government, and satisfaction for the same shall be exacted all in the same way, and with equal diligence and energy as if the same incursions were committed in its own territory, against its own citizens.

It shall not be lawful, under any pretext whatever, for any inhabitant of the United States to purchase or acquire any Mexican, or any foreigner residing in Mexico, who may have been captured by Indians inhabiting the territory of either of the Republics, not to purchase or acquire horses, mules, cattle or property of any kind, stolen within the Mexican territory, by such Indians; nor to provide such Indians with fire-arms or ammunition by sale or otherwise.

And in the event of any person or persons captured within Mexican territory by Indians, being carried into the territory of the United States, the Government of the latter engages and binds itself in the most solemn manner, so soon as it shall know of such captives being within its territory, and shall be able so to do, through the faithful exercise of its influence and power to rescue them and return them to their country, or deliver them to the agent or representative of the Mexican Government. The Mexican authorities will, as far as practicable, give to the Government of the United States notice of such captures; and its expenses incurred in the maintenance and transmission of the rescued captives; who, in the mean time, shall be treated with the utmost hospitality by the American authorities at the place where they may be. But if the Government of the United States, before receiving such notice from Mexico, should obtain intelligence, through any other channel, of the existence of Mexican captives within its territory, it will proceed forthwith to effect their release and delivery to the Mexican agent, as above stipulated.

For the purpose of giving to these stipulations the fullest possible efficacy, thereby affording the security and redress demanded by their true spirit and intent, the Government of the United States will now and hereafter pass, without unnecessary delay, and always vigilantly enforce, such laws as the nature of the subject may require. And finally, the sacredness of this obligation shall never be lost sight of by the said Government, when providing for the removal of Indians from any portion of said territories, or for its being settled by the citizens of the United States; but, on the contrary, special care then shall be taken not to place its Indian occupants under the necessity of seeking new homes, by committing those invasions which the United States have solemnly obliged themselves to restrain.

ARTICLE XII.

In consideration of the extension acquired by the boundaries of the United States, as defined in the fifth article of the present Treaty, the Government of the United States engages to pay to that of the Mexican Republic the sum of fifteen millions of dollars in the one or the other of the two modes below specified.

The Mexican Government shall at the time of ratifying this Treaty, declare which of these two modes of payment it prefers; and the mode so selected by it shall be conformed to by that of the United States.

First mode of payment—Immediately after this Treaty shall have been duly ratified by the Government of the Mexican Republic, the sum of three millions of dollars shall be paid to the said Government by that of the United States, at the City of Mexico, in the gold or silver coin of Mexico. For the remaining twelve millions of dollars the United States shall create a stock, bearing an interest of six per centum per annum, commencing on the day of the ratification of this Treaty by the Government of the Mexican Republic, and payable annually at the City of Washington; the principal of said stock to be redeemable there, at the pleasure of the Government of the United States, at any time after two years from the exchange of ratifications of this Treaty; six month's public notice of the intention to redeem the same being previously given. Certificates of such stock, in proper form, for such sums as shall be specified by the Mexican Government, shall be delivered, and transferable by the said Government to the same by that of the United States.

Second mode of payment—Immediately after this Treaty shall have been duly ratified by the Government of the Mexican Republic, the sum of three millions of dollars shall be paid to the said Government by that of the United States, at the City of Mexico, in the gold or silver coin of Mexico. The remaining twelve millions of

THE TREATY.   7

dollars shall be paid at the same place, and in the same coin, in annual instalments of three millions of dollars each, together with interest on the same, at the rate of six per centum per annum. This interest shall begin to run upon the whole sum of twelve millions from the day of the ratification of the present Treaty by the Mexican Government, and the first of the instalments shall be paid at the expiration of one year from the same day. Together with each annual instalment, as it falls due, the whole interest accruing on such instalment from the beginning shall also be paid.

[Certificates in the proper form for the said instalments, respectively, in sums as shall be desired by the Mexican Government, and transferrable by it, shall be delivered to the said Government by that of the United States.]

[N. B. The first of these modes is rejected. The latter is adopted, with the exception of the last paragraph, in brackets.]

ARTICLE XIII.

The United States engage, moreover, to assume and pay to the claimants all the amounts now due them, and these hereafter to become due, by reason of the claims already liquidated and decided against the Mexican Republic, under the Conventions between the two republics severally concluded on the eleventh day of April, eighteen hundred and thirty-nine, and on the thirtieth day of January, eighteen hundred and forty-three; so that the Mexican Republic shall be absolutely exempt, for the future, from all expense whatever on account of the said claims.

ARTICLE XIV.

The United States do furthermore discharge the Mexican Republic from all claims of citizens of the United States, not heretofore decided against the Mexican Government, which may have arisen previously to the date of the signature of this Treaty; which discharge shall be final and perpetual, whether the said claims be rejected or be allowed by the Board of Commissioners provided for in the following article, and whatever shall be the total amount of those allowed.

ARTICLE XV.

The United States, exonerating Mexico from all demands on account of the claims of their citizens mentioned in the preceding article, and considering them entirely and forever canceled whatever their amount may be, undertake to make satisfaction for the same, to an amount not exceeding three and one-quarter millions of dollars. To ascertain the validity and amount of those claims, a Board of Commissioners shall be established by the Government of the United States, whose awards shall be final and conclusive; provided, that in deciding upon the validity of each claim, the Board shall be guided and governed by the principles and rules of decision prescribed by the first and fifth articles of the unratified Convention, concluded at the City of Mexico on the twentieth day of November, one thousand eight hundred and forty-three; and in no case shall an award be made in favor of any claim not embraced by these principles and rules.

If, in the opinion of the said Board of Commissioners, or of the claimants, any books, records, or documents in the possession or power of the Government of the Mexican Republic, shall be deemed necessary to the just decision of any claim, the Commissioners, or the claimants through them, shall, within such period as Congress may designate, make an application in writing for the same, be assessed to the Mexican Minister for Foreign Affairs, to be transmitted by the Secretary of State of the United States; and the Mexican Government engages, at the earliest possible moment after the receipt of such demand, to cause any of the books, records, or documents so specified, which shall be in their possession or power (or authenticated copies or extracts of the same) to be transmitted to the said Secretary of State, who shall immediately deliver them over to the said Board of Commissioners; provided, that no such application shall be made by or at the instance of any claimant, until the facts which it is expected to prove by such books, records, or documents, shall have been stated under oath or affirmation.

ARTICLE XVI

Each of the contracting parties reserves to itself the entire right to fortify whatever point within its territory it may judge proper so to fortify for its security.

ARTICLE XVII.

The Treaty of amity, commerce, and navigation, concluded at the City of Mexico on the 5th day of April, A. D., 1831, between the United States of America and the United Mexican States, except the additional article, and except so far as the stipulations of the said Treaty may not be incompatible with any stipulation contained in the present Treaty, is hereby revived for the period of eight years from the day of the exchange of ratifications of this Treaty, with the same force and virtue as if incorporated therein; it being understood that each of the contracting parties reserves to itself the right, at any time after the said period of eight years shall have expired, to terminate the same by giving one year's notice of such intention to the other party.

ARTICLE XVIII.

All supplies whatever of troops of the United States in Mexico, arriving at ports in the occupation of such troops previous to the final evacuation thereof, although subsequently to the restoration of the Custom-Houses at such ports, shall be entirely exempt from duties and charges of any kind; the Government of the United States hereby engaging and pledging its faith to establish, and vigilantly to enforce all possible guards for securing the revenue of Mexico, by preventing the importation, under cover of this stipulation, of any articles other than such, both in kind and in quality, as shall really be wanted for the use and consumption of the forces of the United States during the time they may remain in Mexico. To this end it shall be the duty of all officers and agents of the United States to announce to the Mexican authorities, at the respective ports, any attempts at a fraudulent abuse of this stipulation which they may know of or may have reason to suspect, and to give to such authorities all the aid in their power with regard thereto; and every such attempt, when duly proved and established by sentence of a competent tribunal, shall be punished by the confiscation of the property so attempted to be fraudulently introduced.

ARTICLE XIX.

With respect to all merchandise, effects, and property whatsoever, imported into ports of Mexico while in the occupation of the forces of the United States, whether by citizens of either republic, or by citizens or subjects of any neutral nation, the following rules shall be observed:

1. All such merchandise, effects, and property, if imported previously to the restoration of the Custom-Houses to the Mexican authorities, as stipulated for in the third article of this Treaty, shall be exempt from confiscation, although the importation of the same be prohibited by the Mexican Tariff.

2. The same perfect exemption shall be enjoyed by all such merchandise, effects, and property, imported subsequently to the restoration of the Custom-Houses, and previously to the sixty days fixed in the following article for the coming into force of the Mexican Tariff, at such ports respectively; the said merchandise, effects, and property being, however, at the time of their importation, subject to the payment of duties, as provided for in the said following article.

3. All merchandise, effects, and property described in the two rules foregoing, shall, during their continuance at the place of importation, or upon their leaving such place for the interior, be exempt from all duty, tax or impost of every kind, under whatsoever title or denomination. Nor shall they be there subject to any charge whatsoever upon the sale thereof.

4. All merchandise, effects, and property, described in the first and second rules, which shall have been removed to any place in the interior while such place was in the occupation of the forces of the United States, shall, during their continuance therein, be exempt from all tax upon the sale of consumption thereof, and from every kind of impost or contribution, under whatsoever title or denomination.

5. But if any merchandise, effects, or property, described in the first and second rules shall be removed to any place not occupied at the time by the forces of the

United States, they shall, upon their introduction into such place, or upon their sale or consumption there, be subject to the same duties which, under the Mexican laws, they would be required to pay in such cases if they had been imported in time of peace, through the maritime Custom-Houses, and had there paid the duties conformably with the Mexican Tariff.

6. The owners of all merchandise, effects, or property described in the first and second rules and existing in any port of Mexico, shall have the right to re-ship the same, exempt from all tax, impost, or contribution whatever.

With respect to the metals, or other property, exported from any Mexican port while in the occupation of the forces of the United States, and previously to the restoration of the Custom-House at such port, no person shall be required by the Mexican authorities, whether general or State, to pay any tax, duty, or contribution upon any such exportation, or in any manner to account for the same to the said authorities.

ARTICLE XX.

Through consideration for the interests of commerce generally, it is agreed that if less than sixty days should elapse between the date of the signature of this Treaty and the restoration of the custom-houses, conformably with a stipulation in the third Article, in such case, all merchandise, effects, and property whatsoever, arriving at the Mexican ports after the restoration of the said custom-houses, and previously to the expiration of sixty days after the signature of this Treaty, shall be admitted to entry; and no other duties shall be levied thereon than the duties established by the Tariff found in force at such custom-houses at the time of the restoration of the same. And to all such merchandise, effects and property, the rules established in the preceding Article shall apply.

ARTICLE XXI.

If, unhappily, any disagreement should hereafter arise between the Governments of the two Republics, whether with respect to the interpretation of any stipulation in this Treaty or with respect to any other particular concerning the political or commercial relations of the two nations, the said Governments, in the name of those nations, do promise to each other that they will endeavor, in the most sincere and earnest manner, to settle the difference so arising, and to preserve the state of peace and friendship in which the two countries are now placing themselves; using, for this end, mutual representations and pacific negotiations. And if, by these means, they should not be enabled to come to an agreement, a resort shall not, on this account, be had in reprisals, aggressions, or hostility of any kind by the one Republic against the other, until the Government of that which deems itself aggrieved shall have maturely considered, in the spirit of peace and good neighborship, whether it would not be better that such difference should be settled by the arbitration of Commissioners appointed on each side, or by that of a friendly nation. And should such course be proposed by either party, it shall be acceded to by the other, unless deemed by it altogether incompatible with the nature of the difference, or the circumstances of the case.

ARTICLE XXII.

If, (which is not to be expected, and which God forbid!) war shall unhappily break out between the two Republics, they do now, with a view to such calamity, pledge themselves to each other and to the world, to observe the following rules, absolutely, where the nature of the subject permits, and as closely as possible in all cases where such absolute observance shall be impossible.

1. The merchants of either Republic then residing in the other shall be allowed to remain twelve months, (for those dwelling in the interior,) and six months, (for those dwelling at the seaports,) to collect their debts and settle their affairs; during which periods, they shall enjoy the same protection, and be on the same footing, in all respects, as the citizens or subjects of the most friendly nations; and, at the expiration thereof, or at any time before, they shall have full liberty to depart, carrying off all their effects without molestation or hinderance; conforming therein to the same laws which the citizens or subjects of the most friendly nations are required to conform to. Upon the entrance of the armies of either nation into the

territories of the other, women and children, ecclesiastics, scholars of every faculty, cultivators of the earth, merchants, artisans, manufacturers, and fishermen, unarmed, and inhabiting unfortified towns, villages or places, and in general all persons whose occupations are for the common subsistence and benefit of mankind, shall be allowed to continue their respective employments unmolested in their persons. Nor shall their houses or goods be burnt or otherwise destroyed, nor their cattle taken, nor their fields wasted, by the armed force into whose power, by the events of war, they may happen to fall; but if the necessity arise to take any thing from them for the use of such armed force, the same shall be paid for at an equitable price. All churches, hospitals, schools, colleges, libraries, and other establishments, for charitable and beneficent purposes, shall be respected, and all persons connected with the same protected in the discharge of their duties, and the pursuits of their vocations.

2. In order that the fate of prisoners of war may be alleviated, all such practices as those of sending them into distant, inclement, or unwholesome districts, or crowding them into close and noxious places, shall be studiously avoided. They shall not be confined in dungeons, prison-ships or prisons; nor be put in irons, or bound, or otherwise restrained in the use of their limbs. The officers shall enjoy liberty on their paroles, within convenient districts, and have comfortable quarters; and the common soldiers shall be disposed in cantonments, open and extensive enough for air and exercise, and lodged in barracks as roomy and good as are provided by the party in whose power they are for its own troops. But if any officer shall break his parole by leaving the district so assigned him, or any other prisoner shall escape from the limits of his cantonment, after they shall have been designated to him, such individual, officer, or other prisoner shall forfeit so much of the benefit of this Article as provides for his liberty on parole or in cantonment. And if an officer so breaking his parole, or any common soldier so escaping from the limits assigned him, shall afterward be found in arms, previously to his being regularly exchanged, the person so offending shall be dealt with according to the established laws of war. The officers shall be daily furnished by the party in whose power they are, with as many rations, and of the same articles, as are allowed, either in kind or by computation, to officers of equal rank in its own army; and all others shall be daily furnished with such ration as is allowed to a common soldier in its own service; the value of all which supplies shall, at the close of the war, or at periods to be agreed upon between the respective commanders, be paid by the other party, on a mutual adjustment of accounts for the subsistence of prisoners; and such accounts shall not be mingled with or set off against any others, nor the balance due on them withheld, as a compensation or reprisal for any cause whatever, real or pretended. Each party shall be allowed to keep a commissary of prisoners, appointed by itself, with every cantonment of prisoners, in possession of the other; which commissary shall see the prisoners as often as he pleases; shall be allowed to receive, exempt from all duties or taxes, and to distribute, whatever comforts may be sent to them by their friends; and shall be free to transmit his reports in open letters to the party by whom he is employed. And it is declared that neither the pretense that war dissolves all Treaties, nor any other whatever, shall be considered as annulling or suspending the solemn covenant contained in this article. On the contrary, the state of war is precisely that for which it is provided; and during which, its stipulations are to be as sacredly observed as the most acknowledged obligations under the law of nature or nations.

ARTICLE XXIII.

This Treaty shall be ratified by the President of the United States of America, by and with the advice and consent of the Senate thereof; and by the President of the Mexican Republic with the previous approbation of its General Congress; and the ratifications shall be exchanged in the city of Washington, in four months from the date of the signature hereof, or sooner, if practicable.

In faith whereof, we, the respective Plenipotentiaries, have signed this Treaty of Peace, Friendship, Limits, and Settlement; and have hereunto affixed our seals respectively. Done in Quintuplicate, at the city of Gaudalupe Hidalgo, on the second day of February, in the year of our Lord one thousand eight hundred and forty-eight.

N. P. TRIST, [L. S.]
LUIS G. CUEVAS, [L. S.]
BERNARDO CONTO, [L. S.]
MIG. ATRISTAIN, [L. S.]

THE TREATY.

ADDITIONAL AND SECRET ARTICLE *of the Treaty of Peace, Friendship, Limits, and Settlement between the United States of America and the Mexican Republic, signed this day by their respective Plenipotentiaries.* (Expunged.)

In view of the possibility that the exchange of the ratifications of this Treaty may, by the circumstances in which the Mexican Republic is placed, be delayed longer than the term of four months fixed by its twenty-third article for the exchange of ratifications of the same, it is hereby agreed that such delay shall not, in any manner, affect the force and validity of this Treaty, unless it should exceed the term of eight months, counted from the date of the signature thereof.

This article is to have the same force and virtue as if inserted in the treaty to which this is an addition.

In faith whereof, we, the respective Plenipotentiaries, have signed this additional and secret article, and have hereunto affixed our seals, respectively. Done in Quintuplicate at the city of Gaudalupe Hidalgo, on the second day of February, in the year of our Lord one thousand eight hundred and forty-eight.

N. P. TRIST, [L. S.]
LUIS G. CUEVAS, [L. S.]
BERNARDO CONTO, [L. S.]
MIG. ATRISTAIN, [L. S.]

And whereas, the said Treaty, as amended, has been duly ratified on both parts, and the respective ratifications of the same were exchanged at Queretaro, on the thirtieth day of May last, by Ambrose H. Sevier and Nathan Clifford, commissioners on the part of the Government of the United States, and by Señor Don Luis de la Rosa, Minister of Relations of the Mexican Republic, on the part of that Government:

Now, therefore, be it known, that I, James K. Polk, President of the United States of America, have caused the said Treaty to be made public, to the end that the same, and every clause and article thereof, may be observed and fulfilled with good faith by the United States and the citizens thereof.

In witness whereof, I have hereunto set my hand and caused the seal of the United States to be affixed.

Done at the City of Washington, on this fourth day of July, one thousand eight hundred and forty-eight, and of the Independence of the United States the seventy-third.

By the President,

[L. S.]
JAMES K. POLK.
JAMES BUCHANAN, Secretary of State.

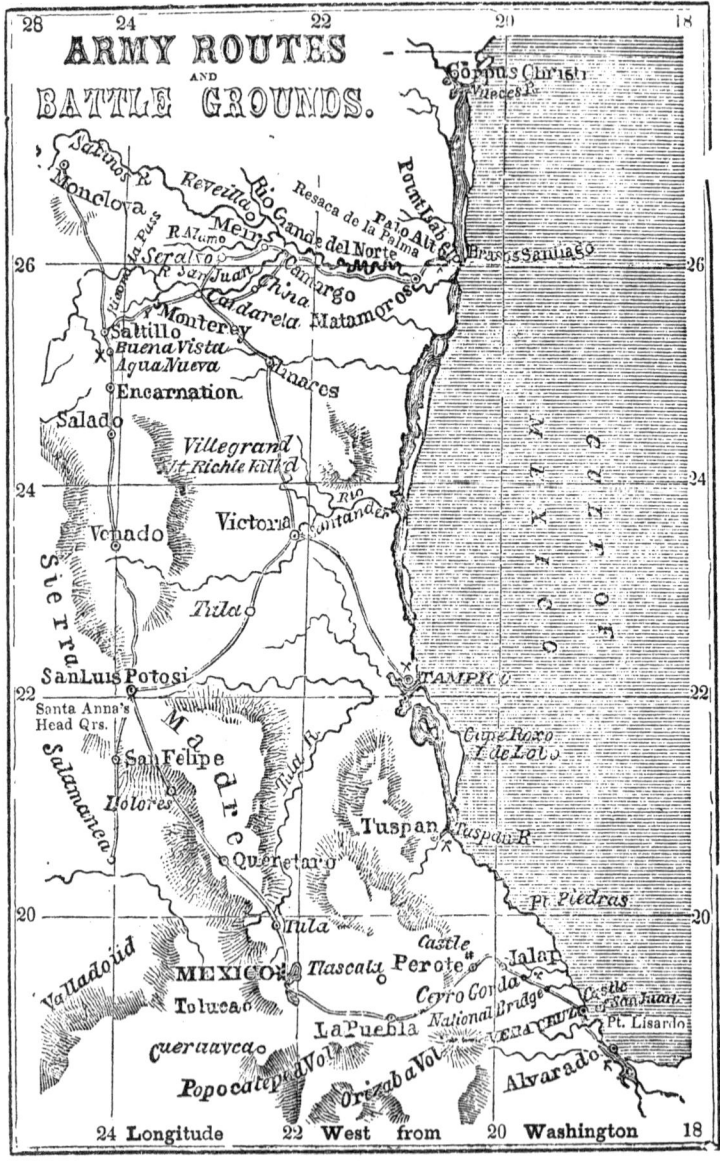

www.ingramcontent.com/pod-product-compliance
Lightning Source LLC
Chambersburg PA
CBHW071314150426
43191CB00007B/616